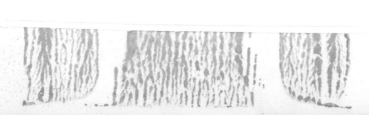

CRITICAL READING
AND WRITING

CRITICAL READING AND WRITING

ALEXANDER SCHARBACH

Portland State College

MCGRAW-HILL BOOK COMPANY

New York   St. Louis   San Francisco   Toronto

CRITICAL READING AND WRITING

TO ALL MY STUDENTS

"America's leadership must be guided by the lights of learning and reason—or else those who confuse rhetoric with reality and the plausible with the possible will gain the popular ascendancy with their seeming swift and simple solutions to every world problem."

Words from the speech President John F. Kennedy had planned to make in Dallas on November 22, 1963.

FOR THE RECORD:
NOTES TO THE TEACHER

As its title suggests, this textbook has two closely related aims: to develop the student's ability to read with a critical eye, and to apply this critical scrutiny to the improvement of his own writing.

Every good teacher provides his composition classes with analytical methods and illustrative examples of effective and ineffective writing as they touch almost every aspect of our daily life. He explains the processes of reasoning underlying all compositional structures. And whatever he can reveal of the effective rhetorical devices in what his classes read and hear as students and citizens, he urges them to apply to their own writing efforts. A textbook such as this one offers the instructor assistance in these endeavors: it goes on speaking for him outside the classroom.

This text also provides a wide and highly varied range of assignment exercises: oral and written discussions, reports, written analyses, brief essays, and extended essays. No principle or concept can be learned until the student makes it his own, at least in part, by applying that principle or concept in his writing. Abstract ideas cannot be taught merely through lectures, a fact that explains why science teachers rely upon laboratory sessions. So it is that critical reading requires critical writing.

Every topic discussed in these chapters is followed by a Critical Focus and a number of assignments dealing directly with the material which has been discussed and illustrated. The Critical Focus provides a summary and, at times, suggests methods for evaluating the kind of language studied in the preceding section. All such suggestions have been led up to; by the time the student comes to them, he is prepared to think in terms of the critical form listed.

This text begins with an inquiry into the nature of our language and the semantic and syntactic meanings of its words and word patterns. It analyzes denotative and connotative meanings of words and their power as the "diction" of effective writing. It next applies these insights to the important, practical affairs of our everyday world—advertising, politics, and journalism. By analysis and example, the student is shown how to recognize and evaluate the workings of these pervasive written forms. Again he is given concrete writing problems which provide practice in exposition as well as experience with the language of advertising, politics, and journalism.

When the student has learned to question the intentions of writers and speakers, he is ready for the more detailed study and application of logic. Many examples show how these are applicable to his own writing and thinking. He becomes aware also of the indirect logic found in literature, especially in poetry. He moves next into the study of literature of several genres. Now he has the opportunity to apply all that he has learned about critical evaluation on the basis of diction, logic, and rhetoric.

Whatever he has learned about language and thought, he can next apply to the language of the sciences. A chapter on compositional structures follows. Summary chapters on tone and style precede the conclusion, How to Read a Book, which encompasses all that this text has tried to do in helping the student to recognize good writing and thinking and to develop a satisfactory writing style of his own.

Despite its plan, *Critical Reading and Writing* remains a book flexible enough to permit the instructor to take up at any time, and in any order, the chapters he deems suitable to the needs of his class.

In addition to all the authors and publishers who generously permitted quotations from their works, I wish to thank especially Professor Freeman Anderson, my English Department colleague, for his enlightening comments and sagacious assistance in reading galleys. I am likewise most grateful to Professor Wilma Morrison of the Department of Journalism and Professor Irving Polonoff of the Department of Philosophy for their help with the journalism and logic chapters.

Alexander Scharbach

PREVIEW:

TO THE STUDENT

Some of you may already be familiar with critical reading. If you can readily understand your reading assignments, see the relationship of ideas, detect poor reasoning, and at the same time appreciate effective expression and compositional structure, you have a good start as a critical reader. But what you say in your written work, and how well you say it, are the best tests of your ability to think analytically.

The critical reader is one who reads to understand, to analyze, and finally to evaluate the qualities of language, reasoning, emotion, structure, and style. By knowing how to read everything from advertisements to novels with good judgment, he develops critical poise and confidence. At the same time, he learns how to apply this critical rigor and intellectual tact to his own written work.

Do not think that to be critical means being "negative" or cynical. No one can judge the writing or speech of someone else without having a scale of values, a means of measuring that expression. You will find critical reading, therefore, a creative process, one appealing to vision as well as to judgment. It is creative as writing class essays is creative. To write well you need to let your imagination and emotions respond to an idea or a possible solution to a problem. Discovering the means to shape and control that emotional thinking is half of our task in this book. It is a process of building, of growing. To be critical, as we see the term here, means to have an expandable knowledge, a growing awareness of how language shapes our lives, and also a developing skill in communicating what we have learned.

Through the many examples and exercise assignments, this textbook provides the means to make you a critical reader and a greatly improved writer. A glance at the table of contents will indicate its organization and scope. In every section of a chapter, you will find in bold print a Critical Focus. Its function is to summarize and emphasize, but on occasion it may also offer a method for evaluating the kind of language and writing that the section has explained. Watch for the Critical Focus. It is your guide to the exercises following it and your reminder of what to watch for in your own written work.

The college reader needs to become critical in self-defense. Off campus as well as on, he finds himself struggling against a semantic flood pouring from a myriad of presses and electronic sound devices. It has been estimated that the average person is now exposed in any one day to some 2,700 "messages." In increasing numbers, electronic eyes and ears "bug" us. More and more, computers interpret our behavior and try to predict it. In this world of changing meanings and changing language, clear thinking through critical analysis daily becomes more essential for the protection of our society and our personal freedom.

Critical reading also opens the doors to literature, for such reading is at once a method of analysis and a form of discovery. It gives us the great delight of testing a fine poem, short story, essay, or novel with every means of critical evaluation and then finding that such a work not only withstands our examination but reveals its merits only to those equipped to question its qualities.

Most important of all, the critical reader soon discovers that when he can detect what is faulty and deceitful he becomes his own best critic as a writer. He comes to prefer the excellent and strives for it in his own writing. And what is more, he acknowledges that it will take time and much effort to apply to his own work the skills and qualities that distinguish good writing.

CONTENTS

chapter 1

LANGUAGE, MEANING, AND DICTION

WHAT LANGUAGE DOES

In a creative civilization, language works as a flexible, responsive agent. It changes and grows with the demands made upon its resources. And in eras such as ours, when new knowledge of every kind challenges the experts, thousands of new words, meanings, and symbols appear, to communicate those findings.

As college students, you hardly need to be reminded of this spate of language. Who can escape the fact that we live in a world of constantly expanding language? Even the householder sprawled before his television set takes for granted the terms representing a swiftly changing world of technology. He watches the launching of *moon shots, communication satellites,* and *intercontinental missiles* during *countdown* and *lift-off* from the *firing pad.* He follows *range tracking* through *radiation belts,* and to the hum and clatter of *electronic computers* thinks of what *Sputnik* started. The householder may also reach for a *tranquilizer* as he thinks of the terms his college-age son brings up at the dinner table to startle his parents: *psychotic, Oedipal, compulsive, anal, oral, introvert, extrovert, masocho-sadist, frustration, affluent society, lonely crowd, motivational research, suburbia,* and *population explosion.* Meanwhile, little brother dawdles in a corner over a *teaching machine,* and older sister upstairs resists *going ape* over the latest *beat* howling from her *transistor* while she wonders how *deoxyribo-*

nucleic acid, as her high school science text says, could have given her a snubbed nose like her mother's.

To cope with this tremendous master-servant, language, in our own writing and to become capable of evaluating what we read and hear, we should have a basic idea of language, of what it is and does:

1. Spoken language differs from writing.
2. Language, in its transmitting capacity, preserves a common culture and thereby perpetuates as well as fosters civilization.
3. Language continually undergoes change. Its old words take on fresh meanings, and new terms multiply during periods of social growth. Sounds, grammatical structure, and usage also change.
4. Language includes special vocabularies, which give man new insights into himself and into nature, as in the fields of the sciences, the social sciences, history, art, and literature.
5. Language gives the individual both his sense of personal identity and his membership in the social community.

It is these shaping aspects of language that justify what at first may be thought to be too bold statements, such as this one:

> Every language offers its speakers a ready-made *interpretation* of the world, a *Weltanschauung,* a metaphysical world picture which, after having originated in the thinking of our ancestors, tends to impose itself ever anew on posterity.

To a great extent, then, everyone is a "prisoner" of his native language.

The languages they speak help to make people characteristically American, Canadian, French, Japanese, Irish, German, Italian, Chinese, Russian, or Nigerian. Each language reflects the history of its people and the institutions or cultural practices that make up their way of life. Its word forms and rituals preserve cherished ideals and principles, as has been shown, for example, in the conflicts in Canada arising between the English-speaking and the French-speaking provinces. In Belgium, similar clashes in language traditions intensify differences between areas of that small country. Here in the United States, we witness our own sectional distinctions, marked both by viewpoints and attitudes and by regional accents in the speech that typifies New England, the Middle West, the South, and such special areas as Brooklyn and Texas.

From childhood on, we daily hear language that teaches us who and what we are as persons; it gives us our personal names and our ideals and goals—our whole sense of values, whether they be those of Los Angeles or Harlem, Atlanta or Toronto.

Such is the protean nature of language. There are two unavoidable difficulties, however, in any approach to the subject: We cannot escape talking *about* language in terms of language; and, as the voluminous scholarship clearly shows, it is a study which by its very nature must be controversial, for it is related to the deep mystery of the human personality. How words and terms, signs and symbols are given their meanings will be taken up in the next section, which defines *meaning* and introduces semantics as the study of meaning.

CRITICAL FOCUS

Characteristics of Language:

It transmits and so preserves the vital part of any culture.
It undergoes continual change.
It may have both written and oral forms.
It nurtures special vocabularies.
It helps give the individual his sense of identity.

**To read and write with judgment, know the workings
of your own language.**

Exercise 1   Discussion assignment. Bring to class printed material (magazine, book, newspaper, etc.) exemplifying three of the six meanings of *language* as defined below.* Be prepared to explain the various meanings in the light of your examples. Consult a dictionary for any terms not wholly clear to you.

> **lan·guage** (lang'gwij)   *n.* **1.** The expression and communication of emotions or ideas between human beings by means of speech and hearing, the sounds spoken or heard being systematized and confirmed by usage among a given people over a period of time. **2.** Transmission of emotions or ideas between any living creatures by any means. **3.** The words forming the means of communication among members of a single nation or group at a given period; tongue: the French *language.* **4.** The impulses, capacities, and powers that induce and make possible the creation and use of all forms of human communication by speech and hearing. **5.** The vocabulary or technical expressions used in a specific business, science, etc.: the *language* of mathematics. **6.** One's characteristic manner of expression or use of speech. Abbr. *lang.* [< OF *langage* < *langue* tongue < L *lingua* tongue, language. Akin to TONGUE.]

* By permission from *Funk & Wagnalls Standard ® College Dictionary.* Copyright 1963 by Funk & Wagnalls Company, Inc.

Exercise 2   Discussion assignment. (*a*) Have you ever noticed in someone else's speech an irritating expression? If so, explain why it is irritating. (*b*) Does any characteristic expression of yours irritate someone else?

Exercise 3   Written assignment. To show that you grasp how language shapes our basic views, write one well-developed paragraph based on the following observation:

> It has often been said that man in the past saw nature, and God, in his own image. It now appears that he saw things in the image of his own language.

Suggestion: How did you regard and speak of things around you and of God when you were a child? Do you know of primitive people who could see only what their vocabulary told them existed? Read the account of an island boy's insights on page 23. Marc Connelly's *Green Pastures*, though a modern drama, also well illustrates a primitive but moving identification of words with the things they stand for.

Exercise 4   Report assignment. Show your skill in classification by arranging the words and terms found in "A Ballad of New Words" according to the field of study in which each belongs: science, social science, education, business, and the humanities. Consult your dictionary if any of the terms are unfamiliar.

A Ballad of New Words
stubble mulch, slop jar
string quartet, stock car
source book, sacred cow
steamer trunk, solemn vow
sudden death, smoke-filled room
sandwich board, sonic boom
silver screen, strep throat
spinner play, straw vote
shish kebab, sandy loam
scandal sheet, soldiers' home
squirrel cage, sour mash
song and dance, swung dash
shelter half, swim fin

state guard, scatter pin
scrub brush, swimmer's itch
service charge, slip stitch
spirit lamp, sucking louse
section hand, solar house
surgeon general, scratch sheet
sweat pants, sliding seat
set point, strawberry roan
spoon feed, strike zone
shore dinner, striped bass
sweetie pie, sung mass
shop steward, skid row
steel band, ski tow

Exercise 5   Written assignment. To some important degree, everyone has been affected—at least in early life—by words of warning. Here are two broad categories of such possible warning sources. Choose one of the items that applies to your experience, and write one paragraph stating, explaining, and illustrating that particular warning.

Family outlook on	**Neighborhood outlook on**
family history	economic conditions
politics	education facilities
social life	recreation
education	social improvement

Exercise 6   Essay assignment. Write a brief essay showing in specific detail of what importance you now think language may be to you in your possible future career or life.

Exercise 7   Discussion assignment. How does the following report illustrate the characteristics of writing?

Chinese characters are singularly illuminating concerning the relations between concrete and abstract. "Benevolence" is "man plus two" (a man who thinks of another beside himself), "happiness" is "one mouth supported by a field," "peace" is "a woman under a roof" (indoors), "home" is a "pig under a roof" (food and shelter), "spirit" is the skeleton of a great man, a "great" man is one who has not only legs to obey but arms to enforce. "father" is a "hand holding a whip."

Exercise 8   Special assignment. In her book *Male and Female*, Margaret Mead describes the language and ritual employed by American parents and adults to teach the child its proper sexual behavior as male or female child. Read the book, and report on how your own observations compare with those of the anthropologist.

Exercise 9   Discussion assignment. To what extent does the following analysis explain why language is an effective preserver of tradition? Have you had experiences which would show that children acquire principles and attitudes in their early years along with their language?

> To constrain a man against his principles—make a pacifist bear arms, a patriot insult his flag, a pagan receive baptism—is to endanger his attitude toward the world, his personal strength and single-mindedness. No matter how fantastic may be the dogmas he holds sacred, how much his living rites conflict with the will or convenience of society, it is never a light matter to demand their violation. Men fight passionately against being forced to do lip-service, because the enactment of a rite is always, in some measure, assent to its meaning. . . . It is a breach of personality.

Note: The key words in this paragraph—*dogmas, rites,* and *principles*—generally involve statements of belief, words and expressions held sacred.

SEMANTICS AND MEANING

As we have seen, language in its broadest sense, both spoken and written, exists in order to convey meaning. The hieroglyphic inscriptions on the Rosetta stone were written language even though none of its finders in 1799 could read the characters, whereas well-recognized typewriter characters printed by untrained chimpanzees are not language. Certain experimental authors may not always seem to be writing with meaning, yet they may be said to communicate significance if their immediate followers find meaning in their works. Whether the meaning is the one the author wished to communicate is another matter. In the visual arts, chimps achieve high praise and good sales with paint and canvas. Evidently, paint may be splashed and smeared about in rhythmic abandon, and yet be accepted for its interesting nonsignificance, or as an "abstraction." Hardly so, words. We expect them to bring discernible meaning.

Semantics is the study of this meaning. A skilled writer—novelist, poet, advertising copywriter, political speech-writer, newspaper reporter, or scholarly researcher—is one who can use language to say what he means. (We shall later examine such writers at work to see how they make words perform to affect our lives, whether to delight us with the tragic-comic struggles of mankind, to sell us deodorants, to win our votes, to give us the daily news, or to enlighten us with a new discovery.) We can see immediately that the study of meaning must form one of the major divisions of language study. As part of its work, semantics deals also with the historic and psychological forces producing changes in the meaning of the words that make up language.

Since a *symbol* is something that represents something else—a cross, a flag, a barber pole—it has meaning, and so also may be included in the study of semantics. It is true that words themselves are symbols; a word stands for the object it names or the concept it represents, which is the *referent* of that word, just as a symbol has a *referent*, the thing it refers to or stands for. For its importance in the discussion of imaginative writing and art, we shall consider symbol meaning as part of semantics. Let's make *symbol* and *referent* clear. The Red Cross banner is a symbol having as its referent the international welfare society that operates under that insignia. Any thing, any word can become a symbol so long as it has a meaningful attachment to a referent. The meaning attached to a symbol is arbitrarily assigned the symbol by a culture; for example, custom is the only reason that black should be the symbol of mourning in the Western world, whereas in the East white is the corresponding symbol. So also in one culture a kiss may be the symbol of affection, and in another the rubbing of noses may be the accepted symbol.

On the contrary, a *sign* can be said to have a direct relation to its referent. We see or smell smoke and at once think of fire; we notice a man weaving his way down a walk and babbling to himself: he is intoxicated, we conclude. When there is a black cloud overhead and the first raindrops splash against the windshield, the driver of a convertible puts his top up in a hurry. He believes in signs. This direct relation may, however, be only in the eye of the beholder, which is the case with many radio evangelists who see every bad turn of events as a sign of Judgment Day's being at hand.

Another kind of meaning which the critical reader and writer needs to know how to appraise is syntactic meaning. *Syntactics* makes up the branch of linguistics devoted to the study of grammar and sentence structure, for words in group patterns make up larger units of meaning. If you have studied a foreign language, you know you must master more than a vocabulary. To write correctly in that language, you require skill in applying its rules of grammar, for every language has its own peculiar and arbitrary forms of expression. We should recognize a non-English pattern in the speech of one who, for example, said, "I could not take off my eyes from her hat." Syntactic meaning will be frequently considered throughout this book along with lexical (or word) meaning and rhetorical sentence patterns.

Before going further with this most complex term *meaning*, let us try to make clear what it usually signifies. Here is the entry from *Webster's Seventh New Collegiate Dictionary.** Note how the synonyms—words having a similar meaning—are carefully distinguished; they give us a glimpse into the process of how words, by distinguishing concepts from each other, make logical reasoning possible.

mean·ing \\'mē-niŋ\ *n* **1 a :** the thing one intends to convey esp. by language **:** PURPORT   **b :** the thing that is conveyed esp. by language **:** IMPORT   **2 :** INTENT, PURPOSE   **3 :** SIGNIFICANCE   **4 a :** CONNOTA-TION   **b :** DENOTATION — **meaning** *adj*
   syn MEANING, SENSE, ACCEPTATION, SIGNIFICATION, SIGNIFICANCE, IMPORT denote the idea conveyed to the mind. MEANING is the general term used of anything (as a word, sign, poem, or action) requiring or allowing of interpretation; SENSE denotes the meaning or more often a particular meaning of a word or phrase; ACCEPTATION is used of a sense of a word or phrase as regularly understood by a large number of speakers and writers; SIGNIFICATION denotes the established meaning of a term, symbol, or character; SIGNIFICANCE applies specifically to a covert as distinguished from the ostensible meaning of an utterance, act, or work of art; IMPORT suggests the meaning a speaker tries to convey esp. through language

As this dictionary entry well illustrates, the problem of how we know what we know is always bound to raise many questions, especially since we are using language to think about and talk about *language*.

Literature abounds with examples of characters in search of significant relationship between words and concepts. One vivid instance is the case of Holden Caulfield in J. D. Salinger's *The Catcher in the Rye*. In his flight from preparatory school to New York, his frantic visit home, and then his return to school, Holden expresses repeatedly his hunger for understanding. He tries desperately to see what bearing the words and expressions he hears at school and at home have on life

---

* By permission. From *Webster's Seventh New Collegiate Dictionary*. Copyright 1963 by G. & C. Merriam Co., Publishers of the Merriam-Webster Dictionaries.

as he is experiencing it. His language abounds with such phrases as *I mean, If you want to know the truth,* and *phonies.* His perplexed examination of the world of school, adult life, and family reflects every aspect of striving for *meaning, sense, acceptation, signification, significance,* and *import.*

We have said that a skilled writer is one who knows how to say what he means. But skilled or unskilled in writing, all of us make constant use of words to express two kinds of meaning: *denotation* and *connotation.* According to some linguistics scholars, denotation and connotation are actually two types of reaction to a symbol, in the sense that all words are symbols. Like all reactions, these two have meanings and, furthermore, as reactions *to* meaning, they are especially related to the workings of language, and thus deserve extensive treatment in an introductory study such as this. Denotation and connotation are key terms for the critical reader, and in the next section we shall begin with denotation.

CRITICAL FOCUS

1. *Semantics* is the study of meaning.
2. The critical reader regards signs and symbols as important expressions of meaning.
3. He looks for both *lexical* meaning (pertaining to words) and *syntactic* meaning (pertaining to grammar and sentence structure).
4. He becomes increasingly aware of the complexity and subtlety of his own use of words, of their *denotation* and their *connotation.*

Exercise 10   Written assignment. To show that we react to words more vividly as they shift from general meaning to a particular meaning, consider the word *table* and the changes in our associations when *table* becomes *dining-room table, operating table, conference table,* or *library table.* Now try this experiment.

1. Select one of the general terms listed below.
2. Copy an appropriate dictionary meaning.
3. As with *table,* list several terms having a more particular meaning, and note your reactions to each.
4. Write a paragraph describing and explaining the changes in meaning the basic word underwent as you moved from the

general to the particular, for example, with *plant: edible plant, garden vegetable, lettuce, butter lettuce.*

weather	shirt	animal	illness	projectile
mail	sandwich	weed	dance	saw
car	game	fish	conflict	instrument

Exercise 11   Written assignment. Write a paragraph giving details of how, when, where, and why the object named by *one* of the following words could be considered a symbol.

automobile	identification card
fur coat	concert
birthday	date
motor bike	painting
lipstick	money
high heels	credit card
library card	signature
greeting	darkness

Exercise 12   Written assignment. Write a brief analysis of how you construe *one* of these popular terms. Give instances to illustrate your interpretation.

Lil in "Lil Abner"	*Pirates* in "Terry and the Pirates"
Mad in *Mad* magazine	*Smilin'* in "Smilin' Jack"
Alley in "Gasoline Alley"	*Smoky* in "Smoky the Bear"
Orphan in "Orphan Annie"	*Bugs* in "Bugs Bunny"
Peanuts in "Peanuts"	*Pogo* in "Pogo"

DENOTATION AS MEANING

Perhaps without being aware of it, you have been thinking in terms of meaning as *denotation* and *connotation* as you worked your way through the last set of exercises. We can say that denotation is the general, nonemotional meaning that a word has; it is the general significance a word gives us as it names or identifies its referent object or concept. In Exercise 10, the denotation for *table* is "an article of furniture consisting of some kind of smooth, flat surface material sitting on legs." *Table* gives a name to a whole class of objects, just as *justice* does to related general concepts or ideas. We need to think of *dinner table* before we perhaps see a specific table. Almost instantly, then, we may also experience a rush of images and memories that *dinner table* suggests. These associated meanings that produce or arouse emotional responses are the *connotation* of *dinner table*. But, as may seem confusing, even plain *table* can have general connotations—associations almost everybody shares. And, as we shall see in discussing connotation at greater length, expressions such as *Come to the table now* may have much more emotional meaning for some persons than for others.

The total meaning of a word is determined by its total range of uses, and (even in only its denotations) a word such as *good* may have extensive meanings. Among the many expressions including the word *good* are these: *good graces, good faith, good folk* (brownies, fairies), *good heart, good nature, good time, Good Queen Bess, Good Samaritan, Good Shepherd, Good Book, good for, good day, good riddance, good time, good going,* and *good-by.* Though *good-by* survives as the contraction of "God be with ye," it now shares the general denotation of *good.*

Dictionary entries make convenient sources for finding denotative meanings, but the definitions are not always satisfactory. At times the reader may find an old term being given an apparently new meaning, or he may encounter a term to which he attaches no lexical meaning. In such situations, he can guess at the denotation through the context in which the word or term appears.

By *context* is meant the sentences or paragraphs which come before and after the term in question. It may be that the whole discourse requires study for one to find the significance of a term. Such is the case in these excerpts from a letter written by a Peace Corps volunteer working in a slum area in Chimbot, Peru. What does the term *culture shock* denote in this context?

> Fed with Peace Corps press releases about glory and rewards heaped on volunteers by loving, thankful natives, and topped by a naïve conclusion that the world really needs less "stuffy old politicians" and more "real folks," some rush to the post office to send in their applications. Volunteers call this the Albert Schweitzer complex. These dreams would not be harmful except for what happens to the volunteer overseas, and to his co-workers, when he joins for these reasons.
>
> I live in a picturesque bamboo mat house I built myself, and I

buy my water from a picturesque boy with a burro loaded down with water cans. I read and write under a kerosene lantern, sleep on a cot, and cook on a camp stove. A recently arrived volunteer is constructing a mat house similar to mine, not because it is the best possible living quarters under the circumstances, but because it is exciting and picturesque and she wants to take pictures of it for her friends back home.

Her mat house will not be picturesque during a 3 A.M. rainstorm, when water gets in her expensive camera, or during the frequent dust storms which stop up her radio so she can't hear the Voice of America broadcasts. Her water boy won't be picturesque either when she sees where he gets his water, or her cot so "outdoorish" when she lies on it doubled up with dysentery.

There comes a day when all this suddenly becomes apparent. Things are no longer picturesque, they're dirty. They're no longer quaint but furiously frustrating, and you want to just get out of there, and go home. This is called "culture shock," and you don't find it mentioned on recruiting posters. It happens to one and all, usually about the third or fourth month. More volunteers quit and go home at this time than at any other time. Others remain, but count the days until their two years are up, hating each day, souring themselves, their friends, and all the Peruvians with whom they talk. What a waste! Two years of their lives ruined by idealistic daydreams and tragic misinformation from unofficial and official sources.

If you're a tough minded realist, willing to work for two long years, not a junior year abroad, you'll have a rewarding, maturing experience second to none. If you think it will be thrilling, picturesque, or a good story for your friends back home, you wouldn't like it. . . .

I was a dreamer once too, and my fall was hard. Now, all things considered, I think I'm doing something worthwhile. I don't think I'll sign up for another stretch, but you couldn't drag me away from this one.

Before tackling the meaning of *culture shock,* let's determine what we make of the letter as quoted here. The writer begins with a description of what he calls the *Albert Schweitzer complex,* an allusion to the celebrated French physician and musician who has devoted his life to operating a hospital in a most primitive part of Africa. The Corps volunteer describes his living conditions and gives some realistic glimpses of the misery he himself must have experienced. It is clear that nothing in the *dreams* of a misinformed volunteer can prepare him for the realities of a Peruvian slum. The writer concludes by telling of those who can't take such hardships and disillusionments, but says that he will finish up his term of service.

A second look now at the immediate context of *culture shock* will suggest why the term was not immediately self-explanatory: "There comes a day when all this suddenly becomes apparent. . . . They're no longer quaint but furiously frustrating, and you want to just get out of there, and go home. This is called 'culture shock,' and you don't find it mentioned on recruiting posters." Note the vague expressions surrounding our term. The pronoun *this* appears twice and has no specific antecedent; "get out of there" has the reader making the effort to recall all of the conditions and scenes described. Yet because of the context of the whole letter, *culture shock* can be given a clear meaning. It includes these six elements of feeling, each of which may have its own connotative meanings:

1. Initial high expectations and opinion of self
2. Physical suffering and misery
3. Bitterness of disillusionment
4. Frustration over problems encountered
5. Resentment and desire to escape
6. Homesickness

Before we try to combine these elements into a denotative statement, let's consult the lexicographers.

Of the five meanings found for *culture* in *Webster's Third New International,* one is particularly applicable.*

> **b :** the body of customary beliefs, social forms, and material traits constituting a distinct complex of tradition of a racial, religious, or social group ⟨a nation with many ∼s⟩ ⟨Plains Indian ∼⟩ ⟨but to many men today the most interesting thing about society is its ∼ . . . that complex whole that includes knowledge, belief, morals, law, customs, opinions, religion, superstition, and art —Preserved Smith⟩

And as for *shock,* no single one of the seven dictionary entries has the desired meaning that denotes the combination of the six interwoven emotions we have listed. But two of the seven approach it.*

> (2) **:** a sudden or violent disturbance in the mental or emotional faculties ⟨the ∼ and elation of victory and defeat —Oscar Handlin⟩ ⟨fresh ∼s of wonder at the unaccountable apparition —George Meredith⟩ (3) **:** a sense of outrage to one's convictions esp. of morality or propriety ⟨terms that in better districts would have caused disgust and ∼ —Ruth Park⟩

Brought together and considered in the light of the context, these several meanings could give us the following definition for *culture shock:* "a state of emotional and psychological disturbance brought on by physical and mental anguish on unexpectedly encountering social conditions contrary to usual convictions and notions of propriety." No wonder the term with some such denotation has become useful in the social sciences; it may some day be included in *Webster's.*

Learning to scan a context for the proper denotation of a word or term sharpens the reader. Try another selection for contextual analysis. This time see whether you can determine the meaning of a term that enjoyed a tremendous vogue in England in the early nineteenth century. For modern readers *sensibility* will hardly hold the significance it did for the audience for whom Jane Austen wrote *Sense and Sensibility* or for her seventeen-year-old heroine. What does *sensibility* denote in Marianne's reply to her mother's question of whether the girl approves of her older sister's choice of suitors?

"Perhaps," said Marianne, "I may consider it with some surprise. Edward is very amiable, and I love him tenderly. But yet—he is not the kind of young man—there is a something wanting—his figure is not striking; it has none of that grace which I should expect in the man who could seriously attach my sister. His eyes want all that spirit, that fire, which at once announce virtue and intelligence. And besides all this, I am afraid, mama, he has no real taste. Music seems scarcely to attract him, and though he admires Elinor's drawings very much, it is not the admiration of a person who can understand their worth. It is evident, in spite of his frequent attention to her while she draws, that in fact he knows nothing of the matter. He admires as a lover, not as a connoisseur. To satisfy me, those characters must be united. I could not be happy with a man whose taste did not in every point coincide with my own. He must enter into all my feelings; the same books, the same music must charm us both. Oh! mama, how spiritless, how tame was Edward's manner in reading to us last night! I felt for my sister most severely. Yet she bore it with so much composure, she seemed scarcely to notice it. I could hardly keep my seat. To hear those beautiful lines which have frequently almost driven me wild, pronounced with such impenetrable calmness, such dreadful indifference! . . .

"Nay, mama, if he is not to be animated by Cowper!—but we must allow for difference of taste. Elinor has not my feeling, and therefore she may overlook it, and be happy with him. But it would have broke my heart had I loved him, to hear him read with so little sensibility. . . .

"Mama, the more I know of the world, the more am I convinced that I shall never see a man whom I can really love. I require so much! He must have all Edward's virtues, and his person and manners must ornament his goodness with every possible charm."

Sensibility appears in the final lines of Marianne's statement of her many criteria for the ideal suitor. She dreams of a man with a striking but graceful figure and eyes that glow with fiery intelligence and spirit, but yet show virtue. He must have such sensitive taste as to be capable of going into raptures over music and drawing—even though the performance be amateur. His voice in reading poetry aloud should resound with the deep feeling stirred within him as he visualizes the beauty expressed by the poet. In short, as she implies, Marianne wants a partner who will match her own *sensibility*.

In its context, this abstract term means a heightened state of feeling characterized by desire and willingness to seek out romantic love with the same glorious abandon given to ecstatic enjoyment of poetry, art, music, and landscapes. On this denotation, Jane Austen based the theme of her comic novel, *Sense and Sensibility*, wherein Marianne represents *sensibility*, and her prudent sister, Elinor, its antonym, *sense*. All of Miss Austen's readers are able to find general connotations for these abstract terms, many perhaps even to the extent of making the two sisters symbols of contrasting ways of life.

As found in most dictionary entries, *denotation* appears as formal definition, which follows the Aristotelian formula of placing the object to be defined into its proper genus and class, and then pointing out the characteristics that distinguish it from others of its kind. Thus, an astrophysicist and a geologist are both scientists, but one studies the physical properties of the celestial bodies, and the other the earth and its rocks. This process of conceptual definition may also be at work in informal definitions, such as the following one for *nation* and *nationalism:*

But what is a nation? No one has ever seen a nation; no one has ever touched one. The nation has no existence in the physical world. Its existence, therefore, while nonetheless real, is entirely metaphysical, or mental; the nation exists only as a concept held in common by many men. It is the emotional loyalty of men to this always changing concept, the nation, that constitutes nationalism. Without the concept, the loyalty would not exist.

Do not let the apparently simple language deceive you about how much the author has done with a definition in a few words. To begin with, he frames the topic sentence of his paragraph as a question. He then shows why *nation* is an *abstract* word—one that refers to a class or a concept—and in doing so defines *abstract* without mentioning it. To explain *metaphysical,* he adds a common, if somewhat inaccurate, synonym. Once he has set up a general concept of *nation,* he moves on to *nationalism* by pointing out how the feeling of loyalty which characterizes *nationalism* depends upon the concept of *nation.* Throughout, he has made careful classification and distinctions. Now, if he wishes, he can go on to illustration and comparison and contrast to amplify his definitions.

As an example of how denotative language can differ from the connotative, compare the following free paraphrase with the original:

But what is a nation? It is the stars and stripes flying over every sovereign state and over every heart dedicated to liberty and justice for all. It is the thoughtful civilian who, while drums beat and gleaming columns parade down the avenues of peace and commerce, recalls his neighbor, patriot, and friend who lies now among the hallowed dead on an alien shore, where he fell fighting that men should be free. These are the nation. And the millions of kindred souls cherishing this heritage of sacrifice, renewing their faith and love for their land, their precious soil, bespeak the universal loyalty that can be proudly hailed as nationalism.

This emotional version abounds with clichés and bathos: It employs connotation in its most exaggerated and excessive form. In the next section we shall explore the skillful use of connotation.

CRITICAL FOCUS

1. *Denotation* is nonemotional meaning that names, points out, and identifies objects or concepts.

2. *Connotation* is emotion-arousing meaning that implies or suggests; as will be shown, it may be general or private.
3. *Context*—the surrounding sentences, paragraphs—always to some extent determines the denotation of a word.
4. *Definition* may be *formal* or *informal*.

Remember: Words may appeal to the intellect or to the emotions and the imagination.

    Exercise 13   Written assignment. Look up *malleable* in a standard dictionary, and decide whether any of the given meanings fit the denotation of *malleable* in the context of the following quotation. Then write a one-paragraph definition explaining exactly what *malleable* denotes herein, and why it is or is not "the proper word in the proper place," as Jonathan Swift defined *style*. Do the same with *world*.

> It seems amazing how malleable the world is and how easily it models and remodels itself according to the inner vision of man, how readily it responds to his "theorizing." Thus the most important advice which an educator can give to his pupils may easily be: Be careful how you interpret the world; it *is* like that.

    Exercise 14   Discussion. George Orwell's *1984*, the frightening novel of a future totalitarian state, contains an appendix entitled "The Principles of Newspeak," which is the name given to the official party language. "The purpose of Newspeak was not only to provide a medium of expression for the world-view and mental habits proper to the devotees of Ingsoc, but to make all other modes of thought impossible." It is said that this control of language also limited all thought by reducing the total number of words.

    One legal term would cover all variations of behavior that once had required perhaps many terms with careful distinctions in meaning. The term *crimethink,* for example, meant the concepts formerly associated with liberty and freedom. *Sexcrime* was the single term applied to all sexual practices, even relations between a married couple, except for procreation. Legally enforced chastity was called *goodsex.*

Questions for Discussion

1. Read the appendix to *1984*. How do you explain that the denota-

tion of the words making up *crimethink* and *sexcrime* differ from those we should give them had we coined the terms?

2. How would it be possible for a new language established by a government but built on the old words to make all the old modes of thought impossible?

Exercise 15   Discussion. Give precise reasons why you would choose or reject any of the following definitions of *nationalism* for inclusion in a textbook.

1. It is a state of mind in which we give our paramount loyalty to one fraction of the human race—to the particular tribe of which we happen to be tribesmen.

2. It is an ideology by which we hold that the highest political good for us is in our own nation's sovereign independence; that our nation has a moral right to exercise its sovereignty according to what it believes to be its own national interest, whatever consequences this may entail for the foreign majority of the human race; and that our duty, as citizens of our country, is to support our country, right or wrong.

3. We shall fight to the limit of our resources and meet intransigence with intransigence, whenever and wherever our sacred freedom and rights are invaded or insulted.

Exercise 16   Written assignment. Fill each blank with the word having the correct denotation, and explain the choice you made on the basis of contextual meaning. Point out also why you discarded the other synonyms.

1. During the _____ immediately following the French Revolution, the slogan of "Liberty, Fraternity, and Equality!" frightened English conservatives almost as much as the Napoleonic conquests did. (period, epoch, era, age, eon)

2. I don't know what to make of Milly's letter. Here it is: "Dear Mack, I understand now. You are the one confused, not me, because you are mixed up without really knowing it. I may seem a little bewildered at times, but really down deep I'm not at all. I know I've got problems, and I know I don't know whether you really are going to be one or not." Now I want to know, is she trying to be *cryptic* or is she only *obscure* as a letter writer (_____)?

3. In the production of *Macbeth*, a literal-minded director had the ghost of Banquo enter and take the seat reserved for Banquo. The appearance of the ghost was _____. (actual, real, true)
4. At religious services her voice could be heard raised high in every hymn; she had little patience for the shortcomings of the younger generation in church social behavior; for the hardships of others she always had an appropriate Biblical quotation, but she attributed her own misfortunes to the stupidity and blindness of everyone but herself. Without doubt she was a _____ person. (pious, religious, pietistic, sanctimonious, devout)
5. No matter how hard he studied, his grades stayed at the _____ of 2.5. (mean, average, median, norm)
6. After reading the letter from her fiancé, telling her that he wanted to break their engagement, Ella went about dry-eyed but looking stunned for several days. Then she howled up a storm, threw records to smash on the driveway, and ended up by giving herself a new hairdo and going about looking as if she enjoyed her _____. (depression, melancholy, gloom, sadness)
7. Joe saw his always-polite mother wince at the salesman's desperate manner and loud voice when he insisted on making the demonstration of the vacuum sweeper. Joe knew she would consider the whole performance _____. (distasteful, repugnant, repellent, abhorrent, obnoxious, invidious)
8. All during the legislative session, no matter how hopeless the outcome seemed, he adhered with _____ determination to the promise he had made. (strong, stout, tenacious, sturdy, stalwart, tough)

Exercise 17   Written assignment. (*a*) Carefully study the following passage from Herman Melville's *Billy Budd*; (*b*) prepare a list of the various meanings that the author gives for the expression— *Natural Depravity: a depravity according to nature*; (*c*) decide what denotation these words have in context; (*d*) write a brief essay explaining in detail the various denotations this expression has in the present context as related to Claggart. (You would need to read all of this short novel to appreciate fully Claggart's depravity.)

In a list of definitions included in the authentic translation of Plato, a list attributed to him, occurs this: "Natural Depravity: a depravity according to nature." A definition which tho' savoring of Calvinism, by no means involves Calvin's dogmas as to total mankind.

Evidently its intent makes it applicable but to individuals. Not many are the examples of this depravity which the gallows and jail supply. At any rate for notable instances, since these have no vulgar alloy of the brute in them, but invariably are dominated by intellectuality, one must go elsewere. Civilization, especially if of the austerer sort, is auspicious to it. It folds itself in the mantle of respectability. It has its certain negative virtues serving as silent auxiliaries. It never allows wine to get within its guard. It is not going too far to say that it is without vices or small sins. There is a phenomenal pride in it that excludes them from anything mercenary or avaricious. In short the depravity here meant partakes nothing of the sordid or sensual. It is serious, but free from acerbity. Though no flatterer of mankind it never speaks ill of it.

But the thing which in eminent instances signalizes so exceptional a nature is this: though the man's even temper and discreet bearing would seem to intimate a mind peculiarly subject to the law of reason, not the less in his heart he would seem to riot in complete exemption from that law, having apparently little to do with reason, further than to employ it as an ambidexter implement for effecting the irrational. That is to say: Toward the accomplishment of an aim which in wantonness of malignity would seem to partake of the insane, he will direct a cool judgment sagacious and sound.

These men are true madmen, and of the most dangerous sort, for their lunacy is not continuous but occasional, evoked by some special object; it is probably secretive, which is as much to say it is self-contained, so that when moreover, most active, it is to the average mind not distinguishable from sanity, and for the reason above suggested that whatever its aims may be, and the aim is never declared —the method and the outward proceeding are always perfectly rational.

Now something such an one was Claggart, in whom was the mania of an evil nature, not engendered by vicious training or corrupting books or licentious living, but born with him and innate, in short "a depravity according to nature."

Exercise 18   Written assignment. In a brief essay define what you think Chekhov meant by *my holy of holies* when he said: "My holy of holies is the human body, health, intelligence, talent, inspiration, love, and absolute freedom—freedom from violence and falsehood, no matter how the last two manifest themselves."

Exercise 19   Report assignment. Which one of the listed terms best describes the character of the speaker in this speech addressed to a young lady by an older woman? (*imperious, arrogant, proud, presumptuous, ostentatious, haughty, bumptious, conceited, domineering*) For full discussion of the terms, consult *Webster's Dictionary of Synonyms.*

"Obstinate, headstrong girl! I am ashamed of you! Is this your gratitude for my attentions to you last spring? Is nothing due to me on that score? Let us sit down. You are to understand, Miss Bennet, that I came here with the determined resolution of carrying my purpose; nor will I be dissuaded from it. I have not been used to submit to any person's whims. I have not been in the habit of brooking disappointment. . . .

"I will not be interrupted! Hear me in silence. My daughter and my nephew are formed for each other. They are descended, on the maternal side, from the same noble line; and, on the fathers', from respectable, honourable, and ancient, though untitled families. Their fortune on both sides is splendid. They are destined for each other by the voice of every member of their respective houses; and what is to divide them? The upstart pretensions of a young woman without family, connections, or fortune. Is this to be endured? But it must not, shall not be! If you were sensible of your own good, you would not wish to quit the sphere in which you have been brought up."

Exercise 20   Report assignment. Bring to class a letter to the editor, found in a daily newspaper or current magazine, that defines, or attempts to define, a term *or* that labels someone with a "bad name." Comment on the degree of accuracy of the denotation in the light of the context.

CONNOTATION AND DICTION

To become perceptive readers and effective writers, we should do well to learn almost as much about words and composition as a professional writer knows. One sure way to recognize the skilled author is by his care in selecting terms and expressions that have connotations suitable to his purposes. In short, he shows himself a discriminating judge of *diction,* as that term is defined and distinguished in the entry that follows: *

> **dic·tion** (dik′shən) *n.* **1.** The use, choice, and arrangement of words in writing and speaking. **2.** The manner of uttering speech sounds; enunciation. [< L *dictio, -onis* speech < *dicere* to say, speak]
> — **Syn. 1.** *Diction, wording, phraseology, vocabulary,* and *parlance* are here compared as they refer to choice of words. *Diction* is applied to the broad aspects of such choice: His *diction* is lofty and sententious. *Wording* and *phraseology* are used of limited passages, and often emphasize the preference shown for a particular word or turn of phrase: the *wording* of a letter, the *phraseology* of a contract. A person's *vocabulary* is the total number of words he knows or commonly uses; by extension, it refers to his broad preferences: Hardy's *vocabulary* was largely Anglo-Saxon. *Parlance* is often used in the sense of jargon: In military *parlance,* this device was called a petard.

He deliberately chooses the special language that will aid him

1. To describe—create impressions of place, person, time
2. To explain—define, give details, analyze
3. To argue—convince, persuade, sell
4. To narrate—tell story, tale, event, happening

(How he may be judged for his skill in use of the structures of these four basic kinds of writing is shown in Chapter 8.)

By now, your own awareness of the powers of connotation must have sharpened considerably. You may already know that concrete terms such as the following can arouse images appealing to one or all of our senses—sight, hearing, smell, taste, touch, and possibly others:

> transcontinental Greyhound bus
> diesel truck exhaust roar
> formaldehyde stench
> acidy tart green grapes
> bone-crunching grip
> subway turnstile
> drive-in theater
> country general store
> homecoming dance

All of these terms probably have both a *general* and a *private* connotation: general, in the sense that almost every one of us will think of or imagine many of the same details on reading the terms. But since

* By permission from *Funk & Wagnalls Standard ® College Dictionary.* Copyright 1963 by Funk & Wagnalls Company, Inc.

language is for each of us also mysteriously fused with what he thinks of as his *self*, any word may also have a unique, private meaning. If you have ever had a dramatic, unusual experience with a referent of any expression listed above, the term can have a distinct impact upon you, one that perhaps no one else can wholly fathom. Any of the everyday names of things can have special meanings that we cannot begin to express: words such as *backyard, carport, tree house, swimming pool, forest, subway, alley, fire escape, basketball, stairs,* and *gutter.*

Poets create poems out of just such private meanings arising from memory and joining with other associations. And the simple words of a poem such as Robert Frost's "Stopping by Woods on a Snowy Evening" may hold very rich connotations; Jawaharlal Nehru, India's great leader, meditated on them during his last weeks.

In his book *In the Castle of My Skin*, George Lamming reveals how experience and meaning can be bound together with words and also be cloven apart. In recalling a boyhood experience in Barbados, this West Indian author shows how private connotation can be.

We walked through the grape vine disentangling our feet from the leaves. We uprooted the patches of moss and fern that covered the narrow dirt swamps. And we didn't look back. It was hours since we had left home. We had talked and talked and talked. We had talked a lot of nonsense, perhaps. But anyone would forgive us. With the sea shimmering, and the sand and the wind in the trees, we received so many strange feelings. And in the village, in the cellar, at the school, in this corner or that corner of the house, something was always happening. We didn't notice it then, but when something bigger appeared like the sea and the sand, it brought with it a big, big feeling, and the big feeling pushed up all the little feelings we had received in other places. We weren't ashamed. Perhaps we would do better if we had good big words like the educated people. But we didn't. We had to say something was like something else, and whatever we said didn't convey all that we felt. We wouldn't dare tell anybody what we had talked about. People who were sure of what they were saying and who had the right words to use could do that. They could talk to others. And even if they didn't feel what they were saying, it didn't matter. They had the right words. Language was a kind of passport. You could go where you like if you had a clean record. You could say what you like if you knew how to say it. It didn't matter whether you felt everything you said. You had language, good, big words to make up for what you didn't feel. And if you were really educated, and you could command the language like a captain on a ship, if you could make the language do what you wanted it to do, say what you wanted it to say, then you didn't have to feel at all. You could do away with feeling. That's why everybody wanted to be educated. You didn't have to feel. You learnt this and you learnt that, and you knew a Jack for a Jack and Ace for an Ace. You were all right. Nothing would ever go pop, pop, pop in your head. You had language to safeguard you. And if you were beginning to feel too strongly, you could kill the feeling, you could get it out of the way by fetching the words that couldn't understand what the feeling was all about. It was like a knife. If you wanted to slaughter the pig, you got your knife. The knife hadn't a clue what was going on in the pig's head, but when you wielded it, the job was done. It was so with language. When the feelings came up like so many little pigs that grunted and irritated with their grunts, you could slaughter them. You could slaughter your feelings as you slaughtered a pig. Language was all you needed. It was like a knife. It knifed your feelings clean and proper, and put an end to any pop, pop, pop in your head. Perhaps we would do better if we were educated. For the time being we weren't going to say a word to anybody. Not a word.

The author is speaking to us directly, telling us what it was like when he and the others were, as boys, still merely creatures of feeling, ones with no ready words. It was a time when "the big feeling pushed up all the little feelings we had received in other places." No sensations, nothing sensed could be named accurately: "We had to say something was like something else." Things went "pop, pop, pop in your head" until you learned other people's speech. If we make the effort to recall our own childhood, we can remember similar situations. And we may have learned, too, as Lamming repeatedly says, that language kills feelings and produces talk that, as social speech, lacks meaning in the sense of its relation to personal experience.

CRITICAL FOCUS

Try this two-minute experiment in introspection. It will show you how sensations and ideas are and are not pegged to words.

1. Closely examine some object you take from your pocket or purse.
2. *In silence* for one minute note as many of its details of size, shape, color, texture, composition, weight, smell, etc., as you can.
3. Concentrate on the use of the object for a few seconds.

4. Write down as fast as you can—if not in class, just speak out—all
   the words that you can find to describe *everything* that you have
   been aware of during those two minutes: every detail of the object
   noted, every sound heard, every uncomfortable sensation, every
   memory however fragmentary, every silly impulse.

Result: You may not have been able even to follow directions. Your
list of words is probably disappointingly flat and dull. You have
discovered there are not enough words to tell *all* that flashed into your
awareness.

Explanation: The human attention span is only seconds long. We
become distracted and, therefore, unable to keep track of all that
passes through our mind. This condition is the basis of "stream-of-
consciousness" writing, which involves a special and psychologically
realistic use of language.

As any attempt at introspection suggests, the process of connotative thinking resembles a swiftly dissolving welter of memories, strange
images, impulses, and desires—even physical sensations and changes
(as also in reading poetry). If the expressions giving rise to such a
process are related to pleasant experiences and sensations, this mélange
may turn into a delightful daydream. If, on the contrary, they are harsh
and painful, they give rise to fears and concerns that, like nightmares
which resist being shaken off, can trouble us deeply.

Shakespeare's dramas offer many instances of this kind of connotative thinking and its effects. Macbeth, for example, after having
commissioned the murder of Banquo, pretends to miss Banquo's presence at the evening banquet. When Macbeth becomes conscious of the
import of the words he is uttering to the guests—"Were the graced
person of our Banquo present"—he imagines that he sees the ghost of
Banquo seated at the table; and, as the audience are meant to, they feel
a chill. Lady Macbeth in the sleep-walking scene reveals that she is
obsessed with the foul associations of the murder of King Duncan,
when she speaks of "blood" on her hands.

We must postpone discussion of how connotation relates to
myth, but it can be said here that some terms have gathered centuries
of historic connotation. One such is "The Fall." Originally, it referred to
the account in *Genesis* of the transgression of Adam and Eve. In the
long passage of time, its signification has expanded to include much of
the mystery of life and human nature. Milton's great epic, *Paradise
Lost,* and Albert Camus's existential novel, *The Fall,* represent only
extremes of the connotations as well as the denotations implicit in that

ancient term. These two works alone take us from Paradise and Hell to the streets and canals of modern Amsterdam, wherein *sin, judgment,* and *penitence* take on most somber shades for contemporary man.

It may seem surprising, but laughter also springs from the connotative process, as it does in this description of the fox by Josh Billings, the humorist of whom Abraham Lincoln said, "Next to William Shakespeare, Josh Billings is the greatest judge of human nature the world has ever seen."

The fox is a fleshy-minded sinner, and his blandness is too much for the quaintness of the goose, the melancholy reserve of the turkey, or the pompous rhetoric of the rooster. They all kneel to the logic of his tongue and find themselves at rest in his stomach.

He loves lambs and green peas—but will discount the peas rather than lose his dinner—and will go a mile and a half out of his way to be polite to a duck or a gosling.

But the most lively trait of the fox is his cunning. He always pettifogs his own case and wins a great deal oftener than he loses. Foxes are not like men, critters of habit. They never do a thing twice with the same figures, and often alter their mind before they do a thing once. This is the effect of too much genius.

There is this difference between genius and common sense in a fox: Common sense is governed by circumstances, but circumstances is governed by genius.

The fox has no moral honesty, but he has got a great supply of political honesty. If another fox in his parish wants a fat goose, he will work hard and get the goose for him, and then clean the meat all off from the outskirts of the goose for pettifogging the case, and give him the bones, and tell his political friend, with a smile in the left corner of his eye, that "everything is lovely and the goose hangs high."

Foxes have learnt this piety from watching the men get geese from each other, and if animals don't want their piety to get sour, they must keep away from the men weekdays. The fox is too much of a politician to invest his religion in any such indigenous trash. He knows that society has claims on him, for some goose, and expects to have for several more.

Foxes come out of the ground through the instrumentality of a hole, but whether the hole begins at the surface and runs into the mountain, or whether it begins in the mountain and runs to the surface don't make a cussed bit of difference.

But philosophers have argued about this hole business for years.

Some of them say it runs in and some of them be darned if it does.
While they stand fighting at the mouth of the hole, the fox is stealing their ducks and goslings.

Foxes are like cunning men—they have but few brains and but a
small place to keep them in, but what few they have got are like
angleworms in hot water—full of anxiety and misery.

Cunning is a branding iron—the letters on it are small but always
red-hot.

Josh Billings relied upon incongruous associations for his
humor—associations arising from the connotations of terms, such as
those in the opening paragraph. To begin with, he calls the fox *a
fleshy-minded sinner,* a term which generally has moralistic meanings.
To call the fox *a sinner* is humorous, since we know that morality
cannot be ascribed to an animal, but we come to this conclusion only
after we have pictured to ourselves images of a *fleshy-minded sinner*
who lusts for pleasures of the flesh. *Blandness* suggests the sly, matter-
of-fact hunting and killing of the fox and contributes to the smile we
give to the connotations of the other terms for the victims of the fox.

Humor arises from the unexpected relationships shown between
things generally regarded as dissimilar, when that relationship is expressed with the concise aptness of wit. We can picture the fox going *a
mile and a half out of his way to be polite to a duck or a gosling.* And in
cunning, we might not expect the fox to be superior to man, but Josh
Billings attributes the fox with brilliance, even *genius.* The fox has
political honesty, which Billings associates with political cunning as
shown in the crafty tricks of the *pettifogger,* an inferior lawyer who
resorts to tricks to win his case. This humor is often satirical in its
comparisons of terms having rich connotations, as in the case of *Foxes
have learnt this "piety":* a term suggesting religious sincerity but which
here implies foxy cunning, which, Billings implies, is superior to the
intellectualism of philosophers. It is clear that for Billings the term
philosophers held unfavorable connotations, which here again contributes to the humor and satire of the description, and we find that on the
whole this little essay is as much a meditation upon human nature as it
is upon the fox.

An often bewildering power of connotation to affect our behavior may easily delude us. It can lead us into thinking that the mere
conferring of a name gives to the referent all the traits denoted and
connoted by that name. In *Science and Sanity,* a pioneer work on

semantics, Alfred Korzybski called this error the *mistaking the map for the territory.*

In today's terminology-conscious civilization, patients suffering only slightly from mental illness will often despair on hearing the label of *schizophrenic, manic-depressive,* or *psychotic* applied to themselves. In Thomas Hardy's novel *Tess of the d'Urbervilles,* the heroine's troubles start when her father begins acting like a lord after learning that his ancestors once had enjoyed a title. This mistaking of the name of a thing for the thing itself lies at the root of much faulty reasoning, as we shall see in Chapter 5, The Language of Logic.

How the reader can learn to recognize and to question effectively the language of those who would convince us that the map is the territory will be taken up in the next three chapters. Each will deal with specific areas of language as they affect our general culture and especially our pocketbooks, our education, our politics, and our mass media sources of information.

CRITICAL FOCUS

Connotation is the sum of the implied or suggested meanings a word has. It also describes the power of words to make us see, feel, hear, taste, smell, or otherwise sense things not physically present. Connotation can be private or general.

What Connotation Does:

1. It creates images in the imagination.
2. It may lead to emotional thinking.
3. It draws upon the associative resources of language.
4. It can awaken memories and their related ideas and feelings, both pleasant and unpleasant.

Exercise 21   Discussion. What reasons can you give for such euphemisms, or shifts in titles, as those listed below—changes that have affected concepts but not the referent? Can you suggest others? (For example, a place where liquors are sold to be drunk on the premises—here the *referent*—was once called a *saloon;* now, since Prohibition, the same kind of place is called a *tavern,* a more dignified term.)

janitor—maintenance engineer
garbage man—sanitary engineer

undertaker—embalmer, mortician
scrub woman—housekeeper
hair dresser—beautician, hair stylist
night watchman—building custodian
publicity agent—public relations counselor
stock salesman—investment counselor
stock broker—account executive
traveling salesman—company representative
grocery store—supermarket
motel—inn, motor lodge
bill—statement

Exercise 22   Discussion. What are the possibilities that a person chosen as one of the following may take the title as meaning all it seems to say?

May Queen	Miss City	Mr. Republican
Rose Queen	Miss State	Mr. Democrat
Cheese Queen	Miss America	Mr. America
Harvest Queen	Miss Appleweek	Mrs. America

Exercise 23   Written assignment. What does each of the following groups of "favorite" connotative words suggest to you about the character or personality of the person who compiled it?

1. Cabin, sugar, country, depression, cookie, lake, pasture, train, mountain range, leaf, perfume, clay, dream, picnic, gooseberry, catfish, autumn, twilight, fire
2. Candle, cadaver, stump, syllogism, ponderous, propinquity, carnation, peanuts, cytoplasm, pipe, philander, scent, death, black knit, machine, master
3. Sea, harbor, hilltop, sub, cop, high school, main street, runaway, senseless, cosmetics, naked, Hollywood, bus, parking lot, under the table, drag, censor, decency
4. Sundeck, tow, filch, marble, glacier, cabin, starlight, deep freeze, exhaust, orchid, slattern, mope, drag, high, translucent, tendril, febrile, procession, Lent, crocus

Exercise 24   Written assignment. Make up a list of connotative words having significant connotation for you. Explain in one paragraph why one of these words particularly affects you.

Exercise 25   Written assignment. Walt Whitman had no lofty opinion of pre–Civil War politicians. Select three terms from his description of convention delegates, and describe the images and sensations you associate with each. (Warning: Some have since changed their meanings.)

> [They] were, seven-eighths of them, the meanest kind of bawling and blowing office-holders, office-seekers, pimps, malignants, contractors, kept-editors, spaniels, well trained to carry and fetch, jobbers, infidels, disunionists, terrorists, mail-riflers, slavecatchers, pushers of slavery, creatures of the President, creatures of would-be Presidents, spies, bribers, compromisers, lobbyers, spongers, ruined sports, expelled gamblers, policy-backers, monte-dealers, duellists, carriers of concealed weapons, deaf men, pimpled men, scarred inside with vile disease, gaudy outside with gold chains made from the people's money and harlots' money, twisted together, crawling, serpentine men, the lousy combings and born freedom-sellers of the earth.

Exercise 26   Writing a paragraph. Here are a number of thematic sentences to help you develop awareness of how connotative words create their impact on readers. First, read through all the statements. Second, select three that most appeal to you and quickly jot down words and phrases that carry out the theme, setting, or action. Third, take the most promising one and write at least one paragraph which adequately develops your theme. Remember, you want concrete nouns and strong verbs that stir feelings and arouse images. Rewrite to improve word choice and economy of language.

1. The elevator door opened on a grim scene.
2. She peered out from behind the living-room curtains to watch the two, who thought no one saw them.
3. The boy stood on the riverbank frantically listening to the gasps and splashings of his friend out in deep water.
4. It was a moldy dirt-floor basement jammed with junk.
5. Her father looked just the way he talked on the telephone.
6. After the first few minutes, I knew I was seeing only an imitation of an Italian art movie.
7. When we were on the very top, the ferris wheel stopped, and our seat began to rock.

8. There's something about a banana split.
9. You could tell before going into the place just what the food would be like.
10. At the next stop, they somehow jammed a half dozen more into the car.
11. It was supposed to be a basketball game.
12. He was in pretty bad shape by the time we got him into the house.
13. His sister was a shy little elf.
14. We were caught in the traffic jam caused by the freight train with the hot box.
15. "This must be a dream," I thought.
16. All systems are "Go!"
17. Let's face it. It'll be a typical family dinner.
18. He always said, "I just take a drink to be sociable."
19. When you're never more than a substitute and used only in football scrimmages, you sometimes wonder why you keep trying.
20. Still, they call it "music."

Exercise 27   Discussion assignment. (*a*) Point out which of these statements are primarily denotative and which are primarily connotative; (*b*) explain whether each is adequate in what it does.

1. *Happiness Is a Warm Puppy.*
2. An executive is any person charged with administrative responsibilities who hires other people to do his work.
3. *A Friend Is Someone Who Likes You.*
4. Obsolescence is when anything wears out.
5. *A Hole Is to Dig.*
6. Pop art is a kind of art of the absurd wherein collages reflect the chaotic hodgepodge of everyday reality and our wild daydreams by combining everything from worn-out socks to soup cans and wadded newspapers.
7. "A Pop-Top Holiday is anywhere you take the Schlitz. . . . They open in your hands."
8. "What do you call a wagon with a 5-year or 50,000-mile warranty? A product of Chrysler Corporation."
9. "Love is where you find it."
10. Good is "the greatest happiness for the greatest number."
11. The art of conversation consists in blending wit, thought, and imagination in a pleasurable ratio.

12. To me a symphony means the building of a *world* with every technical means available.—*Gustave Mahler.*
13. Sonic boom is a scientific name for the house-shaking crash that shatters nerves, makes dogs howl and children cover their ears and scream, causes real estate values to drop to nothing, and turns dreams into nightmares.
14. Insecticides are not bug killers but rather stream polluters, fish killers, song bird silencers, and food poisoners.
15. "Home is where the heart is."

Exercise 28   Discussion assignment. What connotative meanings do the following borrowed foreign words have that are lacking in the English equivalents? (Make your own additions to the list.)

chef—cook	*olé!*—Hurrah!
maître d'hôtel—headwaiter	crepes suzette—pancakes
coiffure—hairdo	*garçon*—waiter
les girls—young women	*couture*—dress style
chapeau—hat	chic—stylish
chauffeur—driver	*au revoir*—good by

Exercise 29   Discussion assignment. In the light of the following remarks and definition by a social psychologist, which denotations of the term *religion* do you think should be included in a dictionary entry? Is there a difference between defining words and defining things?

Recently I sent a questionaire to social scientists studying religion asking them for a definition of it. Of the 68 replies no two were exactly alike, though they could be roughly classified into six groups. Some emphasized the supernatural, others values, still others institutions and creeds, others theology, and so on. . . . In general I think of religion as, most characteristically, the inner experience of the individual as he apprehends a Beyond, especially as he strives to harmonize his life with the Beyond.

Exercise 30   Written assignment. Select one published criticism each of a book, a movie, and a television program. Show by detail, example, comparison, and contrast which excels in clarity and effectiveness of denotative and connotative diction.

Exercise 31   Essay assignment. Analyze each of the terms in the following definition of *liberal education,* and write an essay amplifying and illustrating the definition. If any term seems too broad or vague to you, restate the definition in your own terms and make it the basis of your essay.

> Liberal education is a kind of broad education that frees men of the limitations of ignorance, prejudice, and provincialism.

Exercise 32   Essay assignment. First, analyze the denotative meanings and possible connotations of the terms contained in this letter addressed to the editor of a mass-circulation magazine by a college dean. Take care to keep all meanings strictly related to the context. Second, write an objective summary of your analysis. Third, conclude with your own clearly stated views on the subject.

Morality

J. Robert Moskin's article, *Morality USA,* is timely and first-rate. In the article, I am quoted as being pleased that women nowadays are becoming more independent for many reasons, including the new birth-control information, and that women and men seem to be in a more open, healthier state of comradeship and friendship than be in a more open, healthier state of comradeship and friendship than ever before.

No sensible adult in our society, least of all a college dean, favors or encourages free love. But if we are to develop a sensible and workable code of sexual behavior, we need to see these matters as they are. Our code of sexual behavior must be based less on authority and fear, and more on making clear to our students the social wisdom behind the old rules, the personal consequences of deep emotional involvement, and the enduring value of personal dignity and self-discipline. In all this, I deeply believe that the new found independence and strengthening position of women will, in the long run, turn out to be a force, not for the further deterioration of our moral standards, but for their improvement.

Exercise 33   Written assignment. List the various contextual connotations for expressions and terms such as *the faults of man* in this poem by Thomas Campion. Show also how denotation and connotation intermingle in poetry.

Never Love Unless You Can

Never love unless you can
Bear with all the faults of man;
Men sometimes will jealous be,
Though but little cause they see,
   And hang the head, as discontent,
   And speak what straight they will repent.

Men that but one saint adore
Make a show of love to more;
Beauty must be scorned in none,
Though but truly served in one;
   For what is courtship but disguise?
   True hearts may have dissembling eyes.

Men when their affairs require
Must a while themselves retire,
Sometimes hunt, and sometimes hawk,
And not ever sit and talk.
   If these and such like you can bear,
   Then like, and love, and never fear.

chapter **2**

IMAGE AND AUDIENCE

ADVERTISING: MEDIA, AGENCY, AND CORPORATE IMAGE

Ours has been called the age of *image* and *image makers*. These are terms as rich in connotation as they are vague in denotation. They also represent the *jargon*, the technical terminology, of advertising professionals, whose skills in language we are going to survey. Represented by the advertising executives and public relations counselors of Madison Avenue in New York and Michigan Avenue in Chicago, advertising is a huge American industry. Its more than 13 billion dollar a year "products" affect every one of us in terms of our daily bread, jobs, health, politics, morals, and amusements.

We can begin our inquiry by building on what we have already learned about language in general: how words define and suggest the meanings of human experience. The language of advertising provides a good test of critical thinking, for it demands the following abilities of the reader:

1. To grasp accurately what is said
2. To restate it objectively
3. To evaluate its worth
4. To suggest alternatives
5. To propose fresh, creative approaches
6. To express these matters clearly and concisely in written form
7. To perceive the writer's real intent

Let us start by defining the key terms of this chapter. *Image* in the advertising denotation means a public concept of something or someone that embodies traits and features typical of a class of consumers, a product, a corporation, or a public figure. The *image makers* are the advertising and public relations agencies that dream up both the image and the selling campaign that goes with it. The largest American agencies are now establishing offices in Europe, Asia, South America, and Africa on the principle that "commerce follows communication." They employ every semantic device of picture, symbol, sign, sound, and word to endow everything from dog foods to political candidates with a readily recognizable "personality" designed to appeal to the buyer. And every segment of the mass media engaged in the battle for the advertising dollar boasts that its powers of image peddling are unexcelled.

Magazines, newspapers, radio, and television are the big competitors for the tobacco, beverage, and cosmetic advertising budgets. The magazines and the newspapers especially have images of their own, reflecting a highly sophisticated awareness of markets. Their bids for advertisements appear in trade journals aimed at the agencies.

Here are a few. "*Seventeen Magazine* is read by 3 out of 4 teen-age girls in the U.S.A. . . . [every one] a buyer, gift receiver, family influencer, bride and homemaker." *Life* boasts that it reaches over one-fourth of all adults in the country. And *Reader's Digest* maintains that each month it enters almost two-fifths of our households. It tells prospective advertisers: "The average advertising page in *Reader's Digest* is looked at more than 60 million times." A single article on filter cigarettes, it says, "changed the nation's smoking habits virtually overnight," and another article made the auto seat belt a success. Another periodical modestly states: "A fresh approach to the contemporary executive market . . . 21% of all corporate officers, directors, owners, partners, and general managers in the U.S. earning $25,000 a year or more read *Sports Illustrated* each week."

Presumably, all of these figures and claims, creating images of media efficacy, have been compiled by statisticians on data brought in by trained pollsters making survey researches, much in the same manner as they do for political popularity standings. Now, before going into just what their image is of us as buyers and consumers of these many products, let us first look at the corporate image of the product makers.

"The dominant image of the corporate leadership today is that of the responsible trustee," we are told. Through the widespread sale of their stock, and through combines with component industries, corporations have become impersonal. Through radical changes in executives, corporations may from one year to the other change almost completely in image. It is understandable that some would hold with the famous *gaffe:* "What is good for General Motors is good for the country." There is no doubt that the corporate image can be that of a giant:

> In 1955 the 200 top non-financial companies—most of which dominated their respective industries as price and policy leaders—directly owned 43.0 per cent of the total assets of 435,000 non-financial corporations; this amounted to at least 18.3 per cent of the total national reproducible tangible assets of $891 billion.

Every corporation of this size strives to create a favorable image of itself in the public eye, and does so by means of *institutional* advertisements. It tries to show how its products and facilities benefit the country as well as maintain the stability of the company. Since the institutional advertisement does not sell any particular product, it often appears to be instructional, but its purpose is really promotional in that it aims at conditioning and influencing public thought.

Here is a typical one. It features a picture of a beautiful Northwest forest clearing with a stump in the foreground surrounded by seedling trees. On the stump, a chipmunk is shown being watched by a family of curious skunks while it rips into a seed cone. As a critical reader, what do you make of the language of the headline and the *copy* or text? Is there any "special pleading" or asking for preferential treatment?

How Many Trees Can a Chipmunk Eat?

This pert little ruffian is making his dinner off what otherwise might be useful trees about 80 years from now. Like much of the wildlife that thrives on Weyerhaeuser tree farms, he is a delight to see in the woods. Nevertheless, he and his brethren are a real hazard in this complex business of growing timber as a crop. From scampering squirrels to lumbering bears, they do away with untold bushels of tree seed and damage several thousand young trees every year.

There are other hazards, too. Fire that destroys decades of work. Tree-killing insects and diseases that require heavy investments to control. All of these risks are compounded by the fact that it takes up to 80 years to grow a new tree crop to merchandisable size.

Intensive research and extensive forest protection practices have done a lot to bring some of these risks under control. Even so, tree farming simply isn't practical unless the nation's tax structure takes such long-range risks into account. Congress recognized this in 1944. It then adopted tax legislation specifically intended to provide fair and equitable treatment for all who grow trees as a commercial crop.

Result? More than 27 thousand individuals and firms now grow timber as a crop on private lands—totalling some 64 million acres. These lands are a perpetual source of payrolls and taxes as well as water, recreation and wildlife. They also are the nation's primary source of wood for building materials, pulp, paper, plastics, rayon and many other essential products.

Future generations must not be denied these benefits. Tree farming must continue to be encouraged by a realistic tax climate.

The startling question of a chipmunk's appetite for trees arouses reader curiosity, as does calling him *pert little ruffian*. Yet he and other wildlife, though delightful to see, endanger Weyerhaeuser tree farms by eating "untold bushels" of tree seed, just as apparently the skunks and the *lumbering* bears (this must be an unintentional pun) damage large numbers of young trees each year. Additional details of risks and expenses suggest that the "80 years to grow a new tree crop" are full of hazards despite all modern protective practices.

But if tree farming is to remain a practical economic enterprise, it must continue to have the benefit of the kind of tax legislation that thousands of private tree-farm operators now enjoy. Five general benefits accruing to the country from such farms are listed as essential. The piece concludes with the imperative: "Tree farming must continue to be encouraged by a realistic tax climate." It appears that this one firm has assumed the role of spokesman for all others engaged in the same business. On the whole, it is a persuasive advertisement, full of appeals and warning, yet appreciative of present tax support.

In relation to the bright illustration, the connotations of such expressions as *pert little ruffian, wildlife thrives, complex business, tree farm, merchandisable size, perpetual source of payrolls and taxes as well as water, recreation and wildlife,* and *realistic tax climate* are highly effective. Yet the mood, or tone, of the piece is forced, and sentimental readers especially may dislike thinking the cute chipmunk could be a destroyer who has to have a whole industry allied against him. On the whole, the piece exemplifies what Madison Avenue appropriately calls "the soft sell."

As this advertisement shows and the experts admit, it is very difficult to determine just what results even the most carefully prepared institutional "message" may have. How many readers would be tempted by the headline to read on far enough to make out the desired image? That we readers also have various images will be shown in the next section.

CRITICAL FOCUS

*All organs of the mass media have their own images
as persuaders of consumers. So do great corporations. Advertising
and public relations agencies attempt to create and foster
favorable images.*

Exercise 1   Essay assignment. Examine several issues of a magazine to determine its image, considering the kind of advertisements and the language and subject matter of its articles, stories, editorials, etc. Write an essay to show that image and to classify and describe the features contributing to it. You may want to choose one representative item and point out how it illustrates the general features you found.

Exercise 2   Report assignment. Bring two advertisements to class, one in color and one in black and white. Be prepared to discuss these points: (*a*) What effective use is made of color? (*b*) Are some colors better than others for certain products, e.g., cosmetics, cars, soaps? (*c*) What effective use is made of black and white? (*d*) In each case, does the color add connotation of any kind to the words? (*e*) What kinds of pictures are more effective in black and white than in color?

Exercise 3   Report assignment. An advertisement may have these three parts: illustration, headline, and copy. If it has all three parts, it is called a *standard;* if no illustration, an *all-type;* and if no body text, a *poster.* Bring to class one example of each of these three types. Be prepared to explain the comparative degree of effectiveness of each part in adding to denotation and connotation.

Exercise 4   Discussion assignment. What connotations do brand or corporation names such as the following hold for you?

Heinz	Lady Clairol	American Motors
Kleenex	Polaroid	Zenith
Kraft	Kodak	Minute Maid
Dial	General Motors	RCA
Green Giant	Marlboro	Bell Telephone
Levi	Prudential	General Foods
Keds	Rockefeller Foundation	Ford Foundation

Exercise 5   Special written report. Container Corporation of America sponsors an unusual kind of institutional advertisement series under the general title of "Great Ideas of Western Man." Each one features an original work of art as an illustration of a quotation from some famous thinker. Find at least one of these advertisements, and describe how the denotative and connotative meanings of the quotation are expressed and enhanced by the art work. Comment also on what kind of corporate image this series suggests to you.

Exercise 6   Essay assignment. The following advertisement occupied a full page in at least one magazine having a national circulation. Read the language carefully for its denotation and possible connotation. Frame a thesis sentence summing up your judgment of the view expressed. (You may wish to check your first draft for the seven abilities required of a critical reader, as listed on page 35.)

Attention, Belief, and Believing Action

A point we should not overlook in this review is that readers regard *Good Housekeeping* as a magazine to be *believed*. This probably requires little elaboration except to say that sometimes we seem to treat this as a limited or negative thing, when in fact it goes much further.

Our virtue is not simply that we do not print things which ought to be *dis*believed; it is even more that we incorporate positively a great deal that deserves attention and then belief and finally believing action. Such items range from "Houston's Quiet Victory" to "What Women Really Think About Their Doctors"; from Dr. Carl Jung's "Why I Believe in God" to Dr. John Rock's "We Can End the Battle Over Birth Control!"

Believability, then, cannot be to us just an absence of lies as legislated by the technicians of the Good Housekeeping Institute in recognition of the consumers' guaranty; it must be a courageous and activist presentation of facts and ideas which deserve positive belief and the support of believing people.

(The above is an excerpt from an internal memorandum dated March 19, 1961, from Editor Wade Nichols to the editorial and advertising staffs of *Good Housekeeping*. Its purpose was to restate the basic editorial platform of the magazine. *Good Housekeeping* feels it provides an insight, possibly of public interest, into the magazine's continuing editorial policies and functions as interpreted by its editor.)

Exercise 7   Essay assignment. Analyze this Union Oil Company of California advertisement for its institutional character. Read it carefully several times so that you can include an objective summary in your written analysis. Is every denotative meaning clear? Is there any use of connotation? (If your instructor so recommends, you might try paraphrasing the piece in simple, idiomatic language.) Suggested order for the essay: brief introduction with statement of your judgment as thesis sentence, objective summary, points of your agreement or disagreement and their supporting details, conclusion ending with your strongest point.

THE FUNDAMENTAL FREEDOM

Without It, All Your Other Freedoms Are in Jeopardy

Every schoolboy in America is familiar with the freedoms guaranteed by our Bill of Rights—Freedom of Worship, Freedom of Speech, Freedom of Assembly, etc. But there is one more freedom without which all of our other freedoms would be put in serious jeopardy.

That freedom is ECONOMIC FREEDOM—the right of private citizens to own property; to buy and sell their goods and services on the free market; and to enjoy the rewards of their economic efforts as they see it—all without undue restraint or control by our government.

If a government assumes a dominant role in the economic activity of a country—as it does under socialism or communism or dictatorships—it immediately gains the power to grant or withhold from the individual citizen the basic economic requirements of food, clothing and shelter.

For such a government can tell you—*what* work you will do, *where* you will do it, and *how much* you will be paid. In fact, it must do so in order to implement its national economic planning. Once a government has this economic control, it can control every other aspect of your life. And history proves that sooner or later it does so.

Consequently, there can be no enduring liberty and freedom for the individual without a reasonably free economy. That is, a society in which the bulk of the economic activity is carried on by private enterprise operating in a free market. A free economy is a *fundamental* freedom. Without it most, if not all, of the other freedoms granted by our Bill of Rights would eventually be taken from us.

IMAGE OF THE CONSUMER

Across a double-page spread in the Sunday newspaper, banner headlines proclaim: "Giant Warehouse Clearance Sale! This One Day Special—3 rooms of furniture for only $169!!" This advertisement brings, among others, a furniture-desperate pair of newlyweds to the scene of the sale. On inquiry, they are led to a shoddy, flimsy sofa and chair, a warehouse-scarred bed and chest of drawers, but no mattress: "3 rooms of furniture." After the first disappointment, they are shown and sold a $400 bedroom set for $600. As they leave already worried about the payments, they do not know that they have fallen for a "bait ad" and are victims of a "switch sale." The salesman who closed the deal with every pressure he could exert may be proud of his "hard sell," or will at least rationalize and excuse it with some variation of the old proverb: *Caveat emptor!*—Let the buyer beware!

Our young couple have become *consumers,* for there is little doubt that they will "utilize an instrument of production in such a way that it becomes less efficient with respect to future uses." We are all such consumers. Our clothes, cars, books, records, and homes gradually become "less efficient." Like the young couple, in buying our things we may also at some time or other have been victimized. It is very human to respond to the natural drives and impulses that make us the complex creatures that we are. And it is this emotional, impulsive—often compulsive—nature that advertising aims to utilize.

"Our class had 21% fewer cavities. . . . It's a lively one! Turn 'er on! . . . Smoke light, smoke mild. . . . Only her hairdresser knows for sure." Under the pressure of such slogans, we consumers go on buying the products that keep production lines moving and paychecks well-ventilated. All of us operate according to our basic human needs, the psychologists tell Madison Avenue agencies. Our *id*, which consists of all the biological impulses inherited from our ancestors, greatly troubles our *ego*, the reasoning and self-reflective part of us; the *ego* is often restricted by its conscience or censoring activity, the *superego*.

It is this image of man as a confusion of impulses, thoughts, fantasies, dreams, desires, and guilts that commercial promotion projects as the consumer. What is *commercial promotion?*

> [It] aims to pave the way for the sale of goods or services by making . . . [them] seem more desirable to the potential buyer. This objective involves influencing and conditioning the mind of the prospect in much the same way as agencies with other purposes— home, press, classroom, pulpit, courts, political forums, legislative halls, and government agencies for information.

It is such promotion that makes the Coca Cola emblem one that the sun never sets on, or that has us telling ourselves, "It's Pepsi—for those who think young."

Terms for classifying the forces within us that motivate our actions are vague, but we may speak of the *visceral* drives, such as hunger, the need to breathe, thirst, sex, and bodily comfort; *social* drives, such as desire for approval, recognition, amusement, superiority; and *superego* or *transcendent* drives, such as those for identification, love, mysticism, and art. Put all together, they make the complex *image* that few advertisements ever show. Mostly the visceral provides the appeal, as in this one: A flaming redhead model is portrayed holding an orange in one hand; below the full-color illustration the headline asks: "Who made the orange more tempting than the apple?" The reply comes immediately: "Smirnoff did it—with the famous Smirnoff Screwdriver." So visceral urges combine with a superego myth to sell a brand of vodka.

"Let your neighbors see what kind of up-and-go executive you really are, even if you can't quite afford it! Drive a fast-scat Buick!" The desire for recognition and status is the same one that makes waving lotions and curlers as necessary in the home as the third car in the carport. On the other hand, the same urges that make us desire also seem to give rise to our fears. For every desire, there appears to be a corresponding fear. (See page 62 for a list of paired political promises and threats corresponding to desires and fears.) Insurance companies of all kinds harp on the basic fears of loss of life, security, and protection for family. As a result of insurance advertising, it has been said, women own a large percentage of the country's wealth as widows. Yet insurance policies enable millions of men to sleep more securely at night, "knowing that their loved ones have been taken care of—if." One has visions of car wrecks and bathroom falls, cancer, heart attacks, and all the other melancholy facts of life constantly thrust at him to buy "protection." Scares such as the famous "Always a bridesmaid . . . never a bride" have made many a girl hurry out to buy Listerine and also rush into a marriage just "to be married."

The *consumer image* which is supposed to reflect our personalities usually is only a stereotype. In the television toothpaste and detergent one-minute "dramas," we readily see the stereotype at work. It consists of a few superficial traits of behavior and appearance that are supposed to suggest "average" human beings. The drama is set in the house of a "blue-collar worker," or perhaps even in the kitchen of a "white-collar worker's" home. Wife, husband, and family-dominating children make up the cast. All take most seriously or most happily— depending upon the product—the warnings or the discoveries of the salesman delivering the message. If a character tag-line should become notorious enough to be featured by a television comedian—"Mother, please! I'd rather do it myself!"—the consumer may by that time be so conditioned that he will select the brand item from among its dazzling competitors in supermarket displays. If he does, he has been affected by stereotype images ridiculing his own image of himself.

The consumer may do well to realize that some in the industry regard him as "the enemy" or, at least, "the prey":

> We must break through the attention barrier. The reader is in a hurry. . . . How do we reach him? How do we capture his attention? To every layout, every headline, every illustration, every type face, every lead sentence, every box of summarized points, indeed, to every choice of word, we must bring these questions.

This basic view leads to an effective headline such as this: "Every lady should carry an automatic." Not a firearm, but an automatic camera. Another copywriter for a science magazine recalls his John Milton and captions an electronic color shot of a laser light beam: "Working the light fantastic." Then there is the subtly punning lead such as this one for a "beauty" soap: "Sweet Heart is pure. Not many soaps can say that to your face."

With agency fees running about 15 per cent of the advertising budget, the corporations footing the bill have good reasons to demand results. To sell the products pouring out of their factories and to keep employment high and stockholders content, executives adopt bold policies. The head of one firm, which has been highest among the 100 national advertisers in advertising–sales-dollar ratio, has expressed his company's aggresive policy thus:

1. Make a better product—sold at mass-premium prices and distributed through all possible outlets.
2. Develop a sales force so aggressive they could sell steam heat at the equator.
3. Back salesmen with mass-media advertising—but be sure it's the most effective money can buy.
4. Recognize that the public itself is willing to change, and motivate the public to your brand.

But all these pressured selling tactics have aroused considerable reaction, as the following list of popular book titles indicates:

Vance Packard	*The Hidden Persuaders*
	The Waste Makers
	The Naked Society
J. K. Galbraith	*The Affluent Society*
William Whyte	*The Organization Man*
D. J. Boorstin	*The Image*
Kenneth E. Boulding	*The Image*

Other critics are aroused by the impression that our advertising, like our movies, may be making abroad:

The foreigner's view of the United States has been created in large part by the advertising industry, and by the mass media it has captured, like television, or very nearly captured, like daily press. The advertising industry is the force behind a monstrous mass of anti-intellectualism that inevitably seeps over our borders and comes to epitomize us abroad.

Occasionally a member of the Federal Communications Commission may protest against what has been called "the wasteland" of television programs and excessive commercials, and investigating committees may complain about rating systems. But it appears that the critical reader will have to continue being also his own critical viewer.

There are sporadic attempts on the part of the advertising industry to draw up reform codes urging amendment of language practices on the air and in print. They criticize abuses such as *real* in *real good, miracle* in *miracle deodorant, funtastic, fantabulous,* and what one writer calls the "pneumatic drill school" *fast . . . fast . . . fast relief!* They worry about "piggyback" parades of tortured headaches, bad breaths, and exploited childhood—all pushed on the principle that "The lost sale is like the baby that was never born." They continue to draw up solemn codes, but the industry, being the kind it is, will remain at the mercy of whatever new innovation in picture and language will capture the consumer and his pocketbook.

As one observer has remarked, in our country, where all the networks are privately owned and operated, only the people themselves can bring about lasting improvements:

> The distinction between political liberty and cultural liberty, or taste, worked out well when the issue arose of government control over any of the mass media. Since the political supposedly had nothing to do with the cultural, business interests could in effect say to the government: "Mind your own business! The vote that elected you to office was for political matters. For cultural things the people themselves decide. They use another vote to express their choice, and their candidate is whatever they spend their dollar for."

Because of such attitudes, the programs and the commercial messages that are received in more than 50 million sets in our homes may not always be in good taste or even reliable. The agency copywriters will go on delighting in word sound and rhythm at the expense of word meaning, as when they urge, "Lavish luxury on yourself!" And if the number of Americans buying sets continues to increase at the rate of 100,000 a month, more people are going to wish they had critical skill to distinguish the meretricious from the admirable.

CRITICAL FOCUS

The language of advertising is largely the language of connotation, working in subtle ways to persuade us to believe and to buy. It employs all the resources of effective wordplay to appeal to our visceral, social, and superego or transcendent drives. The best defense against such appeals is the critical mind.

Exercise 8 Report assignment. Study the advertisements in one issue of a woman's magazine such as *Good Housekeeping, McCall's, Town & Country,* or *Seventeen.* Copy out and classify according to type of appeal every advertisement headline found in that issue. Explain how the language of the copy fits the headlines and the brand names in each case. How many different types of drives and urges are appealed to? Which type has the greatest number of advertisements? How is the image of the magazine reflected in them? How the image of the consumer?

Exercise 9 Essay assignment. Pretend that you are a citizen of a foreign country and have just finished looking through three issues of *Life* or *Look* given you by a tourist. Describe the various impressions you would have formed about American people and culture from studying the advertisements. Classify and arrange your impressions so as to give the essay unity and coherence.

Exercise 10 Written assignment. Someone—you, one of your family, a friend, neighbor—has recently purchased a car, a household appliance, or any other such expensive item. Try to determine what feelings and circumstances prompted the purchase, and what language influenced it. Write a "case history" of all that motivated the purchase in terms of the language heard and read.

Exercise 11 Report assignment. Repeat Exercise 8, this time examining the advertisements in one issue of an "outdoor" magazine aimed at male readers.

Exercise 12 Written assignment. Here are two companion advertisements that appeared in *Town & Country,* July, 1964. Choose one, and give all the connotations each of the four questions has for you. Comment also on the types of appeals.

How Can a Woman Know if She's Made for Saga Mink?
(Take the Leo Ritter Test)
1. Does your penthouse have a pug, a Picasso and a Pucci?
2. Would you buy a white sports car just to go with your tan?
3. Do you have a weakness for titles?
4. Did you ski in Scandinavia this winter and fall in love with the landscape?

How Can a Lady Tell if She's Meant for Empress Chinchilla?
1. Do you dodge opening nights in favor of previews?
2. Is your limousine British, your chauffeur Irish?
3. Does your co-op apartment face the park?
4. Would you rather have fresh flowers every day than a box at the opera?

Exercise 13   Report assignment. Study the advertisements in several issues of a science or engineering journal. Make a list of all newly coined or effectively used technical terms found in the head-lines. How does the copy support them? In at least two cases be able to show how the advertisements give the corporation an image.

Exercise 14   Essay assignment. Develop a defense of or an attack on this published statement: "Perhaps the television commercial will become a new art form, the first distinctly *American* contribution to the arts."

Exercise 15   Special written assignment. Read and study carefully the contents of any *one* issue of *Reader's Digest*. As you read, try to be aware of what different types of feelings and ideas the various articles arouse in you. Keeping alert for possible connotative language will help you. Ask yourself: "Just what does this writer want me to think or to feel?" When your notes are completed, classify and arrange the types of desires and fears you may have found aroused in the reading. Consider also how the advertisements fit the image that the magazine enjoys. *Note:* As study of the cover index will indicate, *Reader's Digest* does not print *only* articles that have appeared first in other magazines.

PUBLISHERS' IMAGES OF THE READER

As we have seen, every solvent publisher—perhaps even more so the insolvent ones—has definite notions about the economic and cultural backgrounds and tastes of his readers. From the hometown gossip sheet to the loftiest literary quarterly, the editorial staff must keep before them the complex image of those they hope to please with each issue. The choice of subject matter, approach, attitude, tone, and language depends upon the special audience envisioned.

While *New Yorker* browsers might also read *Playboy* or *Esquire* for their fiction, *Vogue, Harper's Bazaar,* or *Town & Country* sophisticates are not expected to share the same longings as do their sisters who never tire of *True Confessions. Commonweal* readers might subscribe to *Commentary,* and both could read the *Saturday Review. Partisan Review, Paris Review,* and *Hudson Review* devotees might glance at *Harper's Magazine* or *Atlantic,* should either of those publications by rarest chance grace a dentist's waiting room. But both would rather gloom over a toothache than resort to *Saturday Evening Post* or *Reader's Digest.*

It may not be difficult to note differences in reader appeals, but to find terms expressive of those differences is another matter. What are the sources, for example, of each of the following passages? Who are their readers—are you among them? What makes the language of each distinctive?

1.

It happens to everybody. You might say it's in the Christmas cards. A woman who organized her December life in mid-November, who has been pretty much keeping up with her self-directives, who has faithfully appeared at her beauty salon for accelerated holiday appointments—even that admirably collected woman comes upon one evening that starts like this. A party's an hour away, she's tired, her face shows it, and her hair can't get to the hairdresser until tomorrow. Furthermore, her obvious head-saver—her wig or hairpiece—is either out of order or just won't do for the situation at hand. Unless she moves fast and brilliantly, she is about to be no ornament in the eye of her beholding hostess. . . . Assuming that, what with their laboratories and research facilities and experience in such fast rescue work, they would have devised a system to beat the holiday syndrome, we called on Revlon for help. We took with us a face and **a** head of hair (our own) that demonstrated our premise: emergency repair work necessary. They showed us their way of coping in a half hour flat. We pass it on.

Allow at least *a half hour* for pre-party restoration. More if possible, because you'd probably be right to assume that the incandescent light you shed on her guests and her house could be more thrilling to your hostess than your punctuality.

2.

Fanny, in *Le Mal,* is not consciously vicious in spite of all the misery she causes. She flits from pleasure to pleasure in an everlasting search for happiness: "cigarettes, fine foods, stimulants, soporifics, narcotics," all take their turn in the general round of Fanny's searchings. Even rouge, powder, lipstick, and dyed hair come in for Mauriac's reproaches. They are the varnish with which women cover their outer surfaces in order to hide the spiritual poverty within. ". . . The preservation of women arouses disgust and even fear. In the young women of fifty, miraculously preserved, old age betrays itself only by a look, by a certain wavering which has its origin in the soul, by an altogether spiritual exhaustion."

3.

Existentialism's diagnosis has striking relevance in contemporary America. Wrapped in an ethnocentric cocoon, we find ourselves acting as if today's values were permanent fixtures. We are serious about trivialities (electric toothbrushes, sports cars, hair-dos), trivial about reality (life, encounter, death). We insist on convenient categorical pegs on which to hang every conception; despise uncertainty and disorder; and impose both certainty and order where none exists. So it is in suburbia, the market place, the university. Instead of real education we offer adjustment, pressing pliant human beings into patterns, filling curricula with supermarket knowledge conveniently packaged and labeled. Pat answers masquerade as truth. Some bewildered intellectuals have retreated to the eighteenth century's excessive adulation for reason. Fighting flux with formalism, they are reconciled to superficiality in every phase of life. And having only one life to live, our frightened females decide they might as well live it as a blonde.

4.

The deluge of advertising that floods the mails—and never seems so insistent as during the holiday season—sometimes infuriates by its bulk as much as it influences by its appeal. Each year the public is hit by an onslaught of 48 billion direct-mail ads, and the business of compiling mailing lists has become a highly automated industry made up of dozens of firms that spare no effort to capture another name. This year they will gross close to $1 billion rent in names and addresses to anyone who has anything to sell. Lists can be rented with the names of 221,782 doctors, 2,476 patent lawyers, 18 safety-pin makers, 41 zoos, Cadillac owners, and every American named Murphy (50,000). On the average, each mailing nets less than a 2% response, but that is enough to produce $30 billion in mail sales.

There they are: three from current magazines and one from a book of critical essays. What do we have? In the first, glossy realism and pitiless analysis of the needs and superficial yearnings of affluent women—especially those engaged in the charm struggle for pelf and influence—characterize the selection as coming from the pages of *Vogue,* which operates on this principle: "A great party is a pretty girl in a really smashing dress." Besides dropping one advertiser's name and providing apt copy for another one's dress, the piece has dry wit—*it's in the Christmas cards.* It offers a quotable clinical term that explains and justifies the pictured exhaustion—*the holiday syndrome.* The second passage, beginning with references to book title, author's name, quotation, and critical comment, indicates that it comes from a chapter or essay of literary analysis. The third one, which deplores social shallowness by pointing out notable ironies, certainly would appeal to readers of *Saturday Review,* who are culture-watchers. And the consciously incongruous items of a report—ending with mild astonishment at the dollar success of ingenious enterprise—suggests *Time* about its business of recording and viewing. Lastly, the critical reader of this book may also have wondered why its author selected just these four particular passages.

CRITICAL FOCUS

How do you fit the image that publishers may have of their readers? Again be a critical reader, and examine yourself:

1. Do you like to daydream over the contents of any magazine— its stories, pictures, articles, advertisements?
2. Do you change your way of dressing, talking, and acting to

follow the latest trends as found in popular magazines, books,
or movie and television entertainment?

3. Should you feel guilty if your answers are *yes* to such inquiries?

Exercise 16   Essay assignment. Choose one of the statements
in the passage from *The Saturday Review* (page 50) as an essay topic.
Agree or disagree with it as you wish, but develop your views with
supporting details and illustrations drawn from our life and times as
they are affected by advertisements and commercials.

Exercise 17   Essay assignment. The advertising industry
might answer criticism in such language as the following. Write a brief
essay defining the word *progress* as used in this context:

"Advertising, by establishing brand names, guarantees the quality of
widely advertised products, since, to hold his own in a highly competitive market, the manufacturer must be assured of the high
quality of his product. Advertising, by giving products nationwide
distribution, makes possible the mass production that gives consumers the best quality at the lowest possible prices. It also brings
new products to the attention of the public, products that otherwise
might never have a chance to contribute to the health and well-
being of the country. Advertising makes possible the great charitable
and health drives and campaigns on both local and national levels.
It also provides the public, at a nominal cost, with all the interesting,
informative magazines that could not exist without the organized
support of the industry. It forms the financial backbone of the newspapers on which the American people depend for news and interpretation of events. It makes possible the great range of *free*
entertainment offered by radio and television. It underwrites the
informative reports on life in all parts of the world that make television documentaries important in decision making and international
understanding. In every respect, it strengthens the free-enterprise
system that has given our country the highest standard of living
ever enjoyed by any people in history. How can anyone doubt that
advertising, on the whole, is an indispensable agent of *progress* in
our national life?"

Exercise 18   Report assignment. To show how closely advertising is related to all aspects of our daily life: (*a*) Choose a typical

issue of any one of the following types of publications; (*b*) analyze its contents and editorial views, and determine whether these are also reflected in the advertisements.

labor union	national organization
religious denomination	company "house organ"
social club or society	trade journal

chapter 3

THE LANGUAGE OF
POLITICIANS AND POLITICS

IMAGES AND POLITICIANS

Almost every kind of political activity and language is devoted to creating an image favorable in the voters' eyes, whether it be for a ballot measure or a candidate for office. Both a tax measure for a school district and a mayoralty candidate must appear in as appealing a guise as possible. The tax will be described as having highly acceptable precedents, and providing at a very minimal increase great additional benefits in bus service, athletic programs, community service, and faculty. The city hall berth seeker will exude an aura of reform, economy, and accommodating personality. Pretty girls may be necessary to make both ballot items really appealing.

Franklin D. Roosevelt, the great master of political language, as Abraham Lincoln before him, carefully preserved a political image. It is said of Lincoln that he never permitted a picture showing him smiling, although no president was better known for his humor. It is this sad Lincoln that Carl Sandburg's famous biography has enshrined as a symbol of liberator-martyr, and made a hallowed name that all ambitious politicians try to borrow. The winning Roosevelt voice in his *fireside talks* to the nation always presented the President as defender of the ordinary man against those whom he delighted to label as *economic royalists.*

The Roosevelt image shows itself in this very apt summary of his manner:

"My friends, you are interested in greater job security. You want better old age benefits, vacations with pay, and, above all, a fair living wage. We are in agreement on these objectives, I am sure.

"I mention these things because I believe in them, and I think I may have a plan which may make all of them immediately possible.

"Here is the first thing I will do. . . . Here is the second. . . . Here is how I will get this for you. . . .

"Since we all want more security now and in old age, and since I have a plan which I have shown will work, your best bet is . . . vote for me."

This basic image of trustworthy friend and protector emerged in all his pleas for public support during his slightly more than three terms in office. He constantly appealed for voter approval, citing problems and pointing to accomplishments always with promise and hope for the future of the country.

Not all the millions of such words issuing from press and radio in promotion of a national program can be called *propaganda*. This term has many meanings, but as will be seen in the course of this chapter, not all the connotations need be "bad." The millions of voters and the historians who regard President Roosevelt's efforts in behalf of his country as beneficial must consider the propaganda that publicized his program as "good" propaganda. They may not necessarily, however, approve of all the means and methods by which the program was carried out or publicized.

As does advertising, politics requires an always alert critical attention, a fact that leads some observers of the unending battles for acceptance of rival political images to speak out as has this one:

I am equally critical of Republicans and Democrats, of so-called liberals and so-called conservatives. Few and far between have been our political spokesmen who have even tried to give us the basic picture before undertaking to persuade us to adopt one view or another about it.

Frankly, I do not think it is necessary to confuse every issue, baffle every voter, throw a lot of dust in the air to win an argument or an election. I think our politicians could help educate us about economic matters while they try to persuade us. Of course, this would mean that our political leaders would have to find out for themselves just what the basic facts are before they begin to carve out issues. So much the better if they do!

Again, as with advertising, we shall examine some of the means by which this baffling, confusing, and dust-throwing are carried on.

To protect himself as a reader and listener, every citizen would do well to emulate the critical awareness that characterized the framers of our Constitution. Norman Jacobson calls them "realists," and in a fine example of critical analysis of the denotations of their constitutional language points up the evidence for this realism:

> For sustained somberness of mood, the Constitution of the United States is extraordinary. Its authors anticipated little good but mainly evil: war, universal corruption, public insolence and insubordination. Nor did they expect much else of themselves. In addition to formal checks upon the power of those in positions of responsibility and trust, provision is explicitly made against incursions into the public treasury and into the purses of kings and satraps. No sooner is the plan announced for the selection of representatives of the people and their organization into two Houses, than procedures are established for the punishment of members guilty of disorderly conduct and the expulsion of trouble-makers. And why not? Venality and recalcitrance are as natural to men as the air they breathe. . . . Beset by dangers, real and fancied, the authors of the Constitution meant their government to be frankly disciplinary and punitive. Today we call such men realists.

If a realist is one who never forgets that all men have passions that can either destroy or ennoble them, the founders of our government were realists. It is this kind of political realism that can enable us to recognize a good man when we see and hear one. And according to some, that ability itself is a worthy goal of higher education. For only such realism dares credit human nature also with the perfectible reason and the effort for basic goodness that make democratic processes possible realities as well as dreams. It posits, too, an educated, critical citizenry.

For it is not too difficult to deceive ignorant voters or those whose minds are completely governed by habit. It is true, as William James has said, that habit is the flywheel of society and so explains the marvel of Monday mornings, when the travails of commerce and education begin with another turn of the great wheel. Yet habit can blind and cripple even the well-intentioned. It rules those who go through life holding to unvarying patterns of behavior and attitudes on such matters as race, religion, labor, medical practice, and political party. It closes off many possible avenues of personal and national growth and freedom. It stamps life into inflexible stereotypes.

How the habitual responses to images and concepts that we call *stereotypes* operate in political expression is the topic of our next section.

CRITICAL FOCUS

1. *The* public image *is the attitude and manner assumed by everyone—especially politicians—whose fortunes depend upon winning the favor of the general public.*
2. *The word* propaganda *has both good and bad connotations.*
3. *The realist has the best chance of coping with wily deception and of recognizing what is truthful.*

Exercise 1   Written assignment. Describe the *public image* made by one of the following as shown in customary speech, behavior, dress, attitudes, etc.

city office holder, sheriff	woman's organization leader
governor, senator, congressman	business-community leader
student-body leader	local celebrity
religious leader	labor leader
prominent educator	local "rebel"

Exercise 2   Report assignment. *The New Yorker* features a biographical sketch called "A Profile," which is little more than the analysis of the image created by a prominent person. Outline one of these profiles, paying particular attention to how the image was fashioned and what it consists of.

Exercise 3   Essay assignment. Appraise as "good" or "bad" *propaganda* a local publicity campaign being conducted for some public figure or cause. Give detailed reasons for your stand and support the details with illustrations; compare or contrast the campaign with another analogous one.

Exercise 4   Report assignment. Read a biography of an historical political figure written for young readers and determine the image it presents. How does it compare with the one in a biography of the same person but written for adult readers? Write out your report, following some order of comparison and contrast.

STEREOTYPES AND POLITICAL EXPRESSION

Stereotypes represent oversimplifications and frozen concepts. They are found in popular sayings that are taken at full value, such as "Save the pennies and you save the dollars," "Don't count your chickens before they're hatched," "A rolling stone gathers no moss," and "A barking dog never bites." The mind that treasures them as highest wisdom is the kind who deserves G. K. Chesterton's judgment: "He died at 18 but wasn't buried until 65."

Stereotypes, often expressed through clichés, pass for standard conviction on any controversial topic:

> Like mother, like daughter.
> Never trust one behind your back.
> See one and you see 'em all.
> It takes one to know one.
> You want your sister to marry one?
> There are three ways to do anything: the right way, the wrong way, and the Armed Forces way.
> Look out for yourself. No one else will.

> What can you expect? He's a Republican.
> She's a Democrat.
> He's a Catholic.
> She's a Protestant.
> He's a Jew.
> She's not white.
> He's not colored.
> He doesn't live here.
> Anyway, he's not one of us.

In this country there are said to be some 1,300 organizations representing various eccentric views. They are often dismissed with the stereotype condemnation of "screwball." Yet these groups often work with a fanatical zeal born from the oversimplified concepts they cherish as principles. Their creed may consist only of a few basic articles of political belief that generate intense "love" and equally ferocious "hate." Their zeal blinds them to the necessity of cooperation or compromise in the functioning of democratic processes. What they cannot win they seem willing to destroy. In political action their voices grow shrill with vitriolic rancor. Theirs is the political stereotype in its most virulent form. Yet the critical reader, no matter what his own views, should remain also the realist in dealing with these fervent minorities; since—as another cliché has it—like the poor, they will always be with us, we must learn to cope with their language and their logic, or lack of it. Nor will it ever do to reply in kind.

Noting stereotypes at work in other fields than politics, but generally not unrelated to it, reveals how commonplace the stereotype is. Movie studios issue advance stories in connection with the distribution of new productions, which are only press-agent blurbs disguised as news items. The National Chamber of Commerce, the National Association of Manufacturers, national labor unions, the American Medical Association, and all other such bodies will almost invariably take predictable stands on matters affecting their own interests. Many newspaper columnists and especially radio news commentators also give their work recognizable slants. Undoubtedly, human nature is such that we tend to agree with all such voices that most closely echo our own stereotypes or prejudices.

CRITICAL FOCUS

To question the stereotype is the best way to test for truth and reliability. What will stand examination may well withstand attack. Here, are some means of making such an examination:

1. Note how much the writer or speaker relies on general statements that lack solid supporting details and reasoning.
2. Watch for frequent repetition of stock phrases and expressions.
3. Be alert for glibness, for superficial flow of language, for clichés and triteness—almost sure signs of the presence of stereotypes.
4. Suspect notably opinionated persons and publications, those easily stirred to anger: they generally will *mistake the map for the territory.*

Exercise 5   Written report. Do any controversial topics such as the following arouse strong feelings in anyone you know? What forms do the stereotyped responses take? Can you account for their origin? Has the person ever tried to modify these habitual reactions? Would you dare call the person's attention to them?

1. foreign cars	11. athletics
2. sales tax	12. modern art
3. racial integration	13. small farms
4. divorce	14. careers for women
5. religious minorities	15. sectional differences
6. Federal aid to education	16. local government
7. socialized medicine	17. the Peace Corps
8. labor unions	18. alcohol or tobacco
9. ethnic groups	19. going steady
10. twelve-month school year	20. nuclear disarmament

Exercise 6   Written assignment. Write out the monologue of a vehement supporter of a particular stereotype such as one of those listed in the previous exercise. Let the language suggest as closely as possible the speaker's habitual tone, expressions, attitudes, and vehemence.

Exercise 7   Essay assignment. Through analysis of its language, explain the shortcomings of a popular proverb that through personal experience you know cannot be depended on.

Exercise 8   Written assignment. Consider these two stereotyped notions of Americans, both of which are widely held abroad. How would you explain why you preferred being an American to, let us say, a Frenchman who held one or the other of these points of view?

1. "The American character, as described by Europeans, is generally considered to be that of the rather naïve, unsophisticated, clean-cut, innocent young man with a severe superego."
2. "Boy Scout morality . . . a casual assumption of moral superiority. It is this national self-righteousness of Americans that even our best friends hesitate to mention to us."

Exercise 9   Discussion assignment. Bring to class a column written by a political commentator found in a daily newspaper or weekly newsmagazine. Be prepared to point out stereotyped views and attitudes and any connotations clearly slanted in favor of his stand.

> *Exercise 10*   Discussion. What additions can you make to this list of political party jargon, especially heard during party conventions? Can you explain the reason for some of the usages that may not be so obvious?

1. (Not) *The* United States (but) *These* United States!
2. (Not) My state votes (but) *proudly casts its votes.*
3. (Not) *nominate* (but) *name be placed in nomination.*

POLITICAL WORDS AND EMOTIONS

Promises, warnings, appeals, and threats have always provided campaigner and office holder, respectively, with a platform to run on and a program to keep him in office. And in any body politic there is seldom a lack of domestic and international problems that provide issues to be met or ducked.

The language of politics, therefore, has many voices and moods. It may have realistic humor, as in these "short question-and-answer snappers" originating in Poland and Hungary:

Q. "What are the four obstacles to Socialism?"
A. "Spring, summer, fall, and winter."
Q. "Did you hear the Russians have gone to the moon?"
A. (Hopefully) "All of them?"
Q. "What was here before communism?"
A. "Everything."
Q. "Will there be another war?"
A. "No, but there will be such a struggle for peace that not one stone will be left standing."
Q. "What is the solution to the American farm surplus problem?"
A. "Communism."
Q. "Why did Russian scientists try to cross-breed a cow with a giraffe?"
A. "So it could graze in Hungary and be milked in Russia."

Or the voice of politics may be a presidential candidate's televised replies to telephone questions, making a semantic hash of warnings and appeals:

The Alliance for Progress shows no alliance and very little progress.
. . . The Extreme Right is motivated by fear of communist Russia,
and The Extreme Left by the selfish fear of not getting the power to
cut across democratic rights. . . . We need a climate favorable to
job expansion through encouragement of free enterprise. . . . Vital
principles are at stake . . . the role of leadership in the free world
. . . solutions on a sound basis . . . a program to satisfy the aspirations of the people . . . back in the mainstream of American thought
. . . full employment, fiscal integrity, equal opportunity for all human beings, scientific research for the defense of our country . . .
Vietnam—fighting on the frontier of freedom . . . stem the communist tide. . . .

Whether it be the voice of George Washington in *The Farewell
Address,* Calvin Coolidge's laconic "I do not choose to run," or a local
municipal clerk defending *home rule,* the language is essentially emotional. As such it will ring changes on the basic compounds of feeling
suggested in the following outline; it will consist largely of "good"
words and "bad" words.

Negative emotions (threatening)		Positive emotions (promising)	
Disillusionment	Corruption	Hope	Prosperity
Distrust	Poverty	Patriotism	Peace
Disapproval	Defeat	Love	Security
Anxiety	Chaos	Confidence	Morality
Fear	Sin	Admiration	Progress

Threats and warnings speak of impending danger or harm.
Appeals and promises seek to evoke sympathetic responses. Both work
to influence the thinking and the decisions of an uncertain public. For
one audience, words that foment feelings of anxiety and fear may
include these: *left wing, pink, atheist, creeping socialism, radical,
liberal, egghead, professorial longhairs, stifling bureaucracy, UN po-
lice action, graduated income tax,* and *foreign aid.* For an entirely
different audience, a completely contrasting set of epithets will arouse
the same negative emotions: *conservative right, John Birch Society,
right to work laws, isolationism, racism,* and *McCarthyism.*
Whatever their shade of political opinion, all segments of the
public will experience identical hostility or uneasiness on hearing that
their country or community is threatened by *automation unemploy-*

ment, riot, cancer, slums, bankruptcy, atomic fallout, another Korea, missile attack, gangsterism, sabotage, and *depression.* As the political voice also knows, the public in general responds warmly to *our country, the flag, mother, prosperity, freedom, honor, integrity, brotherhood, justice, friendship, peace,* and *morality.*

Through such emotionalism, cleverly exploited by the devices of propaganda and the practice of physical ruthlessness, the dictators of this century—Hitler, Mussolini, and Stalin—captured the will of their nations. Perhaps Albert Camus has best explained the underlying philosophical situation that produced such a general paralysis of the critical capacities of great nations by perverting the terms and concepts of idealism.

> Philosophy secularizes the ideal. But tyrants appear who soon secularize the philosophies that give them the right to do so. Nietzsche had already predicted this development in discussing Hegel, whose originality, according to him, consisted in inventing a pantheism in which evil, error, and suffering could no longer serve as arguments against the divinity. "But the State, the powers that be, immediately made use of this grandiose initiative." He himself, however, had conceived of a system in which crime could no longer serve as an argument and in which the only value resided in the divinity of man. This grandiose initiative also had to be put to use. National Socialism in this respect was only a transitory heir, only the speculative and rabid outcome of nihilism. In all other respects those who, in correcting Nietzsche with the help of Marx, will choose to assent only to history, and no longer to all of creation, will be perfectly logical. The rebel whom Nietzsche set on his knees before the cosmos will, from now on, kneel before history. What is surprising about that? Nietzsche, at least in his theory of superhumanity, and Marx before him, with his classless society, both replace the Beyond by the Later On. In that way Nietzsche betrayed the Greeks and the teachings of Jesus, who, according to him, replaced the Beyond by the Immediate. . . . Nietzsche, at least, foresaw what was going to happen: [. . .] "What we desire is well-being. . . . As a result we march toward a spiritual slavery such as has never been seen. . . . Intellectual Caesarism hovers over every activity of the businessman and the philosopher."

It is noteworthy that when the state becomes this divinity, the rights of critical thinking and speaking are at once remanded by decree, and life approaches that of George Orwell's *1984*, where to think is *thoughtcrime*. How public opinion is pressured into acceptance of tyranny is outlined in the next section of this chapter.

CRITICAL FOCUS

The language of practical politics employs promises, warnings, appeals, and threats.

Exercise 11   Written assignment. Every community has its own local terms and expressions for certain things—expressions that a politician would seize upon to show in a speech that he understands or identifies with a particular locality, that he is *just one of the folks.* For example, in Oregon, item 6 below might be baked Columbia River salmon, or pan-fried rainbow trout, or fresh cooked crab, or Tillamook cheddar cheese, or *crawdad feed.* Substitute a typically regional example of each of the ten items below, and explain the connotation of the "local color" expressions. To begin with item 1, what do your neighbors call a stranger?

1. Somebody who is a stranger to your ways, a "green" newcomer
2. Social affairs for (*a*) males only, (*b*) females only, (*c*) mixed company
3. A special community celebration, e.g., a "shivaree"
4. Men with a marked distaste for steady work
5. Favorite greeting on seeing a long-parted friend
6. Special culinary treats
7. A local tradition associated with athletics, charities, politics, or religion
8. Expressions old folks use
9. Hometown newspaper "society" reporting
10. An historic remark made on a memorable occasion

Exercise 12   Written assignment. The following is a "Let's Look at the Record!" speech which might be made by a local incumbent. (*a*) Analyze the language by classifying its expressions as stereotypes, appeals, and threats; (*b*) now, in straightforward language, write what the speaker might have said in far fewer words.

Let's look at the record, and see what the facts really are! First, on this matter of prosperity. Friends, we've never had it so good! More people have jobs, more families have two automobiles and television sets in this state than ever before. Bank deposits are at an all-time high, and department store sales and bank clearing higher than ever. Sales are up 3 per cent.

Why, we're eating high on that old hog, and saving a penny for a rainy day on top of it. And it's all solid growth, based on sound domestic and foreign policies of our party. We're keeping our economic growth on the uprise and pushing our exports. We're providing a favorable tax climate for new industries. And we're going to bring them here.

Yes, we've taken the big step forward, my friends! Remember when they used to promise you *a chicken in every pot?* Let me tell you, folks, there's not a working man here who can't have cold chicken in his lunchbucket any doggone day he wants it! How about it, folks?

Look at you fine, upstanding people here. Who can say we've not done our best for you? And we've just started. Yes, folks, ours is a proud record. Let no bitter envy besmirch it! And I know the only ones you folks out there are ashamed of in this campaign are the dirty polecats who are trying to throw dirt on us all!

Exercise 13   Written report. A good source for any study of political vocabulary is the *Congressional Record,* which contains all the floor addresses and privileged insertions of our representatives in Washington, D.C. Select two speeches, preferably by members from different parts of the United States, that both deal with the same general topic or piece of legislation. For example, you might choose a Northern speaker and a Southern speaker on civil rights, or a Republican and a Democrat on any partisan measure. Reply to the following:

1. What, in brief (100 words), does each say?
2. What appears to be each one's general mood—anger, pain, approval, indignation, protest?
3. As for the language itself, are there any stereotypes, jargon ("my esteemed colleague"), emotional appeal, threats, highly connotative expressions or terms?
4. Which is the more effective speaker? Why?

AWARENESS OF PROPAGANDA

In India, three American magazines in recent years have reached a vast circle of readers. *The American Reporter,* published in eight languages, has been sent free to almost 400,000 homes; *The American Embassy* to more than 25,000 prominent persons in commerce and public life; and *The American Labor Review* to 17,000 and more trade union and labor leaders. To publish these periodicals requires a highly competent staff of some 600 people, the whole publishing venture being paid for by USIA funds. We call the program *information*. Our Communist opponents, who compete with the same kind of service, call ours *propaganda*.

In this era of international turbulence, when billions of people in Europe, Asia, Africa, and South America are undergoing sudden and tremendous social and economic changes, the fight for influence over minds grows critical. Every country copes with unexpected new problems and, to solve them, weighs variations of the two great economic-political systems—democratic capitalism and socialistic totalitarianism—which vie with one another to provide needed answers. Besides alliances, they compete with one another to give loans and counsel. We call any such deliberate attempt by an organized group to program and disseminate self-favorable policies, ideals, news, etc., or to provide goods and services likely to win friendship *propaganda*.

Although the information provided by press, radio, and television may have the format of news, the dissemination of propaganda is not journalism. News reporting and publishing, as will be seen in the following chapter, deal with current happenings and strive for accuracy, fairness, and completeness. Not so propaganda. It presents only items that will create the desired image and arouse the planned response—at least such is the intention. It repeats and repeats the same points. In this war of words, the Soviet Union and Red China have been devoting 3,000 hours weekly in 55 languages, and the United States under 600 hours and in only 36 languages. Both sides monitor one another's broadcasts, and the Soviet Union has resorted to "jamming" to prevent such programs as those from Radio Free Europe from reaching intended audiences. Likewise, Iron Curtain countries forbid the entry of American magazines and newspapers, but through *cultural-exchange* agreements, both sides carry on propaganda by means of the arts of the dance, music, and cinema.

In 1622, when Pope Gregory XV established the College of Propaganda, the term held the pious significance of *the propagation of the faith*. In our century, the term has become almost synonymous with Nazi and totalitarian control over all means of mass communications in order to arm a people, make them hate "the enemy," and, once at war, keep them fighting. As a result, the term has come to be considered in this light:

> I include under the term "deception" the whole art of propaganda, whether it consists of half-truths, lies, ambiguities, evasions, calculated silence, red herrings, unresponsiveness, slogans, catchwords, showmanship, bathos, hokum, or buncombe.

This definition by Walter Lippmann makes all propaganda self-condemnatory and would seem to include every form of persuasion that men have found necessary for preserving civic peace or defending themselves against outside attack. According to this definition, every civic leader, local or national, would always have to tell "the whole truth and nothing but the truth" in trying to legislate, enforce, and judge laws necessary for governing the passions of men in any form of society. In securing national support for military expenditures for defense, the President would have to reveal secrets that would aid the enemy.

This broad condemnation of all reserve in public matters by responsible leaders does not distinguish between *deception* and *prudence*. In no social situation can anyone speak out fully and openly. Society seems to make "liars" of us all. "How do you like my new hairdo?" a proud wife may ask her husband, as she preens before him with a coiffure that required three hours of beauty parlor anguish and $10 of grocery money. What is he to reply if he honestly thinks the hairdo resembles a bird's nest or a cone of county-fair cotton candy? His *calculated silence* or an ambiguous evasion, such as "Everything looks good on you, Hon," may preserve domestic tranquility. Nations, too, must preserve their domestic tranquility. The Declaration of Independence and the Preamble of the Constitution are both masterpieces of persuasive argument to gain such peace and happiness for the American people. And all institutions and organizations—whether political, military, social, religious, or aesthetic—exercise prudence and even "showmanship" to attain the ideals their members desire. Is it utopian to expect them to do otherwise?

In *War and Peace*, Tolstoy's main characters, Pierre and Prince Andrew, both suffer as idealists trying to find a social life that would satisfy their desires for living in full truth and love without any deception. Doctor Zhivago in Boris Pasternak's courageous novel repeats this same quest in the chaos that was the Russian Communist experiment in utopia founded on Marxist idealism and carried out by ruthless force and propaganda devices.

Creative societies strive for human ideals of justice and freedom and try to employ fair means to attain them. In context, Walter Lippmann's words are protests against all those who would employ the basic appeals and persuasion methods only in order to cheat and rule the people. He condemns those who would impose their rule and views upon society in order to subordinate and enslave a people by means of propaganda devices.

Here are some examples of such devices and means of persuading masses of people that have been used for good and for evil throughout the ages:

1. The golden promise
2. Prestige borrowing
3. Identification with the crowd
4. "The red herring" subterfuge
5. Public demonstration of unity
6. "Join the winner"

As will be shown in Chapter 5, these devices also involve faulty reasoning and fallacious persuasion in argument. But for the present let us examine them as instruments of political action: whether they be "good" or "bad" in any one application in the political party wars will, as the old cliché has it, depend on *whose ox is being gored*.

The golden promise is the vague *glittering generality* that flatters or tries to inspire and hold the loyalty of followers. It may be sincere and largely achievable hope or false and deliberately deceptive illusion. It makes tactical use of "good" and "hateful" words: those known to induce benevolent or angry responses. People in iron curtain countries hear every variation of *imperialist exploiters, Wall Street warmongers,* and *capitalist puppet labor unions.* While witnessing parades of military might, they listen to promises of success and a millennium of plenty. Before World War II, Hitler and Mussolini promised their nations great empires. In attempts to persuade other powers to support his conquest plans and concentration camps for genocide, Hitler also promised he would destroy communism and the Soviet Union. Then, as he began his war, his first move was to form a pact with the country he had reviled. Soon again in a rash of promises he led the invasion against his temporary ally. In Asia, Japan's militarily dominated government was making similar *golden promises.* Threat as the opposite of promise makes a further strong force working for a determined program and is often present as a "left-hand" partner to promise.

Prestige borrowing is the deliberate adoption of powerful symbols and persons to support a cause or campaign. It explains why every movement features flags, dignitaries of church and state, and every kind of popular hero that it can acquire. Mayors cut ribbons for the openings of supermarkets; distinguished citizens lend their names to national committees; labor leaders, high churchmen, and congressional members grace speaker platforms; foreign rulers and executives visit the White House and have their pictures taken with cordial Presidents in order to shore up shaky support in home countries. At every election, "name" politicians come to the aid of aspirants in other states and hope that endorsement will transfer some of the winning glory to the newcomer in the political wars.

Identification with the crowd includes all attempts to identify the person or program with the needs and interests of the audience. It enables the people hearing such beguiling appeals to feel that they are dealing with a neighbor, a good friend. Among *just plain folks,* a shrewd campaigner can talk in a neighborly way about local employment problems, roads, welfare, and the efforts of *my good friend and your good friend,* the local party leader who stands at his shoulder and smiles. The same campaigner may deliver the same speech, but in a totally different style of language, to a select gathering of hardheaded business men or, differently again, to an assembly of union members. This device can readily be seen at work in kissing babies, cheering at sports events (for both teams!), thanking cooks at church socials, and playing happily with animals and little children.

The red herring subterfuge, as its terms denote, is any form of evasion, any deliberate attempt to escape being pinned down. It consists of *ignoring the issue* and also of *character* assassination (see page 132). Anyone on the defensive in an argument who tries to avoid losing by bringing up another matter is *drawing a red herring across the trail.* The more dramatic the *herring,* the more likely the speaker is to succeed in diverting the attack on him. This device may be recognized in speakers who attack their questioners' personal character and demand a *yes* or *no* answer to the old question: *Are you still beating your wife?*

A *public demonstration of unity* employs mob psychology to win and hold support. Its commonest appearance, perhaps, is in the cheering sections at athletic contests, where the group no longer consists of lone individuals, but instead has become a cohesive, united, fellow-spirited mass. It works also, of course, in campaign rallies, parades, and mass meetings. The civil-rights efforts, as well as their counterefforts, witnessed new variations of this powerful device in the forms of *passive resistance* (borrowed from Gandhi in India), *sit-in, school boycott, prayer meeting, freedom march, picketing,* and other kinds of demonstrations—all employing signs, chants, songs, and various forms of persuasive speech.

Join the winner takes advantage of the general desire to be on the side of the winner. And every campaigner tries to act like a winner, even down to the last, desperate effort to forestall defeat. This device urges audiences to *climb on the band wagon* and be happy winners who share in the joys and fruits of victory. It explains the omnipresence of bands and music, parades, victory hats, and cheering followers ready to shout themselves hoarse at every appearance of their hero.

How the two broad kinds of emotional language so far studied—advertising and political—affect our news media, the sources of our information, is part of our inquiry in the next chapter.

CRITICAL FOCUS

All propaganda, whether used for noble or ignoble ends, requires the alert attention of the critical reader. Among the devices of propaganda are the following:

1. *The golden promise* (of success and plenty)
2. *Prestige borrowing* (from symbols and people)
3. *Identification with the crowd* (such as *we're just plain folks*)
4. *The red herring subterfuge* (or dodging the issue by switching the issue)
5. *Public demonstration of unity* (or the *united front* of mass meetings)
6. *Join the winner* (the band-wagon psychology)

Exercise 14   Essay assignment. Select one of the following writing directives, and write your own speech directed to a particular audience whom you describe or identify in the opening. To be honest in your appeals, write on a subject you believe in. Use only solid evidence and fair reasoning.

1. Encourage, raise the spirits and morale of a group who you know are feeling low.
2. Ask the audience to tolerate or to accept a view or interpretation contrary to the one they now hold. (You belong to the group that you wish to influence.)
3. Remind a group of ideals and standards they have overlooked or forgotten.
4. Defend the character of a person in the news who you believe is being subjected to character assassination.
5. Persuade a group to act contrary to the way they intend.
6. Reveal defects or shortcomings in someone or something greatly admired by the audience, meanwhile trying to avoid incurring their displeasure.
7. Excite a group to action.

Exercise 15   Discussion assignment. Find current examples of propaganda devices at work in these situations and point out their effectiveness, especially in the use of connotation.

1. College sports reports from coaches before a big game
2. A local press release or letter to the editor by a controversial figure
3. A statement by a social or political organization criticizing a public figure
4. A recent attack on a campus organization
5. Defenses of or attacks on television commercials
6. A peculiar use of opinion polls
7. Predictions regarding women's styles, men's styles
8. Newspaper editorials and a local issue
9. Support of government bonds
10. Public health pronouncements

Exercise 16   Essay assignment. Thomas Mann, the famous German novelist who chose exile rather than remain in a Germany ruled by Hitler, once said: "In our time the destiny of man presents its meaning in political terms."

What do you think he meant by each of the key terms in this

statement? Does the Albert Camus passage on p. 63 throw any light on their meaning? Does the explanation of propaganda have any bearing on them? In what sense could the Mann statement be applied to you?

Exercise 17   Analysis assignment. Discuss the awareness of propaganda in this letter appearing in *Izvestia*.

Boring vs. Jolly

First of all, may I introduce myself, so you will not think the discussion is being started by a prodigal, so to speak, who has nothing but entertainment on his mind. I work as a mechanic at the Rostov Farm Machinery Plant in a brigade that is fighting for the title of Communist Labor Brigade. I am 25 years old. I study in the evening university, am an athlete and head the worker-correspondents' post of the Young Communist League newspaper. I often write about the work in our shop, but today I take pen in hand to tell about something else: recreation, amusement, interesting ways of spending time, entertainment, in brief, the problem of "after six o'clock in the evening."

The working day is becoming shorter and, as the Party Program says, there will be more and more free time. The working people are grateful to the Party and the government for their concern. No country in the world offers such conditions as ours for obtaining a job and an education and for acquiring culture. Marvelous clubs and stadiums, palaces of culture and libraries, theaters and concert halls, art studios and universities of culture, where one can devote one's free hours to any pursuits, diversions and interests, have been built for millions of Soviet people.

But in this letter I would like to talk about such a sphere of recreation as the entertainments in palaces of cultural rest: parks, suburban zones, clubs, cafes, dance halls, etc. Many people, after a working day filled with interesting affairs, are bored there, that is to say, they are bored in places created precisely for amusement and rewarding rest. In my opinion, we are still far from well off in all these matters, and a great deal of imagination, efficiency and wit has to be applied in order to drive boredom and drabness out of places of cultural rest, out of television programs and concerts, out of everything that surrounds us and is being created for us.

Truthfully, I personally do not always have time for entertainment, and I consider this a shortcoming in my life. One must be successful in everything. One day my friend Viktor Sorokin dragged me, as the saying goes, out into the world.

"Where should we go?"

We looked at the Rostov evening paper. Movie? We had already seen "Arshin Mal-alan." Theater? But one does not go there every day. Lecture? But I had already heard this lecture, and besides, today was a difficult day for our shift, we were devilishly tired to start with and then there was a production meeting, so now I just wanted to rest, to be entertained and to laugh.

We went to the dance pavilion. There were slogans and appeals along the alley leading to it. I understand when there are business exhibits and diagrams at the plant; we Y.C.L. members put them up ourselves. But I think this practice should not be abused in parks. After all, people go to parks to rest, not to work. Rest, like work, requires a certain state of mind.

The culture officials of the parks must themselves be people of taste, imagination and wit, if you will.

We went to a cafe. We sat down. A couple at another table were whispering; after all, they may have secrets, or is it bad to have secrets? No, there is nothing bad about it, of course. What is bad is that there is no music in the cafe. A depressing silence, and in this atmosphere even a little laughter may appear indecent. We ordered something. We waited. A few fellows came in, drank a glass of vodka each, ate a few sandwiches and left. When there is no entertainment a person who is not hungry has nothing to do there, so he is bored. But this is still cultured, to have a drink in a cafe. But in some places people will gather in a bar and sit, and sit some more.

Is it not clear that this is not an atmosphere for unrestrained relaxation? People run away from the rubber stamp, from officialese, from stupid and standardized "wit."

Young people like poetry, music and athletics. Once in a while we are invited to meet poets and writers, but for some reason or other these meetings degenerate into formal sessions: A presidium is elected, the esteemed poets formally read their poems and modestly disappear. For some reason the poets do not come down from the rostrum among the Valayas and Petyas to tell them simply about their life, to read their poems, to joke.

No, the "evening out in the world" was clearly not a success. . . . The propaganda of rest is in a bad way.

Exercise 18   Discussion assignment. Analyze this Christmas Day *message,* which appeared in a black-bordered newspaper column.

How do you interpret this mixture of religion and economics? What is its purpose? Who would be impressed by it? What terms of political connotation are obvious in it?

Born into a Tax-burdened World

Jesus was born into a world where people were taxed.

The tax edict of Caesar Augustus which brought every subject to his home town for registration and taxation brought Joseph and Mary to Bethlehem. They found the town so crowded with tax payers that there was no room for them in the local inn.

And today as the world celebrates the birth of the Saviour who was born in a lowly manger, the hand of the taxgatherer lies heavy upon us. In the United States the average citizen must pay taxes which are equivalent of working for the government three months and sixteen days out of every year.

The public debt is in excess of $300,000,000,000.00—three hundred billion dollars! . . . We are not only being burdened with taxes ourselves, but if there are to be children's children unto the third and fourth generations, they too will be saddled with the burden and folly of free-wheeling government spending.

Necessary taxes for the maintenance of minimal government are right, and the Scripture enjoins us to pay tribute to whom tribute is due—to render unto Caesar the things which belong to Caesar. But oppressive taxation is an integral part of the burden which sin imposes upon the race. . . .

The Lord Jesus Christ beckons to an overtaxed world to come to Him for relief. . . . Who among us would not rejoice to have his tax bill forgiven, especially if it were of a size we could never pay? How much greater cause for rejoicing to be delivered from the burden of sin! . . . Will you receive him now? Write us that you have made this all-important decision.

Exercise 19   Essay assignment. What meaning does this Lao Tze saying hold for you? Try to see the connotative meanings in every phrase, in every sentence as a whole. Think of what relation the images may have to one another. Of what importance is the question *Who is their author?* What are the *rash endeavors?* Does this saying relate at all to the concerns of this chapter?

Only simple and quiet words will ripen of themselves. For a whirlwind does not last for the whole morning. Nor does a thundershower last the whole day. Who is their author? The heavens and earth. Yet even they cannot make such violent things last. How much more true this must be of the rash endeavors of man.

Exercise 20   Report assignment. By consulting *The Reader's Guide* and *The International Index to Periodicals,* write a report showing the validity of this statement: *The art of politics is the art of communication.*

Exercise 21   Discussion assignment. Here are a number of quotations from newspapers that had comments to make on Governor William Scranton's entry in the 1964 Republican Convention nomination race against Senator Barry Goldwater. What does their language tell you of the political orientation of these newspapers? What are the connotations of the language? Are there any propaganda devices evident?

1. A new and refreshing voice is calling the G.O.P. from the land of make-believe. *Washington Post*
2. Rally Round Scranton. *Chicago Sun-Times*
3. His cause is right, and he can do his nation and his party a historic service by waging unreserved battle for it. *St. Louis Post-Dispatch*
4. Will add a bit of glamour. *Kansas City Star*
5. The long sleep has ended for the Republican chiefs who feared Senator Goldwater would lead the party to disaster but feared even more doing anything to stop him. *The New York Times*
6. The shattered moderate leadership of the party may be unable to pick itself up off the floor and do serious battle. *Milwaukee Journal*
7. Scranton the boy at the dike. It will take a miracle to make his effort more than a sad exercise in futility. *Nashville Tennesseean*
8. Wishful Willie Scranton closed his eyes, screwed up his courage and dived. The only trouble is that Barry Goldwater might have pulled the plug. *Detroit Free Press*
9. Watch The Lip, Governor. *New York Daily News*
10. A platter of cold fish, garnished with clichés. *World Herald* (Omaha)
11. An insult to the intelligence of the American public and a disaster from which our nation would be long in recovering. *Union Leader* (Manchester, N.H.)

Exercise 22   Written report. A famous letter by Congressman Morris K. Udall, appearing on page 213, provides an excellent opportunity to study the deliberate use of political slanting through connotative diction. Show how favorable and unfavorable connotation can give contrary meanings to the same referents.

chapter 4

THE LANGUAGE
OF THE NEWS

As private or "free" enterprises, American newspapers have big stakes in both advertising and politics. We have already noted their understandable absorption with these two fundamental forces in our national life. The newspapers—like the newsmagazines, radio, and television—depend almost wholly upon the revenues received from advertising; and the vast size of their audiences, as well as the political interests of their owners and publishers, makes participation in politics irresistible.

It is just these two major concerns, advertising and political action, that require the newspaper readers and new listeners to remain constantly alert to the language they read and hear. The critical reader realizes how much he must depend upon the media for his information and news interpretation. And by all traditions of good journalism, he has a right to demand objectivity, full coverage, and accurate reporting. Also, according to that tradition, he expects to find expressions of opinion and favoritism—*bias*—only on the editorial page or in the signed columns of news analysts and commentators.

We come now to some personal questions. What do you think makes a good newspaper? Do you consider your local newspapers to be satisfactory? On what principles do you base your judgment of journalism? These are some of the inquiries an observant reader should be able to answer intelligently. To do so, as we shall see, he needs a lively social-civic awareness, knowledge, principles, and imagination. These are the qualities that go into the making of good editors and reporters.

WHAT GOOD NEWSPAPERS DO

Newspapers are particularly essential to our democratic way of life. Without them, democratic government, industry, charities, cultural activities, and education would be seriously crippled. Though some readers regard them only as sources of daily dramatic news, the best newspapers devote as much as 60 per cent or more of their print columns to their role of service to the community, such as the undramatic documenting of tax, schoolboard and welfare commissions, and election and legislative reports and analysis. They also provide the routine information expected of them regarding weather and stock market reports, items on the social calendar, and sports events.

In addition to this service role, our newspapers enjoy the privilege and duty of acting as watchdogs of human rights and freedoms for the community at large. It is this role, this public trust, that has repeatedly led the Supreme Court to protect the press with libel rulings in favor of news organs. As a result, the American press has unequaled powers and freedom. It is then up to the critical reader to examine his local papers for the manner in which they exercise, or fail to exercise, these great powers. For a newspaper is not only the ear and the eye of the community but also something of its collective conscience.

One cause for growing concern is the rise of *oligopolies*. These are the groups of national corporations that continue to buy up newspapers and television and radio stations once owned by private families. Among these multiple owners is the Newhouse chain, which, perhaps more benevolent and permissive than the William Randolph Hearst kind of proprietorship, nevertheless makes for increasing conservatism and quietism. Cities such as Atlanta, Minneapolis, St. Paul, and Portland, Oregon—to mention only a few—know what it is to lose local ownership of their most potent means of community expression. Large sections of this country are dominated by chain ownership. Here is an historian's view of the situation:

> Few people outside the business understand the extent to which the American press is monopolistic. Where there was once a healthy, competitive variety, only 10% of the dailies in the United States now have competition. As of 1962 there were 1,769 English-language dailies, but only 155 were in competition and many of these were

losing money. Experienced observers believe that by 1970 there may be no more than twenty competing newspapers, and these will be confined to our ten largest cities.

Monopoly extends to the other means of mass communications as well. Newspapers presently own more than 750 radio and television stations, and in 76 American cities the only daily also owns the only radio station.

Such dismal prospects alarm the thoughtful reader. To form his opinions he requires an alert, competitive press. Yet it is true that negligent, indifferent newspaper readers eventually will receive only the kind of poor papers they have always tolerated. But let us next examine that most important element in journalism—the reporter.

CRITICAL FOCUS

Newspapers have great stakes in advertising and politics.
Competition with the news media of radio and television
has sped the growth of oligopolies.

     Exercise 1   Written assignment. What are the derivation, denotations, and connotations of the word *oligopolies?*

     Exercise 2   Essay assignment. In the April 13, 1964, issue, *Time* comments as follows on the fact that as of that date only three cities in the United States have two separately owned dailies that are not part of chains: New York (six), Boston (four), and Washington (three): "The dwindling statistics are the one more indication that the news-hungry public no longer need rely exclusively on its daily news-papers—whose dominion has been seriously challenged by news maga-zines, radio and TV." Explain your views on this statement in the light of your own community's experience with private ownership of news-papers.

     Exercise 3   Essay assignment. *Newspapers are the mirror of society.* On the basis of this observation, describe the image of your city and its people as they are *mirrored* in a local newspaper. You may wish to classify your findings into such categories as crime, charity, amuse-ments, education, political life, industry, business.

Exercise 4   Discussion assignment. In what respects does your campus newspaper succeed or fail as a mirror of the various aspects of the academic and social life of campus *society* (give this term its meaning in the previous exercise)? Support your views with references to current issues of your campus newspaper.

Exercise 5   Discussion assignment. *What is the political position usually taken by a local newspaper on political party issues, local as well as national?* To support your conclusions regarding the political leanings of your local newspaper, bring to class news stories, editorials, headlines, or columnist commentary showing unmistakable signs of *bias*. Remember to consider both denotative and cannotative meanings as the basis for such an analysis.

Exercise 6   Discussion assignment. Who are the major advertisers in your local newspaper? How much advertising space do they average in a week? Have you any clear evidence that these advertisers at all influence the editorial policy of the newspaper? Has the paper featured cigarette advertisements? Has it at the same time shown relaxed views on government health warnings on the smoking of cigarettes as a cause of lung cancer?

THE REPORTER AND THE NEWS

Good journalism features reporting that is accurate, balanced, fair and objective, clear, concise, and current. Many reporters daily meet such tests. They represent the "ideal" reporter as he is aptly described herein by a veteran journalist:

> He isn't concerned with his own position in the matter at all. The only thing he wants to do is to get the story, get it all, wring it dry, not leave any questions unanswered, not leave any angle for the P.M.'s or the A.M.'s as the case may be, to follow up, not have a character on the copy desk, or a crab in the bull-pen be able to ask a single question that isn't answered right there in his story, or challenge a date or a name or a quote or a description or a fact of any kind, most especially a conclusion, that he can't back up with black and white or unassailable logic, as the case may be.

Still, even this exemplar is a human being with strong likes and dislikes, one also often dependent upon his "news beat" as sources of his news.

The longer he has covered his beat—politics, industry, education, etc.—the more important he becomes to his paper as an authority in his field. At the same time, he tends to become too friendly with, or at least dependent upon, his customary sources. At best, a conscientious reporter has no easy time in living up to journalistic ideals.

The reporter in America has advantages but also some handicaps when compared with the European reporter. Here he is inhibited from writing interpretations or making subjective, personal comments on the meaning of the news event he is reporting, whereas newsmen abroad are expected to write "essays" rather than "objective" news stories. If he writes for such famous newspapers as *The Times* of London, *The Guardian* of Manchester, or *Le Monde* of Paris, the reporter knows that his account will be judged not by a businessman publisher, but by an editor who is responsible for the "tone" of all the news that goes into the paper, and who, moreover, gives the paper a consistency of attitude by determining also the meaning of the news as seen by that paper. In the United States, the publisher controls the news sections as well as the advertising, and very often he is a hard-headed businessman rather than a journalist chosen as editor because of his breadth of background and perceptive attitudes and judgment. The American reporter may also be handicapped in being forced to write in concrete, specific terms that even grade school children can read with interest.

He has also the problem of determining just what is most important in the event he is covering, what will most appeal to the readers, and around what central point he can organize his news story. To begin his account, he must write a *lead summary*. This statement gives all the essential who-what-when-where-why-how information, as well as setting the tone of the whole article. It is a personal statement only in that it expresses the reporter's judgment as to what facts are basic.

Following that lead sentence come the parts of the first main point and its supporting summary detail, then elaboration of point two. He writes the piece keeping in mind that the most important items must appear first and the minor details last, so that the city editor and rewrite staff can, if necessary, cut off the lower section to make the story fit into the space available on the page and in the column selected for that particular story. It frequently happens that everything but the lead summary will be thrown away. Cutting a story thus makes also for censorship, as does burying it in the back pages.

How personal even the most expert report is can be seen in the summary leads of the Associated Press, the United Press International, and *The New York Times* in their respective stories on President John F. Kennedy's famous December 31, 1962, press conference, on the occasion of the Russian decision to remove missiles from Cuba.

The Associated Press lead was this:

> President Kennedy intends to follow up his Cuban success by exerting stronger leadership over the West's Cold War policies—even at the risk of offending sensitive allies.

The United Press International lead:

> President Kennedy feels the Cuban missile crisis taught Russia a lesson and may have improved slightly the chances for keeping the world at peace in 1963.

The New York Times service lead:

> President Kennedy believes the onrush of Communist influence in the world was checked in 1962 and that the outlook for peace is slightly better in 1963.

To judge which of these three leads best represents the essence and tenor of the President's announcements, one would have to study the entire transcript, but even that would not convey the nuances of voice and manner that gave varying emphasis to the many points and replies to questions. British and French newspapers chose the AP lead.

In London, *The Times* carried an evidently approving headline:

> **Tough Leadership Resolution**
> **By President Kennedy**

In Paris the headline of *Le Monde* was indignant:

> **President Kennedy Has Decided to Direct**
> **The Western Alliance without Worrying**
> **About Objections of Allies.**

Thus even presidents are at the mercy of reporters and of rewrite men. Any hurried reader trying to determine what was actually said at the conference would have to consult several different newspapers, for each paper usually carries only one press service account. And very few papers would have had their own reporters at this Palm Beach conference, or would have given them space to write a complete report as well as carrying the full transcript itself. How unsafe especially are headlines!

Here is another dramatic instance of the problems encountered by some of the 515 American foreign correspondents in reporting and interpreting news events puzzling to editors and readers at home. (The incidents related may be outdated, but they well illustrate the reporter's constant difficulties.)

Setting the Record Straight

After the coup in South Vietnam, *Editor & Publisher* commented: "The reporters on the scene might well say now, 'We told you so.'" And E. & P. added: "There has been some pretty fast flip-flopping in this country among people who were saying that U.S. correspondents were giving an overly pessimistic view of the military situation and the Diem government."

Months before the Diem government was overthrown, dispatches from Saigon by American reporters reflected the rapidly deteriorating situation in South Vietnam. The facts were unwelcome in many quarters, and the American press corps became the center of controversy. As long ago as Feb. 15, Richard Dudman in the St. Louis *Post-Dispatch* reported that the State Department was unhappy with the work of news correspondents on the scene. The Department said that the American reporters assigned to Saigon were too young and immature to comprehend the subtleties of the situation. In the Department's view, the reporters were over emphasizing our military defeats and the disputes between Diem and American officials.

The attack on the Saigon reporters was taken up by influential sections of the American press itself. *Time* blasted the work of the correspondents, and two of *Time's* reporters resigned on the spot in protest. Several writers with well-known news bylines went to Saigon to expose the press corps. Among them were Frank Conniff, national editor of the Hearst newspapers; William Randolph Hearst, Jr., and Columnist Bob Considine. They agreed that Diem was strong enough to defeat the Communists, while reporters in Saigon unanimously held a contrary opinion. Conniff said that "the assignment of young reporters, most of them in their twenties, to decipher an involved story reflects small credit on the prescience of American editors."

The record should be set straight. The reporters in Saigon were right; their critics were wrong. It is as simple as that.

The chief target of the attack on the Saigon press corps was David Halberstam of the New York *Times,* but Halberstam's performance made his detractors look like clumsy amateurs. Halberstam's reporting from Saigon, especially his brilliant summary of the coup in the Nov. 5 *Times,* deserves a Pulitzer prize.

If by now you have become a more or less critical reader, you will already have raised significant questions: "How do I know that this article is correct? Are the facts and conclusions really as solid here as they appear to be?" Perhaps the best way to answer such inquiries is to raise others:

1. What exactly does this article say or maintain?
2. What data are given as facts?
3. How sound is the reasoning based on those data?
4. What attitude or intention does the article reveal?
5. Who is the author, and what are his qualifications?
6. What are the reputation and character of the publication in which the article appears?
7. What other evidence supports the writer's views?

Except for question 5 (which refers to the "bylined" article), these questions can be applied to all news stories.

We can hardly expect total agreement as to answers regarding "Setting the Record Straight." Some who might readily agree that *Editor & Publisher* is the respected trade organ of the news publishers and that the quotations are accurate in context, might stop dead at the fifth question and be greatly perturbed at the sixth. For in an era of "hot" and "cold" wars, when national and local problems reflecting foreign issues foment fierce oppositions and equally fierce loyalties, the name of any magazine may itself produce some hard breathing from dissidents. In this particular case, however, only history will be able to determine how "straight" the record has been set.

Karl E. Meyer, of the *Washington Post & Times Herald* editorial staff, has noted that the *old style* kind of editorial writing, which *boiled with indignation,* has given way to the *new style,* which relies upon ironic wit rather than upon emotional protest; it also regards politics and politicians as an art and a profession rather than as a patriotic endeavor. Mr. Meyer confesses that at times, in order to avoid passing judgment, he resorts to one or the other of what he calls *the four D's.* These four devices make excellent checkpoints for the critical reader of editorials and columns:

1. *Dichotomy:* State two views on any situation and seem to imply that the truth lies somewhere between them.
2. *Distribution:* In appraising an event or situation, spread out the praise and brickbats evenly.
3. *Description:* Make it appear in describing a figure in the news that a definite judgment is being passed on him, but then gradually negate what was said or suggested earlier in the piece.
4. *Displacement:* Discuss a bad situation, and in analyzing it, make everyone equally responsible for it.

If such are admittedly journalistic practices of news commentators, it is clear that the reader must be highly alert to detect evasions and contradictions where, by tradition, he should not have to expect to find them.

CRITICAL FOCUS

Good reporting is objective, full, and accurate. But even the best report contains subjective elements of personal judgment. A reporter necessarily must decide what facts to emphasize. Summary leads are an important element in a reporter's story and are often the surest guide to the slant of his thinking.

Exercise 7　Written assignment. Analyze the language found in the headlines of five newspaper stories for their clear and accurate bearing on the opening lead sentence. (Cut and mount on paper the headlines and the story columns.) Do headlines at times have a *tone* (see page 143) different from that of the rest of the story? If so, can you account for the difference? (What is the purpose of a headline? What are its special problems regarding word choice and space?)

Exercise 8　Written assignment. The reporter's basic questions are Who? What? When? Where? Why? and How? and the quality of his reporting depends upon his answers to them in his story. To determine the quality of reporting in your campus newspaper, read a story in that paper for which you have first-hand knowledge. Apply the questions to the situation and check the published story for its adequacy of coverage as well as for its language.

Exercise 9   Report assignment. To determine its aura of respectability, rate a local city newspaper according to the average publication of sex-violence incidents noted in the following analysis.

> The 10 newspapers devoted a total of 29,841 column inches to news. Of this total, 1,518 inches, or 5% of the total, dealt with descriptions of incidents of violence. *This surprisingly low total is one of the significant findings of the study.* Of the separate [subordinate] categories, War Violence was highest with an average of less than one percent (.8%) of all news being devoted to this topic by the papers surveyed. This was followed by news of Accidental Violence (.5%) and news devoted to killings (.4%).
>
> The figures cited represent an average of all papers surveyed with the exception of the New York Daily *News.* Inclusion of the averages of this tabloid in the summary would have resulted in a marked distortion of the results. For example, the New York *Daily News* devoted 3.3% of its total news to subjects dealing with sex. Of the papers surveyed, the Philadelphia *Evening Bulletin* was next highest with only .42% of the total news content dealing with this topic. The New York *Daily News* therefore devoted seven times the amount of news space to this subject. . . . The newspaper study presents markedly different results indicating that a representative segment of the American press is not as preoccupied with themes of sex and violence as are some of our other mass media of communication.

Exercise 10   Report assignment. Compare and contrast the Associated Press report with that of the United Press International on some currently important news event. (If it is possible to procure *The New York Times* and *The Christian Science Monitor* in addition, add their accounts to your comparisons.)

Exercise 11   Essay assignment. Test your ability to detect underlying views and attitudes by comparing the pronouncements and language of two columnists who deal with the same problem in the current news. *Suggestion:* Refer to the check list for critical reading, pages 35 and 84.

JOURNALISTIC LANGUAGE
AND NEWSMAGAZINES

Those who rule by the consent of the governed must take care of their image as it appears to the electorate. In Washington, D.C.—as in all state capitals and even county seats—political figures have devised a number of discreet devices for sounding public opinion as well as making friends of newsmen. These means include *backgrounders, leaks, trial balloons,* and *off-the-records.* They have in common the fact that they are opinions or information given by important personages who must remain nameless.

Each term has its special meaning. A *backgrounder* may be a full-sized lecture and presentation of military or other plans and proposals which members of the press will need to know in order to report on the scheduled events yet to come. It resembles the *off-the-record* remarks that, although perhaps revealing and important, must never be ascribed to the one who said them. They usually are the spice of "news chats." A *news leak* is some confidential information that someone sworn to secrecy considers expedient to whisper to a friendly reporter who can be trusted to publish the item but keep its source concealed. Columnists such as Drew Pearson are often given such items, generally intended as *trial balloons,* responses to which may tell politicians which way the winds of public opinion are blowing.

All of these devices, however, involve the reporter in the predicament well summed up in this statement: "If reporters want to use something the nonspeaker has not said at the unmeeting, they must paraphrase the nonspeaker and attribute his ideas to their own intuition or some nameless source." And the reader will recognize these devices at work whenever he spots "according to well informed sources" or "according to responsible authority," and other such euphemisms. At times these phrases may also mask a reporter's desperate guesses.

The news sources enjoyed by the weekly newsmagazines give them advantages that daily newspapers cannot have. Being allowed a week to develop, write, and rewrite a news story should make the article thorough and accurate. For newsmagazines draw not only upon their own large reporter staffs but also upon the wire press services. No wonder many readers consider *Time, Newsweek,* and *U.S. News & World Report* as news "bibles." Much of this reader impression comes from the tone of authority pervading these magazines, which in turn derives from their distinct editorial policies. *Time* boasts of its special editorial viewpoint, and the other two clearly have views governing the selection and import of the events reported.

How do these three weekly newsmagazines compare in approach and diction when reporting a most significant news event? We should be able to form some opinion, however tentative, regarding their respective styles by examining their reports on the signing of the Civil Rights Law on July 2, 1964, and the results of its first tests. To begin, we need to explain some apparent discrepancies of publishing dates on the covers of these three magazines: that for *Time* is July 10, for *Newsweek* July 13, for *U.S. News & World Report* July 20. Though dated July 20 on the cover, *U.S. News & World Report* notes inside that the issue is "Distributed during week of July 13." In reality, then, all three are issued on approximately the same date.

Newsweek made the signing of the bill into law its opening and main story on page 17. Under a picture of President Lyndon B. Johnson's hand signing the document is this caption: "The President used 72 pens to sign the law that reaffirms equality." There follows this three-column headline: "'. . . Shall Now Also Be Equal. . . .'" And the story's opening strives for tense drama reported in hushed tones:

> President Lyndon B. Johnson strode into the chandeliered East Room of the White House at precisely 6:45 P.M., nodded perfunctorily to acknowledge the applause that greeted him, then sat down at a specially installed mahogany desk on which lay the crisp pages of The Civil Rights Act of 1964. The television lights went up and a prompter intoned, "Thirty seconds." The President mopped his brow, cleared his throat, and then delivered a moving, simply cadenced 1,000-word address on the scope and significance of the historic measure he was about to sign into law. . . .

Note connotative phrases: *specially installed mahogany desk, crisp pages, mopped his brow, cleared his throat, moving, simply cadenced 1,000-word address.* This story of four brief parts summarizes as surprisingly favorable the initial response to the law and ends with two short paragraphs under the heading "Testing" which present opposing views of the law.

Because of its usual opening features and a thirteen-page article devoted to the presidential race between Senator Barry Goldwater and

President Johnson—before the Republican convention—*U.S. News & World Report* began its civil-rights story on page 44. The page was made dramatic by the appearance of two news pictures, one showing a favorable and the other an unfavorable reaction, and a cartoon. The bold-print headline reads: "The Civil Rights Law Goes into Action." Three short paragraphs in heavy print summarize the results of tests of the new law, and then comes this opening:

> All across the South, testing of the new Civil Rights law is under way on a broad scale.
>
> The first legal test started on July 10 when Attorney General Robert Kennedy asked a federal court in Atlanta to rule on the constitutionality of the law's public-accommodations section.
>
> By then, Negroes in dozens of localities had applied for admission to hotels, motels, restaurants, swimming pools, bowling alleys and pool halls, nightclubs, theaters, and libraries.
>
> Results varied from quiet desegregation to violence and bloodshed. . . .

This style is a terse, detail-packed summary in paragraphs consisting often of only one sentence. As in the third paragraph, all the language is denotative, but every term in the list is also highly connotative for millions of readers who regard the referents of these words as emotion-arousing symbols to such an extent that the *map* almost becomes the *territory*.

Time's report, on page 26, follows one on "The Presidency," bearing the typically lively *Time* title of "Doin' the Bird," which describes a White House teen-age twist party for Luci Baines Johnson. *Time* emphasized the "testing" aspect of the Civil Rights Law and placed the Presidential signing and speech episode toward the end of the one and one-half column story. It began with a picture of a Negro boy in a barber chair with the caption underneath: "Haircut in Kansas City—End of a Sorry Era." Also in typical highly mannered language, the article opened with Drama after the title, "Time of Testing":

> In the barbershop of Kansas City's Muchlebach Hotel, a 13-year-old Negro boy, Eugene Young, hopped into a chair, opened his fist to display two $1 bills, and ordered a haircut. Without hesitating, Barber Lloyd Soper covered the lad with a white apron, took out his clippers and went to work. . . .

This article exemplifies *Time*'s practice of seizing upon a dramatic but representative incident, and making it tell the story of a whole and perhaps complicated action. The narrative device makes a forceful introduction to the details that follow.

The *Time* manner often includes a breeziness of diction seldom found in the other news weeklies. Here, for example, is a passage from a *Time* report on "show business" under the headline, "Readings—Something to Write Home About":

Dear Mother,

I'm sorry I haven't written, but it has taken me days to get over the wonderful thing that happened. Earlier this week, I saw Elizabeth Taylor and Richard Burton do a poetry reading at the Lunt-Fontanne Theater on Broadway. Mother, I don't care what you say about them, I want to tell you it was really beautiful. . . .

The Burtons read verses alternately in a sort of ping-poem match (hah-hah!). Many of the items had apparently been selected for their meaning to the Burtons. Richard, for example, started off by reciting *To His Coy Mistress* by Andrew Marvell, and one of the poems Elizabeth read was Thomas Hardy's *The Ruined Maid:*

"And now you've gay bracelets and bright feathers three!"
"Yes, that's how we dress when we're ruined," said she.

Elizabeth read that one in a very accomplished cockney accent and showed herself to be more of an actress than I thought she was. She read William Butler Yeats's *Three Bushes,* about two women who loved the same man, and really belted out the line, "What could I do but drop down dead if I lost my chastity?" All evening, as she read, Richard's foster father sat behind her mouthing every word she said. He was just afraid she would make a mistake, but he looked like a ventriloquist.

Together, the Burtons read T. S. Eliot's *Portrait of a Lady,* which, in case you have forgotten, Mother, starts off with a quote from an Elizabethan play: "Thou hast committed fornication, but that was in another country." You see what I mean about courage. . . .

The evening was especially fun because there was so much pleasant banter between Richard and Elizabeth. Once she stopped a poem and said, "Sorry, may I start again? I got all screwed up."

"I could say that in *Hamlet* every night," said Richard. . . .

P.S. I don't miss college one bit.

Newsweek also reviews books and movies, though in more reserved language. Here is a portion of a review of John Houston's movie "The Night of the Iguana":

> . . . The main title runs over shots of iguanas. The Blake's Tours bus passes swarms of Mexican boys holding their captive monsters high. The iguana under the porch is really there, really to be cut loose and allowed to scamper away.
>
> The symbol is the more powerful for its concrete and non-symbolic existence, just as Williams' vision of the dark night of the soul is more effective running without intermission from disaster through despair to the bleary but unmistakable dawn of acceptance and survival.
>
> **M-G-M English:** The cast of human monsters, too, is changed, but with considerable shrewdness. Richard Burton, the big draw, turns out to be quite right as the Rev. T. Lawrence Shannon, for his British diction contrasts with his seedy appearance as effectively as the Southern gentility Williams first had in mind, and Patrick O'Neal used on the stage. Burton, moreover, is a fiery performer who can blaze with anger or smolder in torment, and it is thrilling to watch him act well in a good movie, probably for the first time in his career. Ava Gardner would be an improbable Maxine, except that Houston has had her get rid of what he calls her "M-G-M English" and return to her original North Carolina drawl. Her vowels are wind-blown, like her hair, and she is all high blood and blowziness. . . .

U.S. News & World Report in this issue, as usual, devotes itself only to the sterner stuff of economics, politics, and foreign policy as they affect the nation's business, though on a final page there is information on "vacation precaution," wasps, and tests on how to tell when the cleaner does a good job on a coat. In general, each magazine has its own tone and diction, as has been suggested.

CRITICAL FOCUS

1. As with newspapers, each newsmagazine has its own basic editorial or publishing policy, which governs what will and will not be printed.
2. This policy determines the characteristic tone and diction of the magazine as a whole and of each of its departments.
3. Also as with newspapers, "censorship" can consist of omitting mention of any news event, giving it little space, and/or burying a brief account of it on some obscure back page.

Exercise 12   Essay assignment. To determine for yourself the differences and similarities between newsmagazines in reportage and diction and tone, as well as in editorial or publishing philosophy, compare the various treatments of the same news event as found in *Time, Newsweek,* and *U.S. News & World Report.* You may wish to compare treatments of some event of art, finance, crime, theater, music, ballet, drama, literature, movies, politics, or education.

Exercise 13   Discussion assignment. Discuss *freedom of the press* as related to campus publications. Freedom of the press is zealously guarded by all the media and supported by numerous Supreme Court decisions. Media are allowed and encouraged to publish and interpret the news. Do campus publications enjoy the same freedom on your campus? Should they? Why or why not?

TV NEWS, PRESS WIRE SERVICES, AND RELIABILITY

Like the other news media, television broadcasting companies have their own corps of reporters in addition to AP and UPI services. Editing and rewriting of news items for broadcasting raise problems, as pointed out by a news editor:

> Can the most important story or stories of the hour be fitted into the opening section of 105 seconds? Should one of them be given greater play and dropped down to the second main section? What news should be held for the third and fourth main sections?

The manner in which such edited news stories are preceded or followed by commercials will also have some bearing upon their impact. When split-second reports of tragedies and grave turns of events are framed by raucous jingles or pompous pronouncements of pain relievers, listeners will have to remain highly alert to weigh the reports; this is especially difficult if the broadcasts are watched during the family dinner hour.

All editors and publishers have reasons to keep a wary eye on the press wire services. Not all of these national reporting services have spotless records. Senator J. W. Fulbright, for instance, has disclosed that a Senate committee learned in 1958 that a foreign country's agency "paid fees to the International News Service to gather and distribute material of special interest" to a late dictator. And recently the Securities and Exchange Commission, in an eighty-eight page chapter of a report, attacked public relations men who "seriously mislead stockholders and potential investors" and who "have also tended to corrupt the media of communications upon which the investing public must rely for its information." What is significant here is that public relations copy may make up press release stories handed out by press agents. The reporter on the beat, whether for a national press service or for his local paper, usually can be depended upon to exercise his own critical judgment and recognize such stories for what they are worth.

As competition among the news media grows more intense, the reader-viewer must inform himself of the ways in which those changes affect the quality of reporting. Papers and television are fighting for the sustaining advertising dollar. To survive, the newspaper industry is investing 100 million dollars a year in new machines. According to one expert, by 1973 editors will be working thus with automation:

> By pushing the proper buttons on your keyboard, you will be able to retrieve material from the computer's tape file, news library or morgue, and project it on the display screens in front of you. You will be able to control the entire format of your paper and alter it in a matter of minutes.

Apropos here are the pungent comments of *Grassroots Editor,* spokesman for weekly newspapers across the country:

> Journalism is turning more and more to gadgets. Every time a publisher buys a new machine he thinks he can eliminate another brain from the editorial staff. Witness the passing of the local cartoonist. Witness the decline of the local feature story in favor of something cast from a mat or run off a tape.

But in the future as in the past, the quality of journalism will continue to depend upon the critical demands of free citizens who insist upon receiving good reporting.

We have discovered so far how denotation and connotation work in our language, especially in the areas of advertising, politics, and journalism. We have noted the need of logical reasoning. Now it is time to consider what the critical reader should know about logical thinking in order to judge and evaluate.

CRITICAL FOCUS

For our opinions on foreign, national, state, and local matters of all kinds, we must depend upon news sources furnished us by the wire services such as the Associated Press and United Press International, and the news bureaus of newspaper and broadcasting chains. So long as reporters and news editors maintain their professional integrity, we can be certain to remain an "informed electorate."

Here are some critical attitudes for readers and viewers of and listeners to news:

1. Is the report objective and complete?
2. Does it contain editorial or personal comment?
3. Judging from past performances, what is the general reliability of the source of a disturbing news item?
4. What authoritative source is quoted? What are the unsaid implications?
5. How adequate is the reporting of views and acts of "the other side"?
6. When does news reporting become *propaganda?*
7. What columnists, what editorials interpret a controversial issue or incident?
8. What is the prevailing tone of the letters to the editor?

Exercise 14   Written report. Every television *documentary* has an editorial point of view. As a report story it has also a beginning, a middle, and an end, with a concluding statement which sums up the point of view that has governed the selection of the pictures and the comments. Watch a scheduled documentary and write an analysis of it in the light of this formula.

Be certain to give sufficient details and summary to make the report intelligible to someone who may not have watched it. Do not merely retell the story, however; analyze and classify its parts.

Submit an outline along with the finished report.

List the key words most often repeated, and give their denotation and connotation in the context of the documentary.

Exercise 15   Essay assignments. Keeping in mind your local newspaper-radio-television situation, read the following comments made on American newspapers. Discuss the validity of one of the first four, by a British critic, and one of the final two, made by Americans.

1. What is acceptable to all will invariably have a place; what is hostile to some will need further consideration; what seeks to alter the *status quo* may never get to the point of being given a public airing.
2. The most significant feature of the American newspaper industry, apart from the lack of nation-wide circulations, is the number of cities with a non-competitive daily newspaper situation. . . . So the danger is that the one-newspaper town becomes the one-opinion town, where few alternatives beyond the fashionably accepted ones are discussed.
3. In such cities, television stations can censor any national network program they locally deem "objectionable," and each with its own news teams, who are sensitive to local opinion, can impose a blackout on all "undesirable" issues and questions.
4. Alan Gould of *The New York Times* is quoted as saying: "All the major advertising agencies have testified at FCC hearings that this is the basic policy in television: you do not offend."
5. I submit to you that nowhere in the United States has the press been muzzled by the government or had conformity pressed upon it. It has simply, out of a sense of "responsibility," silenced itself and supported the powers that be. I think that American newspapers are in little danger of having freedom of the press taken away from them. But many of them are in serious danger, I think, of losing their freedom through disuse, through atrophy.
6. The greatest sin of the American press is the sin of omission—the sin of refusing to take a stand on issues that might become too "hot" to handle.

chapter 5

READING FOR LOGIC

DEDUCTIVE REASONING AT WORK

By now we have some idea how through denotative and connotative meanings our language can instruct and delight us, as well as move us to buy and vote. Our language can give us the riches of civilization; it can also cheat and deceive us. But it must be assisted by *logic*, the science of reasoning, or through its misapplication. After all, a person may be well intentioned, but if his thinking is illogical, he can do us as much harm as if he were deliberately malicious. A big-hearted but impulsive and often careless soldier may make a good companion in a PX, but would you like to have him as your sergeant in a mined Southeast Asia rice paddy?

There is no easy way to become a clear thinker, either as reader or writer. Desire helps. So, too, does beginning to ask ourselves questions such as these: Where do ideas come from? How can I be expected to write—on demand!—an interesting essay when I don't seem to have anything much to say? What is the difference between my thinking and that of those who write or speak very well? Not all I hear and read sounds right or reasonable; how can I put my finger on what's wrong? How can I grow sharper as a thinker?

If properly "instructed," a clicking, humming computer might reply in part to these questions: "The more talent, previous training, drive, and basic sense of values you have, the better you will perform." No surprise here. Everyone in college perhaps assumes that much. But the "brain machines" have proved by their functions in doing everything from translating languages to calculating moon shots that the *logical methodology* of their designers and builders—mathematicians, scientists, and engineers—is necessary to all who would think clearly and, therefore, write or speak effectively.

In brief, all fields of thought and inquiry depend upon the processes of logic. So learn these well enough to apply them to your own reasoning, and you may learn how to think coherently. But you have to be willing—more than that, anxious!—to detect your own flaws in reasoning. Once you know how to think, you can properly develop the mind you have been given to its best capacity. (Again, perhaps no one really knows what that *capacity* may be until he has tested it over a lifetime.)

Anyone who has some basic views to begin with can move forward, if trained, step by step to some definite conclusions. Such is the nature of *deductive* reasoning. It begins with a general idea or principle and goes on to apply that principle to a particular case to reach a conclusion: an acceptable one if the logic is correct, and if the principle applied is a sound one.

One of the basic forms of deductive reasoning is the Aristotelian syllogism. Until A. N. Whitehead and Bertrand Russell's *Principia Mathematica* appeared in 1910, the syllogistic method flourished as the leading one, but since that day many other systems of logic have arisen and now function in computer operations. The syllogism remains, however, a useful means of demonstrating basic logic, as we use or misuse it daily.

A syllogism is a form of logical argument with a conclusion which is necessarily derived from two premises. The following are examples of syllogisms:

1. All automobiles are fuel burners. (*major premise*)
2. All hot rods are automobiles. (*minor premise*)
3. All hot rods are fuel burners. (*conclusion*)

1. No habitual criminal is trustworthy. (*major premise*)
2. He is an habitual criminal. (*minor premise*)
3. He is not trustworthy. (*conclusion*)

As can be seen, each of the three statements of a syllogism must be worded in a certain manner for the identifying relationships between the terms of the premises and the conclusion to be wholly correct. These are the *terms* of a syllogism: the major premise has a *major* term, which appears once in the major premise and once in the conclusion (examples: *fuel burners, trustworthy*). The minor premise has a *minor term*, which appears once in the minor premise and once in the conclusion (examples: *hot rods, he*). A third term called the *middle term* appears once in the major premise and once in the minor but not at all in the conclusion (examples: *automobiles, habitual criminal*). These three terms—major, minor, and middle—must be present and retain their same meaning throughout to form a valid syllogism.

These same three terms also play important grammatical roles in each of the three syllogism statements. If a *statement* is an assertion or declaration, it has, like all other sentences, a subject and a predicate. You cannot have escaped noting that each premise and conclusion had a subject and a predicate, and that the terms making up that subject and predicate appeared also in the conclusion. Here is our first syllogism marked so as to show how the minor term and the major term form the statement subject and predicate of the conclusion:

(predicate)
1. All automobiles are *fuel burners.*   (*major premise*)
(major term)

(subject)
2. *All hot rods* are automobiles.   (*minor premise*)
(minor term)

(subject)   (predicate)
3. *All hot rods are fuel burners.*   (*conclusion*)
(minor term)   (major term)

This syllogism has *validity*, for the reason that its conclusion has been properly *inferred* or *deduced* from the major and minor premises; its conclusion consists of subject and predicate, which are, respectively, the minor term of the minor premise and the major term of the major premise. But the *truth* of the syllogism will depend upon the general acceptance of the facts in the premises.

For a concrete illustration of how the syllogistic method may be applied, let us consider certain possible military decisions regarding jungle warfare in South Vietnam. Our military advisers there found that jet-powered planes were not the aircraft most suitable for fighting in such a terrain. Jets flew at too high speeds for the kind of tactical bombing and strafing required. In syllogistic form, the reasoning took some such shape as this:

> (predicate)
> 1. All low-speed bombing planes are desired tactical planes.
>   (subject)
> 2. All old B-26 bombers are low-speed bombing planes.
>   (subject)   (predicate)
> 3. All old B-26 bombers are desired tactical planes.

The major term is *desired tactical planes,* the minor term is *All old B-26 bombers,* and the middle term is *low-speed bombing planes.* It was such reasoning that led to several other conclusions, ending up with the orders to update all B-26 type of bombers at hand and to hurry along new versions of such planes, as yet on the drawing boards.

To study all the intricacies of syllogism constructions and their rules is the work of a course in logic, but for our purposes of learning to examine the deductive reasoning of what we read, we can profit from running through some basic guidelines useful in checking the validity of syllogisms; for we need to learn to construct syllogisms out of the reasoning found in what we read and hear.

> 1. Rules regarding *negative* premise statements.
>   *a.* No conclusion can be derived from two negative premises. Example:
>
>   No men are immortal.
>
>   No women are men.
>
>   *b.* If one of the premises is negative, the conclusion must be negative.
>
>   Example:

Valid	*Invalid*
All good citizens are voters.	All good citizens are voters.
John is not a voter.	John is not a voter.
John is not a good citizen.	John is a good citizen.

> *c.* A negative conclusion cannot be derived from two affirmative premises.

Example:

Valid	*Invalid*
All music is rhythmical.	All music is rhythmical.
All Bach's works are music.	All Bach's works are music.
All Bach's works are rhythmical.	Some of Bach's works are not rhythmical.

2. Rules concerning *particular* premise statements. (A premise is *particular* when it refers to only a part or portion of the members of a class, usually indicated by the word *some*.)

   a. If one premise is particular, the conclusion must be particular. Example:

Valid	*Invalid*
All teen-agers buy rock 'n' roll records.	All teen-agers buy rock 'n' roll records.
Some girls are teen-agers.	Some girls are teen-agers.
Some girls buy rock 'n' roll records.	All girls buy rock 'n' roll records.

   b. A syllogism cannot have two particular premises. Example:

Valid	*Invalid*
All daydreamers are self-centered.	Some voters are U.S. citizens.
Some plans are daydreams.	Some French citizens are voters.
Some plans are self-centered.	Some French citizens are U.S. citizens.

3. Rules regarding *distributed terms.* (A distributed term is one which includes all members of a class; for example, the term *all U.S. citizens* is distributed because it refers to *all* of the class *U.S. citizens.* The term *some U.S. citizens* is *undistributed,* since it does not include *all* U.S. citizens. Of course, a distributed term may also have a negative construction and thus *exclude* all members of a class, as does the term *no U.S. citizen.*
   a. The middle term in at least one of the two premises must be distributed. Example:

Valid	*Invalid*
All carnivorous animals are meat eaters.	Some meat eaters are lions.

Some lions are carnivorous animals.

Some lions are meat eaters. (In this example, the middle term, *carnivorous animals*, is distributed in the major premise.)

All men are meat eaters.

Some men are lions. (In this example, the middle term, *meat eaters*, is not distributed in either premise.)

b. No term can be distributed in the conclusion if it is undistributed in the premise from which it comes. Example:

Valid
All good citizens are voters.
Some men are good citizens.
Some men are voters.
(No term is distributed in the conclusion.)

Invalid
Some women are voters.
No men are women.
No men are voters.
(In this example, the major term, *voters*, is distributed in the conclusion. It is undistributed in the major premise, however, for it does not refer here to *all* voters.)

Such are the rules that govern the validity of a syllogism. But remember that even a valid syllogism must have acceptable or true premise statements to be judged a good syllogism by the critical reader. He challenges assumptions since he knows they lead to conclusions; and if he accepts the premise assumptions, he may have to accept the conclusions.

One means of increasing critical sharpness in detecting assumptions and forming syllogisms is to become aware of *enthymemes*. An enthymeme is an abbreviated syllogism, one in which a premise is omitted or unexpressed, as in this example: "Joan is a great swimmer. She made the Olympic team." Here is the enthymeme filled out as the syllogism:

All who make the Olympic team are great swimmers.
Joan made the Olympic team.
Joan is a great swimmer.

The above syllogism and enthymeme are both valid and true, but what about this one? "John must be a U.S. citizen. After all, he lives in America." It forms this syllogism:

All who live in America are U.S. citizens.
John lives in America.
John is a U.S. citizen.
Both the enthymeme and the syllogism are unacceptable for the reason
that the major premise is not true.

Now that we have some idea of syllogistic reasoning, let's try our
hand at evaluating the reasoning in the following newspaper editorial.
What enthymemes or syllogisms do you find in its reasoning?

> Of late, however, there has come a really disturbing development.
> The RCA 301, described by its manufacturers as a completely tran-
> sistorized, general purpose electronic data processing system, turns
> out to have a wholly unexpected talent for writing blank verse. This
> was discovered by Clair Phillippy, who is employed by the Radio
> Corp. of America to instruct its customers in the use of RCA computer
> equipment.
>
> Mr. Phillippy gave his electronic sidekick a basic vocabulary of
> 100 words, of which 10 were designated as "starters"—those to be
> used at the beginning of each line. He instructed the machine to
> concentrate on a format of four-line verses, with each of the first three
> having seven words and the final line only three. Then he punched
> the starter button and sat back to await results.
>
> The RCA 301 hummed and gurgled and clicked and blinked
> briefly and then its high-speed electric typewriters started kicking out
> blank verse at the incredible rate of 150 complete four-line poems a
> minute. Some of them were a bit obscure—but then, in modern
> poetry as well as modern art, incomprehensibility is highly admired
> by some critics. Take the poem No. 929:
>> "While dream flowed blindly on broken hopes
>> Still space drained sickly o'er broken loves
>> Your light driven slowly from furtive men
>> No heavens slept."
>
> Not bad, if you're a fan of T. S. Eliot, who wrote:
>> "Garlic and sapphires in the mud
>> Clot the bedded axle-tree."
>
> Or:
>> "We, content at the last
>> If our temporal reversion nourish
>> Not too far from the yew-tree
>> The life of significant soil."
>
> While we suppose some serious poets will scorn the thought the

RCA 301 could be considered one of their number, Mr. Eliot seemed to endorse the concept of electronic versifying when he also declared:
"Poetry is not a turning loose of emotion, but an escape from emotion; it is not the expression of personality, but an escape from personality."

By this definition, the wholly impersonal and emotionless RCA 301 ought to be an ideal poet. But let it not extend its ambitions to editorial writing. If we see the thing rolling into our ivory tower, waggling its potentiometers ingratiatingly, it's going to get this typewriter right in the multiplexer.

Will we agree that although this piece says it with a smile, the writer seems pleased to equate the tape-fed computer with T. S. Eliot and others as a modern poet? On the basis of six lines ripped out of the body of T. S. Eliot's poetry and one sentence taken out of context in criticism, the editor reasons thus: Much of modern poetry is obscure or incomprehensible but still is admired; this machine "blank verse" poem is obscure and, therefore, admirable. Next, modern poetry is impersonal and emotionless; this machine poem certainly is impersonal and emotionless; therefore, the machine poem is modern poetry. Also, then, the RCA 301 is *an ideal poet.*

We can now restate some of the editor's basic ideas about poetry and machine-made verse in the form of a syllogism:

> Much obscure verse is admirable.
> This machine blank verse is obscure verse.
> This machine blank verse is admirable.

Putting aside the question of whether we find the premises acceptable, let's examine the syllogism for its validity. Applying our third guideline on distributed terms, we can say that the syllogism is invalid because the middle term—*obscure verse*—is not distributed in either premise. In other words, *much obscure verse* does not account for *all obscure verse,* and we have no way of knowing whether the machine-made verse is part of that verse considered admirable.

It is evident, then, that to question logic, to examine syllogistic reasoning, implies inquiry rather than cynicism. It means we must consider and weigh other people's thinking as well as our own. We must examine our own writing carefully for invalid conclusions and unacceptable assumptions.

Young science students are gradually led to see that the most basic "laws" of their vast systems of knowledge are often only theories. Instructors know that through fresh visions of the obvious, new discoveries can be made. Social science researchers constantly work at techniques and approaches giving them fresh insights into common social behavior. Disquieting as it may be at times, liberal arts students also need to question assumptions in their intellectual disciplines. In fact, all trained, thinking readers and writers try to penetrate the facade of language to glimpse the framework of logic that gives solidity, or its appearances, to argument.

CRITICAL FOCUS

A *syllogism* is a form of deductive reasoning wherein a *conclusion* is inferred from two *premises.*
Each syllogism has a *major premise,* a *minor premise,* and a *conclusion;* these are the three *statements* of a syllogism.
Warning: Do not confuse syllogism *premises*—assumptions—with syllogism *terms*—major, minor, and middle.
Do not accept a syllogism or an *enthymeme*—an abbreviated syllogism—unless it has both *validity* and *truth.*

   Exercise 1   Written assignment. (*a*) List as many as you can of the current assumptions regarding your college or university held by your fellow students and those held by the surrounding community. (*b*) Give an example of both groups of assumptions, and analyze each for the logic behind it.

   Exercise 2   Written assignment. Without regard for their *truth,* but with care for *validity,* state in syllogistic form the premises and conclusion to be found in each of these groups of statements.

   1. When the days begin to grow short and the winds chill, we see again that all songbirds are migratory birds. Then we learn once more that the robins, which have sung and chirped the summer through, obey the instincts of all migratory birds.
   2. In the distorting mirrors of the carnival fun house, all fat people are thin people, and all children are fat people. Don't ask me how that happens. It just does. So what do you know? All children looking in the fantastic fun house mirrors are thin people! How is that possible?
   3. All salmon will return to their hatching waters to spawn. It is hard to believe, but even the fingerling fish hatched in the upper reaches

of the Columbia River will, when fully grown, return to those exact hatching waters to spawn. Even those fingerlings hatched in a university pool-basin with access to the sea will return to that pool in due time to spawn.

4. Some nylon hose are snag-proof, they say. You couldn't prove it by me. But Joe's wife claims she has worn a pair for six months and given them hard wear, too. Well, if a pair lasted that long, maybe what they say is true.

5. On August 10, 1964, the eve of Herbert Hoover's ninetieth birthday, the AP quotes as follows from his statement: "I have searched in these travels—and sought to learn from books and from the leaders of other nations—what it is that has given America this super-abundance. What is the key to it?

"The key, I am convinced, is that among us there is greater freedom for the individual man and woman than in any other great nation. In the Constitution and in the Bill of Rights are enumerated the specific freedoms. . . . Freedom is the open window through which pours the sunlight of the human spirit and of human dignity. With the preservation of these moral and spiritual qualities, and with God's grace, will come further greatness for our country."

Exercise 3   Written assignment. To be able to distinguish premises from conclusions in an argument requires care and practice. This exercise consists of a number of deductive statements, each of which includes several premises and a definite conclusion. You are not asked to put the statements into syllogistic form. Nor are you required to prove or disprove premises or conclusions. *Simply pick out the premises and the conclusion for each of the following statements.*

Example: "It is disgusting to read the products that ooze from the typewriters of the New Frontier columnists, such as Marquis Childs, Walter Lippmann, Stewart Alsop, Max Freedman and other propagandists, thrust at us in the daily newspapers in support of the Johnson Administration, when the people want Barry Goldwater." Possible premises: Some columnists and newspapers are propagandists for the New Frontier. But the people are all for Goldwater and against the Johnson administration. Possible conclusion: Some columnists and newspapers are against the people.

1. For ten years I was a supervisor of freshman English courses and came, cautiously to be sure, to think of myself as something of an expert in "the female in academe"; that is, I came to consider

myself a practical expert, not a philosopher about her or the environment she creates. I also found her quite likeable, the sources of her problems being rarely the self-love and the sense of injured merit that seem to explain so many men.

2. The subversive image of Mark Hopkins and his wretched log has the power to blind us to a good many truths about the educational process—among them the simple fact that decent education and research must be expensive undertakings. To discourage an open and intelligent concern for money—for salaries, grants, endowments, research funds, and amenities—is to invite mediocrity.

3. The basic functions of a college or university are to preserve, augment, criticize, and transmit knowledge and to foster creative capacities. These functions are performed by a community of scholars who must be free to exercise independent judgment in the planning and execution of their educational responsibilities. The government of an institution of higher education should be designed to allow the institution to select and carry out its responsibilities with maximum effectiveness and integrity.

4. A group of Portland architects said Saturday the "garish, gaudy" color of Northwest Tower Center had wreaked "aesthetic havoc" on the neighboring community and likened its bright yellow paint job to a bad smell or a loud noise.

But Gene W. Rossman, executive director of the Housing Authority of Portland, said the tenants at the community project . . . disagreed. "They think it's bright and sunshiny. They like it," he said.

5. After reading your article on . . . [mathematics] I was reminded of a new method of reading. These same types of people with Ph.D. behind their names introduced that, too, and they called it "Sight Reading." . . . It seems I will have to teach my grandchildren how to do math, the same as I had to teach my children how to read by using phonics.

6. . . . As a journalism educator, I am obliged to insist that the mass media be included in your study as an institution that has the power and the responsibility to influence. Thanks to you and your enlightened editors, *Morality U.S.A.* may well stir the American conscience to an examination and betterment of itself. And if such be the case, then we can be grateful that *Look* is exercising the kind of influence and journalistic leadership our country so desperately needs.

7. . . . If every mother and dad believed there was a heaven to gain and a hell to shun, and would take the time to teach their

children this, the morality of our America would be unquestionably high.

8. The immorality of which you complain is grounded in the very philosophy which permeates the approach to your article. You say the bad morality of Mr. Average American is the fault of the government, business and churches. You add the weight of your influence to the already prevalent opinion that " 'everything I do that's wrong is someone else's fault.' "

   I have not abandoned my faith in the capacity of the individual to be morally responsible—nor am I willing to absolve myself of my failings on the grounds the government tempted me, and the church failed me.

9. J. Edgar Hoover, writing in the FBI's Law Enforcement Bulletin: "Morality is one of the more perplexing and controversial problems facing our nation . . . because of individual and collective moral cowardice in society. We do not have the courage to stand in conflict with the mad rush for material wealth, indulgence and social prestige. Many persons are so preoccupied with selfishness and greed they no longer know—nor care for that matter—where honor stops and dishonor commences. Others are simply confused. Rationalization and double standards have so clouded some moral principles that right and wrong are no longer clearly distinguishable."

10. You know the end [of the world] is coming. . . . Communistic leaders are getting ready to push the launching buttons that will fill the skies with missiles. China is getting ready to march with its millions. Africa is shaking itself from sleep like a mighty giant. South America is rumbling like a panther. Crime, delinquency, drug addiction, sex, hate and fear are spread around the world like a cancer.

Exercise 4   Written assignment. Supplying the missing premise in an enthymeme is of fundamental importance in determining its validity and truth. Set up a syllogism and supply the missing premise in the following enthymemes, as in this example.

Example: "So you're buying a foreign car, huh? You're not very patriotic, I'd say." Major premise (missing): All who buy foreign cars are unpatriotic. Minor premise: You are buying a foreign car. Conclusion: You are unpatriotic.

1. To have great football, college coaches need many scholarships and good jobs for their players.

2. He used to smoke cigarettes. Now he smokes a pipe.
3. Some people think they know everything. Oh, I'm sorry! I didn't know you were a junior.
4. There is said to be no real difference between all these advertised pain-relieving pills. I'll take this bargain bottle of aspirin.
5. In the United States we have a mess of measurements, like the inch, pound, foot, mile, pint, teaspoonful, bushel, fathom, and all those terrible fractions. We ought to adopt the metric system of weights and measurements.
6. You don't look very perky today. What's the matter? Too much partying?
7. I'm letting my hair grow out. It's the style now.
8. What—another parking ticket? Dear, when are you ever going to learn to watch out for the meters?

Exercise 5   Discussion assignment. Bring to class three mounted newspaper or magazine clippings of letters or articles. Outline the syllogisms or enthymemes which you have found in them, and be prepared to discuss their logic.

Exercise 6   Written assignment. List any of the assumptions, unproved propositions, or erroneous conclusions found in *one* of the following quotations:

1. Susanne Langer, page 6, Exercise 9.
2. Peace Corps volunteer, pages 11 to 12.
3. *Sense and Sensibility,* pages 14 and 15.
4. *Billy Budd,* pages 19 and 20.
5. *In the Castle of My Skin,* pages 23 and 24.
6. "Never Love Unless You Can," page 34.
7. "How Many Trees Can a Chipmunk Eat?" pages 37 and 38.
8. "Attention, Belief, and Believing Action," pages 40 and 41.
9. "The Fundamental Freedom," pages 41 and 42.
10. *Vogue,* page 49, passage 1.
11. Passage 3, page 50.
12. "How Not to Read a Book," page 132.
13. Mutability, pages 134–144.
14. *Boring* vs. *Jolly,* pp. 72–73.
15. "Born into a Tax-burdened World," page 74.
16. Congressman Morris K. Udall, page 213.
17. "Setting the Record Straight," pages 83 to 84.
18. "Sex-violence Reporting," page 86.

Exercise 7   Discussion assignment. Quote and analyze five unwarranted conclusions, unquestioned assumptions, or facile propositions heard in TV commercials or found in advertisements.

Exercise 8   Discussion assignment. What is the logic leading to the conclusion stated in the final paragraph of this newspaper editorial?

Hang Tight on Loose

Hurray for the women of Loose, England, who refused to recommend changing the name of their village. They don't mind a bit being called Loose women.

The town's name does not refer to the morals of its inhabitants, but is supposed to derive from several streams which lose themselves under ground. Coincidental double meanings like this add a lot to the fun of language, and it would be a shame to stamp them out.

For example, it is possible to go to Yale University on a particular kind of scholarship and be known as a Sterling Fellow, for the John Sterling who established the grant. Down in California there is a whole college called after a man whose name was Mudd, and no one thinks the less of him or it. And we have sometimes pondered the problem which would face the people of Remote, Ore., if they should ever form a chamber of commerce and try advertising their well-named community as being right on the beaten path.

Plenty of ugliness in this world masquerades under a pretty name. It is refreshing to find people willing to let their actions speak louder than their label.

Exercise 9   Written assignment. This sonnet by John Donne has several basic assumptions that serve as premises leading to a conclusion. What are they, expressed in your own words? What is there about such a poem as this that makes the assumptions in context satisfactory?

Death, Be Not Proud

Death, be not proud, though some have called thee
Mighty and dreadful, for thou art not so;
For those whom thou think'st thou dost overthrow
Die not, poor Death; nor yet canst thou kill me.
From rest and sleep, which but thy pictures be,
Much pleasure; then from thee much more must flow,

And soonest our best men with thee do go,
Rest of their bones, and soul's delivery.
Thou art slave to fate, chance, kings, and desperate men,
And dost with poison, war, and sickness dwell,
And poppy or charms can make us sleep as well
And better than thy stroke; why swell'st thou then?
One short sleep past, we wake eternally;
And death shall be no more; Death, thou shalt die.

THE LANGUAGE OF INDUCTIVE THOUGHT

Where do new ideas come from? To be really new, like the discoveries of a Galileo, a Newton, a Curie, or an Einstein, they evidently cannot be deduced from already established propositions through inference alone. Someone of genius and scholarship and, above all, courage and perseverance is the one most likely to hit upon the new concept. But first he must feel a keen need of new approaches. He will be acutely aware of gaps and holes in existing knowledge—vacancies crying for fulfilling answers.

This kind of discovery is made in that mysterious fashion that poets call *insight* or the *intuitive glimpse,* and that others might call the *hunch* or *informed guess.* It is generally termed *inductive* reasoning. Here is how, together with deduction, it worked a revolution in American law.

In the 1870s Oliver Wendell Holmes, then a jurist in his thirties, became increasingly dissatisfied with the theory of law dominating the legal thinking of his age. That theory came from Roman law as that ancient legal system was interpreted by such thinkers as the German philosophers Kant and Hegel. Their interpretations placed the basis of all law upon the individual and his will. Holmes came to see that Kant and Hegel had imposed their own notions of moral principle on legal theory. At the same time, he felt that laws framed only in the light of this unchanging moral theory must be both unrealistic and too often fallacious. Any theory that favored letting a thief keep possession of his stolen goods on the grounds that the theft was "the objective realization of the will" must be false, he reasoned, and he began looking for a better principle.

In his time, when the foundations of American law were not wholly established, he felt he had the right and the duty to look further for realistic and satisfactory concepts of law. He began rereading the great philosophers on law among the Greeks and the Romans. Not finding what he wanted among them, he went on to English common law of the Middle Ages. In the records of the practical decisions of the medieval English courts, he sensed the solution he was seeking. He gradually realized inductively what may now appear to be an obvious fact: "The life of the law has not been logic; it has been experience."

Holmes resolved afresh the problem of the relation of personal morality to acts of law by realizing that "though the law starts from the distinctions, and uses the language of morality, it necessarily ends in external standards not dependent on the actual consciousness of the individual." The thief should be judged on how much he stole and how he stole it, not on how he had made up his mind and directed his will to stealing. Using this proposition as a premise, Holmes worked out the conclusion that the function of law is to protect society from harm, and that the standards it sets up should be observable by any average person having foresight enough to see that his possible actions might produce harm.

There was no need generally for courts to probe into the intentions of the accused. The thief stole, and since everyone knows that stealing is a crime, the criminal should be punished. Although Holmes is said to be not always consistent in his arguments, he admits that the thief, though guilty of violating an "objective standard," may under extenuating circumstances be excused by the court. In any case, punishment is not to take revenge on the lawbreaker, but to prevent harmful crime. Thus largely through inductive processes, Holmes revolutionized legal theory and made possible the further changes and growth characteristic of American law.

As will be shown in The Language of Science (in Chapter 7) and in Reading Imaginative Expression (Chapter 6), the kind of thinking called *inductive* ("leading into, toward") goes on constantly and is intermingled with deduction and feeling. As many others have said elsewhere, John Dewey in his *Art as Experience* states it is only psychology that has separated thought from feeling in the first place. Psychologists, in their effort to define and distinguish, often classify and separate things that may be inseparable. Thus, Dewey points out, scientists and philosophers have come to be classed as thinkers, and poets and artists as ones who *feel,* whereas in reality both are comparably engaged in *emotionalized thinking.*

For the sake of clarity and emphasis, then, we deal here with inductive thinking as though it were separate from the deductive or from emotion. All three may often be blended in moments of revery or meditation—but probably seldom as richly—as they are in this portion of *Meditation XVII* by John Donne:

> The bell doth toll for him that thinks it doth; and though it intermit again, yet from that minute that that occasion wrought upon him, he is united to God. Who casts not up his eye to the sun when it rises? but who takes off his eye from a comet when that breaks out? Who bends not his ear to any bell which upon any occasion rings? but who can remove it from that bell which is passing a piece of himself out of this world? No man is an island, entire of itself, every man is a piece of the continent, a part of the main. If a clod be washed away by the sea, Europe is the less, as well as if a promontory were, as well as if a manor of thy friend's or of thine own were. Any man's death diminishes me because I am involved in mankind, and therefore never send to know for whom the bell tolls, it tolls for thee. Neither can we call this a begging of misery or a borrowing of misery, as though we were not miserable enough of ourselves but must fetch in more from the next house, in taking upon us the misery of our neighbors. Truly it were an excusable covetousness if we did; for affliction is a treasure, and scarce any man hath enough of it. No man hath affliction enough that is not matured and ripened by it and made fit for God by that affliction. If a man carry treasure in bullion, or in a wedge of gold, and have none coined into current money, his treasure will not defray him as he travels. Tribulation is treasure in the nature of it, but it is not current money, in the use of it, except we get nearer and nearer our home, heaven, by it. Another man may be sick too, and sick to death, and this affliction may lie in his bowels as gold in a mine and be of no use to him; but this bell that tells me of his affliction digs out and applies that gold to me, if by this consideration of another's danger I take mine own into contemplation and so secure myself by making my recourse to my God, who is our only security.

The famous phrase, *no man is an island,* may blind one to the complex fusion of assumptions and conclusions given most solid substance herein by the fervent faith and poetic power of their author. He "speaks" to us with conviction that stirs us by the vast scope of its vision. From the beginning, when he first questions the import of the bell's tolling, he is led—and through the powerful connotations of his language leads us—from one intuitive discovery of meaning to another.

He sees and feels and discovers, guesses, and concludes all at one and the same time. By his genius and art he also enables us to share that rich experience of mixed realizations leading to the conclusion that in living and dying all mankind are one because of their Christian immortality. Some modern readers may consider this persuasive essay as being too emotional, but they can hardly deny the genuineness of the poetic conviction that gave it utterance. (For an example of the overuse and illogical use of emotionalism see page 163.)

But let us now return to separating the inseparable in order to see just how *induction* is the opposite of *deduction*. Deductive thought, we know, begins with the general and goes to the particular. For example, if we assume that all freshmen are likely to have times when they feel discouraged about college, we may conclude on seeing Mary, a freshman, looking down at the mouth, that Mary may likely be discouraged about something related to college life as a freshman. We have jumped from *all* freshmen to Mary; whether the conclusion is justifiable in fact is another matter, but the logic is correct.

Turn the situation about. You are a freshman newly arrived on campus. After a series of mishaps continuing through the first two months or more of classes and campus life, you feel very much discouraged and blame yourself. Then, to your relief, you learn from talking to others like yourself that practically everyone else is in the same boat. Through induction you conclude: All freshmen are likely to feel discouraged at times.

Take a more complex example of inductive thinking, mixed, of course, with deduction. A psychologist, curious about what makes some dogs of the same breed better pets than others, works out a method that he hopes will lead to some general conclusion. He will observe a large number of litters and record everything he notes about their behavior during a ten-minute period each day. He is on the watch for the kind of behavior called *imprinting*, which is *the phenomenon of primary socialization*. In oversimplified terms, he is trying to learn what makes puppies sociable. He records four groups of basic behavioral abilities: sensory, motor, social, and learning capacity. After many experiments, he finally arrives at the conclusion that the best time to adopt a puppy as a pet is when it is between six and eight weeks old. It also must have been reared in contact with human beings. This discovery is an inductive one; it is a generalization from specific observations.

Trained observers who are also skilled writers even adapt the inductive method to their writing style. They lead the reader to the general principle, usually expressed in a topic sentence, as is exemplified in this paragraph:

> For the foreigner who goes to Africa expecting to find the élite busily engaged in building a new nation, the first meetings with African officials are likely to be disappointing. One of my first acquaintances in Dakar was a top official in the Ministry of Rural Economy, whom I will call M. N. He held a French law degree, spoke French perfectly, and was clearly in the higher reaches of the élite. His salary was $4,000 a year—more than the average peasant earns in a lifetime—plus government-supplied housing and other privileges. Like almost all African officials, M. N. was graciously hospitable to a foreigner, whether in his office or in his home. When he said "drop in any time" he meant it. He was patient with my questions, though he skirted any subject that suggested any conflict among the Senegalese, but it soon became obvious that talk about peasant problems bored him. He wanted to show me his new slide projector or talk about cars. M. N., I sensed, was profoundly conservative, and with good reason: he had suddenly made it to the top of the heap, and he was mainly interested in enjoying his new position.

The main point is suggested by the opening, but the final sentence makes the specific charge general. The danger in reading excerpts such as this one lies in the possibility that the realism here of the reporting may beguile the reader into accepting without further proof that this one example proves that all African leaders are like this one, a generalization that no mere assertion or suggestion based on one case can justify.

CRITICAL FOCUS

1. *Inductive thinking fuses with emotion and deduction.*
2. *It may work with the startling immediacy of a* hunch.
3. *It leads or jumps from particular facts to conclusions.*
4. *It may require being checked by the careful demands of logic yet to be presented.*

Exercise 10   The following little drama of a domestic crisis in a modern Hungarian household offers the analytical reader a number of revealing inferences and conclusions regarding the economy, the family, and other aspects of life and people under strained conditions. List at least six conclusions derived from reading this dialogue. (*Note:* "Three to four thousand forints [$150 to $200] a month is a fair salary for two people in administrative work in Hungary.")

The woman said: "Even the Kelemens have a car. It's high time we got one."

"Maybe you can tell me where we're to get the money?"

"The Kelemens together earn only 3,500 forints a month. We earn 4,200!"

"And you want to buy a car with this 4,200? You want us to exchange our apartment for a laundry room, as the Kelemens did?"

"We can sell other things besides the apartment."

"Like what?"

"Well, the bookcase. It's a beautiful piece. The State Second-Hand Store would give four grand for it. We could get another four for the books."

The man got angry. "I won't sell my books! And anyway, what good would eight thousand do?"

The woman took pencil and paper. "Listen. We've got seven thousand forints in the bank. The colonial bookcase and the books would bring eight. Mother will give us four—that makes nineteen."

"I won't part with my books!"

"Yes, you will. Anyhow we've got another bookcase in that set of furniture from Czechoslovakia. Which gives me an idea! What if we bring down grandmother's furniture from the attic and—"

"You mean you'd sell the Czech living room set?"

"To buy the car, why not?"

"You want to be like the Gomoris? They're sleeping on ironing boards because they sold everything they owned to buy that car of theirs."

"Grandmother's furniture is the finest walnut."

"Yes, but it was made in 1890."

"But by a real craftsman! A private enterprise product. Anyway, the Czech set is worth at least fourteen. And that gives us a total of thirty-three thousand. We can borrow the rest from the National Savings Bank."

"And how are you going to pay back the loan?"

"We'll cut down on our expenses. You like one-dish dinners; so do I."

"But not every day! And to have to sit in that shaky, old, motheaten plush chair again! And on the old sofa with the china buttons!"

"You can stand it if you've got your own car to sit in."

"You can't even drive."

"If I can run a household, I can run a car. I'll learn. Mrs. Kelemen can drive. I saw her yesterday in their new Skod *Felicia*."

"What! They traded in their Trabant on a Felicia?" The husband was surprised. "Where did they get the money for the difference?"

"They got a price for their laundry room."

"But that's where they lived! Where do they sleep now?"

"In their car, naturally. And it's not a bad idea, either. At least no one can steal the tires during the night."

Exercise 11   Writing challenge. Can you write a similar dialogue that suggests certain features typical of an American household trying hard to *keep up with the Joneses?*

Exercise 12   Discussion assignment. Test your comprehension of inductive reasoning by arranging the items making up the following confusions of raw data, facts, and ideas into a proper logical sequence having inductive order. Also, make up a "bundle" of your own.

1. Speedometer last night showed about 6225. Both doors unlocked. Now 6249.8. No key in ignition. Somebody "borrowed" it. Filter cigarette butts in ash tray. Parked a little closer than usual to this cement pillar. Gas gauge might be down. Did I lock the door on her side last night?

2. Latest *Life* was lying on the coffee table. Some kind of synthetic rug. Served a red wine with the roast beef. Twin-speaker hi-fi secondhand but marvelous bass. Tomato aspic salad. Middle class? Scotch and soda. Swedish blonde bookcase full of *Book of Knowledge*. Both wear dark horn rim specs. Didn't try to sell me insurance policy. Talked about some stock he just bought. Upper middle? Two kids, both under eight—cute and already know it.

READING FOR ANALYSIS OF REASONING

A newspaper banner over a column bearing a Washington Associated Press dateline reads: "Critic Claims Professors Lazy." The article is a report of a meeting of the American Council on Education and begins:

"College professors are lazy, tradition-bound, inefficient, conceited and devoted to their own comfort, a former colleague says."

In news style, this opening is the conclusion of the argument as the AP reporter analyzed the speech. The speaker was a vice president of the Ford Foundation's fund for the advancement of education, and his audience was one thousand college professors and administrators at their Washington meeting. He complained that after the foundation spent 60 million dollars on attempts at improving schools and colleges and saw some success in experiments, the institutions returned to traditional teaching procedures. Particularly, they refused to teach by television, and they still preferred, as surveys showed, to continue teaching small classes by the lecture method. He was highly displeased that out of thirty teaching procedures included in the survey questionnaire, teaching by television rated no higher than eighteenth.

Readers of the AP summary of the probably long speech would be left wondering what portions had been left omitted and what their bearing would have been on the part reported. They would have to remember that newspaper reports of learned society meetings are generally colored by the reporter's eagerness to find a dramatic story that might make headlines, as did this one.

The conclusion opening the report is inferred from two basic syllogisms:

1. Whoever underwrites TV experiments can expect college professors to adopt new methods.
2. The foundation spent 60 million dollars on such experiments!
3. The foundation can expect the professors to adopt new methods.

1. All those not living up to foundation expectations are lazy, tradition-bound, etc.
2. College professors did not live up to foundation expectations.
3. College professors are lazy, tradition-bound, etc.

Both syllogisms reveal assumed premises in their first statement. It would appear to an uninformed reader that perhaps the foundation took too much for granted when it gave the huge sums for the experiments. What solid evidence of possible success did it have to justify expending such amounts? How successful, really, were *the many cases* deemed such by the speaker, and would the new methods bring savings? Must teachers who do not feel convinced by the new methods necessarily be *lazy, tradition-bound,* etc.? Perhaps faulty communication may be the cause of this professorial intransigence. We are not told whether the questionnaire was given to only participating institutions or to others as well.

A proposition that unwisely includes all of a class or kind is called a *hasty generalization.* This fallacy in reasoning appears in the newspaper headline and opening lead: "College professors are lazy." It does not say *some* or *a number,* or even *many.* On the contrary, it implies that *all* are such. (Incidentally, the report lumps all levels of college and university teaching staff into one rank—*professors.* Now, everyone knows that the low men on the totem pole—the instructors and the assistant professors—who are engaged in teaching composition are not *lazy.* Look at the mountains of papers they have to correct!)

CRITICAL FOCUS

Watch out for the sweeping statements, broad claims, and seemingly reliable statistics that make up the hasty generalization.

Exercise 13   Discussion assignment. Point out any *hasty generalizations* to be found in the following statements. Suggest what would be required to make the deductions valid ones.

1. Out of the twelve persons that the district attorney has prosecuted for criminal negligence, in cases where a death resulted from drunken driving, eleven have been convicted. Of the eleven drivers convicted, nine were in their twenties. So, one can say that in one prosecuting attorney's district, at least, the young drivers are the dangerous ones.
2. If colonies of staphylococci are attacked and destroyed by microscopic fungi, the fungi must secrete some antibacterial substance. Alexander Fleming proved this happened with penicillium fungus. So penicillin can be used for most cases of bacterial infection.
3. I have attended drag races steadily for the past five years and have as yet to see either participant or spectator injured as a result of a drag meet. In these five years, I have seen but one accident, and this occurred after the meet. It was pure coincidence that the accident happened to a participant, for it could have happened to anyone. So I say drag racers don't drive fast

and recklessly on all highways because drag-strip racing makes them that way.

4. It's a poor history book: no insights, no value judgments, no drama.

5. There is too much bureaucracy these days. They litter the space above our atmosphere with copper needles; they spray our fields and yards when we don't want it done; they take our homes for freeways and cloverleafs; they've got organizations to run everything and everybody.

6. As *The Feminine Mystique* says, there is one basic reason why our American society is a mess of nervous breakdowns, lung cancer, divorce, undisciplined children, adultery, and all else. It's the fault of the American woman who has let herself be trapped and chained in marriage and housework and who resents it!

7. Of course, Hawaii is about the healthiest spot in the world. Life expectancy there for men is 69.5 years, as compared to the 66.5 years for men on the mainland. And a woman can expect to reach 73.3.

8. What's wrong with the country? Just one thing. There are 11.5 million adult women who started but never finished high school, and less than half of all women over twenty-five are high school graduates. And these are the mothers of our families!

9. Somebody is trying to make atheists and pagans out of our children in school. In the public schools, they won't let us distribute Bibles or any other kind of religious literature. In her classroom, a teacher can't talk about the Bible except as some kind of literature. They can't even play Handel's *Messiah* or show pictures of "The Last Supper" except as samples of art. At Christmas they won't let a crib with angels be set up, and nobody at any time had better be caught talking about religions unless in the way of history. Yes sir, I'm telling you. There's something behind all this.

10. Many people have extrasensory perception. They can make people turn around and look back just by staring at a person's neck. I experiment with it riding on the bus, and when I really concentrate, I can make someone turn around every time.

Exercise 14   Essay assignment. By this time you may be willing to grant that poems can have a highly logical pattern of emotional thought. Paraphrase these stanzas from a section of Alfred, Lord Tennyson's *In Memoriam* by giving in your own words not only the emotional meaning of the language but also the clear sequence of his thought. It is inductive.

I envy not in any moods
  The captive void of noble rage,
  The linnet born within the cage,
That never knew the summer woods;

I envy not the beast that takes
  His license in the field of time,
  Unfettered by the sense of crime,
To whom a conscience never wakes;

Nor, what may count itself as blest,
  The heart that never plighted troth
  But stagnates in the weeds of sloth;
Nor any want-begotten rest.

I hold it true, whate'er befall;
  I feel it, when I sorrow most;
  'Tis better to have loved and lost
Than never to have loved at all.

RECOGNIZING TYPES OF ARGUMENTS

Syllogistic analysis can spotlight the skeletal logic of any lecture or
reading assignment developing a proposition. It can reveal flaws and
strengths in inferences and conclusions. But a convincing argument
needs the shaping features of rhetoric as much as it does those of logic.
These rhetorical qualities are best seen in the basic forms or outlines
that tradition considers effective for convincing speech and writing.

To begin with, remember that argumentation is one of the four
kinds of discourse—exposition, description, and narration being the
other three, and each having techniques of its own. Its purpose to
convince and persuade implies that there will be those who will disagree. More than likely, they will not disagree with everything, only
with certain points. These chief points of difference on which the
argument stands or falls are called *the issues.* Issues raise the questions
that have to be answered, and every type of argument has certain
standard inquiries to determine its chief issues. Skilled debaters know
them by heart and become expert in applying them.

Before listing any types and their formula issues, let's see what
happens in one typical argument. In this passage, what is James Boswell asking himself?

I was deeply offended with the behaviour of this nobleman. I had resolved to give up all regard for him; and now, by our coming to an explanation, I am perfectly convinced that he was not to blame. I hope this acknowledgment is not owing to mere goodness and easiness of temper. For his facts and arguments, which are all just, are very strong in his favour. I think my candid soul is to be admired for yielding my resentful feelings to truth. This even makes me very happy. I shall now enjoy his elegant company and conversations as fully and freely as formerly. We shall be intimate companions.

Paraphrasing, we can say he had been angered by a nobleman and was ready to break off all dealings with him. After hearing an explanation based on facts and reasoning, however, young Boswell gladly changes his plans and will become the other's close friend. In brief, this is a *change of policy* argument and illustrates the various issues to be found in that type. These are the general issue questions:

1. Is the old policy just and beneficial?
2. Can its defects be remedied?
3. Is the new policy just and beneficial?
4. Will it work under the conditions proposed?

James Boswell ran through these classic questions, it would seem, to prove to himself and the future readers of his *Journal* that his earlier plan to be hostile to the nobleman was neither just nor beneficial. He told himself that it was not just his good nature and desire to be at peace with a possible benefactor which made him change his mind. No, the nobleman had good reason and facts on his side. So Boswell can congratulate himself on his own open mind and his good heart and look forward to enjoying a delightful, beneficial friendship. If he was *rationalizing*, he would not admit it to himself (see page 134).

Change of policy arguments naturally abound in the many volumes of the *Congressional Record*. Also, thanks to the custom of *inserting remarks*, an occasional bizarre argument shows up among the serious debates over proposals to eliminate luxury taxes on furs, to build new power dams, to decrease foreign aid, and to make other such weighty changes in policy. One unusual argument comes with the insertion in 1950 of an article written by a physical culturist who proposed a new policy: The American people should stop eating and wearing anything derived from *down deep in the earth*. His issues and their answers can be stated thus:

1. Is the old (or present) policy of what people eat and wear just and beneficial? No. Everybody knows what harmful effects mineral oils, chemicals, and gases can have on the human body.
2. Can the old policy be retained and remedied? Not at all. It has to be done away with. All synthetics are harmful.
3. Is the new policy of diet change just and beneficial? Absolutely! "I believe that since we live on top of the earth, foods, etc. taken from the top of the earth, or near the top, are best for the human body."
4. Will it work? Of course. There are cotton, wool, and linen enough to clothe everybody. Enough food also.

Asking such basic questions quickly reveals the essential ludicrousness of such an argument, but the same questions can be applied to arguments proposing changes in student body rules, in personal life, and in government at all levels.

Argument of analogy is most persuasive, and perhaps sells products and convinces unquestioning minds more easily than do the other forms of argument. *Analogy* can be defined as the likeness between two things consisting of similarity not of the things themselves but of some features. In logic, analogy is a form of inferring that if two or more things agree in some respects, they probably also agree in others.

Analogy works in all manner of situations. After World War II ended, many cautious people looked at shipyards and industries that had been geared to the war effort and began thinking in terms of comparison thus: "After World War I there was a bad depression and much unemployment because there was no more need of war equipment. So now we had better prepare for another depression." Those who acted in such a fearful fashion lost wonderful opportunities to invest in firms that since the war have climbed to record heights of business. These skeptics failed to ask the issue question: *Are the points of similarity stronger than the points of difference?* Or if they asked the question, they were unable to answer it correctly. At the time, it was an inquiry that many respected economists also found it difficult to answer.

Some people allow even a single common term to confuse them

into viewing totally different situations as being analogous, as in the following letter to an editor:

> Really, there is nothing new under the sun. We have the Crusade of the Students Non-Violent Co-ordinating Committee today. We had the Children's Crusade to the Holy Land in 1212. Will they be equally futile?

No possible analogies could be made between two such dissimilar situations; only *crusade* relates them, and the referents are not at all identical in the two instances.

Argument of cause brings in the profound matter of causation: Can A cause B to come into existence? If A is always seen as appearing prior to B in a phenomenon, does A cause B? These are some of the puzzles that bother unthinking persons not at all; they take a cause-effect world for granted, as they do their language. For them, clouds in the sky *cause* rain; warm air *causes* milk to sour; strikes *cause* higher prices. Even the somewhat scholarly persons who write learnedly of baffling subjects can be confused about *cause*. Dr. Immanuel Velikovsky's *Worlds in Collision* is a book providing excellent illustration of the argument of cause.

Velikovsky was evidently trying to find the natural cause or explanation for two stupendous events recorded in the Old Testament: the dividing of the waters of the Red Sea, enabling Moses to lead the Israelites dry-shod across it, and Joshua's feat of commanding the sun to stand still so that he could finish his great battle for the Promised Land. Through a complex fusion of inductive and deductive thinking and feeling, Velikovsky finally arrived at his cause. Despite all refutation, he still holds that a comet split off from the planet Jupiter and, on two different occasions, passed close to Earth, was drawn into the orbit of Mars, and finally, after producing many smaller comets, ended up as the planet Venus. On the first pass near Earth, it providentially made possible the dividing of waters, and on the second the halting of the sun. The comet likewise accounts for the storm on Mt. Sinai when Moses was given the Commandments and for the manna which kept the Israelites alive in the desert.

His *argument of cause* can be and has extensively been questioned on these issue points:

1. Is the assumed cause the only possible one?
2. Is not the cause perhaps only a factor in the conditions?
3. Could the cause produce all of the phenomena observed?

Scholars have given Dr. Velikovsky's comet theory severe criticism on the grounds of the inadequacy of the evidence he offers in geology and astronomy as well as the fallacies of his reasoning upon that evidence. These issue questions indicate the care readers must take in considering arguments.

The *argument of fact* also has its basic issues. Paperback thrillers and television courtroom dramas have popularized the standard inquiries: "What was the condition of the body, Doctor?" "Mr. Crosseyes, where were you standing at the time? Are you sure you saw it all?" In every case, the questions concern the facts of evidence and the competence of the witnesses:

1. Are the facts in evidence relevant and unquestionable?
2. Are the characters of the witnesses reliable?
3. Are the witnesses competent to testify on the subject in question?

The same issues apply to attempts at proving that Homer's Troy has been located, that man's ancestors were carnivorous, or that someone other than Shakespeare wrote "Shakespeare's" plays. They apply as well to interminable efforts to establish before law whether an aluminum plant in the vicinity is directly responsible for the death of a dairy farmer's cows and the ruination of pasture grass. The issues relate also to questions of fact about value judgments such as this one: Is it reprehensible for a student newspaper to publish the statement: "Grades are your means of getting into graduate school; your means of keeping your parents happy; your means of avoiding the Army. . . . [But] Do not give the professor reason to suppose that your interest is in the grade. You must always act like an interested intellectual, no matter what your motive"?

To avoid undue controversy over examples, let's examine how argument-of-fact issues can be applied to a magazine article dealing with this question of fact: "Does the violence of television shows harmfully affect children viewers?" These are the conclusions reached:

A child who watches violence on a screen is not necessarily going to attack the first person he sees. But if he is provoked enough on some future occasion, he may very well copy aggressive patterns of behavior that he has learned from a pictorial medium like television. This is clearly illustrated by an episode in which a boy was seriously wounded during the reenactment, with a friend, of a switchblade knife fight seen in a television rerun of the movie *Rebel Without a Cause*. The impact of the scene upon the boys did not become apparent until the day after the program, when one of them adopted the James Dean role and challenged his friend to a fight. Only after the fight had begun did the *Rebel*-style knife play emerge. . . .

We now see clearly that violence on a television or movie screen affects viewers by:

1. Reducing their inhibitions against violent, aggressive behavior.
2. Teaching them forms of aggression—that is, giving them information about how to attack someone else when the occasion arises.

And, third, let us keep in mind that the ethical ending, in which the villain is punished, may keep viewers from reproducing villainy right away, but does not make them forget how to do it. The ethical ending is just a suppressor of violence; it does not erase.

Since the amount of time that children are exposed to television makes it one of the most important influences in their lives, these laboratory findings do not present a pretty picture—unless our society is interested in increasing the aggressive tendencies of a growing generation.

Now the issue questions: Are the facts relevant and unquestionable? Are the witnesses reliable and competent?

The author of this report is a prominent university psychologist; he carried out a series of experiments with ninety-six boys and girls, most of them four-year-olds, from middle-class homes in the Palo Alto, California, area. In this *Look* article he explains in some detail the experiments wherein children were exposed to patterns of violence "shown by adult models in three different situations: in real life, on film, and as cartoon characters on film." Since the conclusions were arrived at through experiments, other investigators can repeat the tests and check the findings reported. It is evident that the author-experimenter anticipated just such questions. How well his conclusions have held up may possibly be learned by consulting *The Psychological Index*.

As has been suggested, value judgments become the ones most

difficult to establish as facts, such as, for example, this judgment by Montaigne:

> Experience has taught us to rank the virtue of housekeeping above all others in married women. I put my wife to it, as her own concern, leaving her during my absence the entire government of my affairs. It is the most useful and honorable occupation for the mother of a family. Nevertheless, though I have seen many an avaricious woman, I have seldom known a good manager. It is the supreme quality a man should seek in a wife—the only dowry that can ruin or preserve our houses.

Montaigne's is an *argument of values*. Before trying to discuss issues for it, let us consider an even more extreme statement of values, or interpretations, by Oscar Wilde:

> It is the imaginative quality of Christ's own nature that makes him this palpitating centre of romance. The strange figures of poetic drama and ballad are made by the imagination of others, but out of his own imagination entirely did Jesus of Nazareth create himself. The cry of Isaiah had really no more to do with his coming than the song of the nightingale has to do with the rising of the moon—no more, perhaps no less. He was the denial as well as the affirmation of prophecy. For every expectation that he fulfilled there was another that he destroyed. "In all beauty," says Bacon, "there is some strangeness of proportion," and of those who are born of the spirit—of those, that is to say, who like himself are dynamic forces—Christ says that they are like the wind that "bloweth where it listeth, and no man can tell whence it cometh and whither it goeth." That is why he is so fascinating to artists. He has all the colour elements of life: mystery, strangeness, pathos, suggestion, ecstasy, love. He appeals to the temper of wonder and creates that mood in which alone he can be understood.

An *argument of values* almost always involves personal beliefs, both those of the writer and of the reader. They relate to such private matters as religion, philosophy, art, and literature. Because they are intangible, they may often be difficult to appraise fairly. Unlike sciences such as astronomy and geology, wherein experts can agree on many basic facts because they are establishable in laboratories, the liberal arts subjects seldom have experts who are at all universally accepted as infallible. Even the language of the arts of human values differs from that of science, which is mainly mathematical symbols, permitting no errant connotations.

But in a democratic society where citizen often lives elbow-to-elbow with citizen, it is difficult to dismiss all subjective values as merely peculiarities of taste. For as the Constitution founders long ago realized, we remember, men are easily aroused in their passions, and violence may quickly flare. Still, we stand on the rights guaranteed us of freedom of speech and belief. At the same time we are equally bound to respect those rights in others.

What, then, as a critical reader, should one demand of persuasive statements of values? What does he owe himself, the author, and his fellowman? Perhaps a few general questions of issues may provide some answers. (It is better yet if you can provide your own criteria for judgment.)

1. What exactly are the beliefs herein advanced? (Use Critical Reader's Check List, page 135.)
2. Do the views offered propose physical or mental harm to anyone?
3. Do they make daily life more meaningful to the author? More agreeable to others?

These are broad measurements written with the realization that our American civilization has cherished such individualists as Thomas Jefferson, Benjamin Franklin, Henry David Thoreau, Abraham Lincoln, Walt Whitman, and Robert Frost.

To ignore values, stated or implied, in what we read is to miss basic meanings. We must learn to be as quick to detect shoddy half-truths and unacceptable doctrines as we are to note the fallacies in reasoning. Unfortunately, however, as one college entrance examiner was shocked to discover, too many entering college students seem unable, or are unwilling, to detect the unacceptable:

The students who wrote them [the comments on the test paragraph] know how to put sentences together; they come close to knowing how to read. What they don't know is how to evaluate what they read, how to see it in terms of who they are and the other things they know, how to test on their pulses the real assumptions beneath the ostensible ones. Most of the students, I suppose, would have been ready to condemn totalitarianism if they had seen it. The problem is to get them to recognize it *when* they see it.

It could not be said better: critical readers *test on their pulses the real assumptions beneath the ostensible ones.* Logic can show you how to find the assumptions, but your family and you, with perhaps some outside help, must provide *the testing pulse.*

CRITICAL FOCUS

Learn to recognize types of persuasive arguments: change of policy, use of analogy, cause and effect, fact, and value. Challenge the views on basic issues. Remember that tolerance does not imply the surrendering of all one's own personal views.

Exercise 15   Discussion assignment. (*a*) Analyze the following propositions. (*b*) Indicate which ones are statements of personal values and hardly debatable in their present form. (*c*) Restate any debatable topics in need of rephrasing and give your reasons for the changes.

1. "The winds men fear most are those that blow open their cloaks." *Ariston*
2. "There is not a woman, however ill favored, who doesn't think herself worth loving and who doesn't pride herself on her youth, the color of her hair, or the grace of her step." *Montaigne*
3. "Drunkenness is a brutish vice." *Montaigne*
4. "In science, extremes are as vicious as in morals." *Montaigne*
5. "Conventionality is not morality. Self-righteousness is not religion. To attack the first is not to assail the last. To pluck the mask of the Pharisee is not to lift an impious hand to the Crown of Thorns." Charlotte Brontë in Preface to *Jane Eyre*
6. Grammar deals only with word-to-word relations by showing how words are put together in sentences.
7. The athletic policy requires no changes.
8. There is absolutely no doubt about it. Christ is coming soon!
9. "Who profits most from Union Oil? GOVERNMENT."
10. "The matter can be stated flatly: this is the best book on John Keats that has ever been done."
11. "He [Paul Goodman] is by now our only creative social thinker."
12. "Humanist, idealist, poet, dreamer, and reformer, Dr. Karl Menninger, with the help of his two colleagues, has given us a book which is a challenge and an affirmation to everyone concerned with man in health and man in illness."

13. Everyone is either "one-up" or "one-down" in the life game of "one-upmanship."
14. There is no person who is perfectly sane, perfectly "adjusted."
15. When a scientist of genius has discovered an original method opening up new paths for research, many other scientists, tempted by hopes of relatively easy discoveries, immediately try to use this new tool for the most different purposes.
16. "Poverty in America in the 1960s is a shocking and unnecessary irony."
17. Twenty people with adjusted gross incomes in 1959 of over $500,000 paid no taxes at all. Fifteen with incomes over $1 million each didn't pay a cent. One man with $28.7 million in 1960 went scot-free. How did they get away with it? Loopholes.
18. Survey courses should be replaced by more specific courses.
19. "Impulses of love and hate for the same person often coexist in the unconscious, even when one or the other is consciously denied."
20. Our whole culture is based on the desire and need to buy.

Exercise 16 Essay assignment. (*a*) From the following list of broad subjects choose as a topic an argument of either change of policy or a question of fact. (*b*) Frame a debatable proposition fairly stating the argument, and apply the proper issue questions to it. (*c*) Write the argument appealing to the reader's mind and feelings. (*d*) Check the first draft for fallacies or unsubstantiated appeals, and rewrite.

Example: On the topic *lack of privacy* the proposition could be: "Every person should be protected by law against unwanted intrusions of his privacy either by camera or listening devices." This argument is a change of policy; the issues to be applied to this proposition can be found on page 121. The answers to the issues would provide also a coherent outline order.

modern art	space exploration
teacher-training courses	synthetic fabrics
used-car dealers	sports cars
baby sitting	high school athletics
television drama	medical insurance
musical comedies	campus politics
foreign films	marriage
folk music	psychological tests
breakfast foods	legal justice

current etiquette	FM radio
adult behavior	"creepy peepies"
travel abroad	professional football
field trips	foreign languages
urban renewal	air travel
government service	scholarships
Olympic competition	student parking

Exercise 17   Written report. As a measurement of your improved ability as a critical reader, study the following paragraph. Then write a brief report on each of three different experiences you yourself have had, or observed, that may support the points made in the paragraph.

> However, this very dishonesty, this persistence in a proposition which seems false even to ourselves, has something to be said for it. It often happens that we begin with the firm conviction of the truth of our statement; but our opponent's argument appears to refute it. Should we abandon our position at once, we may discover later on that we were right after all; the proof we offered was false, but nevertheless there was a proof for our statement which was true. The argument which would have been our salvation did not occur to us at the moment. Hence we make it a rule to attack a counter-argument, even though to all appearances it is true and forcible, in the belief that its truth is only superficial, and that in the course of the dispute another argument will occur to us by which we may upset it, or succeed in confirming the truth of our statment. In this way we are almost compelled to become dishonest; or, at any rate, the temptation to do so is very great. Thus it is that the weakness of our intellect and the perversity of our will lend each other mutual support; and that, generally, a disputant fights not for truth, but for his proposition, as though it were a battle *pro aris et focis.* He sets to work *per fas et nefas;* nay, as we have seen, he cannot easily do otherwise. As a rule, then, every man will insist on maintaining whatever he has said, even though for the moment he may consider it false or doubtful.

THE MOCKING LANGUAGE OF FALLACIES

That not all which appears sound and reasonable as such has been indicated in the previous chapter. The smokescreens, mousetraps, false appeals, and misleading use of the devices of propaganda somewhat overlap with the errors—deliberate or otherwise—made by many writers and speakers in logic. These errors in reasoning are called *fallacies;* we have already noted the examples of *hasty generalizations* and *false assumptions,* but there are others.

False analogy misleads and beguiles by painting a picture wholly lacking in truth but seeming to be what it claims. *Analogy,* we have said, is "a form of inference in which it is reasoned that if two (or more) things agree with one another in one or more respects, they will (probably) agree in yet other respects." A *false* analogy, therefore, will be one wherein the points of resemblance between two things may seem striking enough to warrant identifying the two as wholly alike, but further examination will show that the points of difference are stronger than the points of similarity. For example, an opponent of Federal aid to state education may contend: "Giving Federal funds to the states for their schools won't work out well for anybody. It will be the case of a father's putting himself into the embarrassing position of handing out money to his children, and then not being able to stop them from wasting or misusing it." The homely comparison may win a delighted chuckle from an audience identifying itself with the nonplussed parent, but the Federal government looks quite awkward in the role of "Dad." Orators fall into analogies as naturally as rain into puddles. "The battle of Waterloo was won on the playing fields of Eton" is a famous progenitor of the many faulty comparisons of sports to the "game of life," which generally confuse one about sports and life.

A writer or speaker *ignoring the issue* may suddenly grow long-winded when challenged on a touchy point. If unable to answer, he may turn nasty and abusive, resorting to name-calling. In other eras he might have evaded the issue by challenging the questioner to a duel—as if being able to slice up an opponent proved a point of logic. The skilled issue dodger has a whole bag of tricks. He may cite undisputable facts, one after the other, but the facts may not be *evidence* relevant to the issue. In arguing that automation really is no monster but a servant, he might give examples and figures of the many new jobs and industries that automation has produced, but he would neglect the charge that it has also brought increased unemployment. Or he might resort to *ad hoc* defense of automation by limiting his explanation to the description of one particular plant or industry which had achieved a remarkable record of employment expansion, ignoring the fact that a neighboring city might consequently have been adversely affected.

Ignoring the issue may take many different forms, but it becomes a particularly bitter charge in a situation wherein what one person feels are his "convictions" others call his "prejudices." Recently *The New York Times* editorially took a congressman to task for ignoring the issues of the merits of a book and attacking instead everyone connected with it:

How Not to Read a Book

Behind the immunity of the Congressional Record, Representative James B. Utt, a rightwing California Republican, has made a McCarthyite attack on the Columbia Broadcasting System, the American Booksellers Association, The New York Herald Tribune, Simon & Schuster and Jessica Mitford, author of the current best seller, "The American Way of Death." Mr. Utt indicts the network, the newspaper and the booksellers because in one way or another they are helping to publicize Miss Mitford's book.

The fact that her discussion of the flamboyance and high cost of funerals has evoked high praise from Catholic, Protestant and Jewish clergymen, as well as from reviewers and other commentators in all parts of the country, is of no concern to Mr. Utt. What makes the book intolerable to him is that Miss Mitford a dozen years ago was accused of membership in subversive organizations and that someone once identified her husband as a Communist.

The Congressman's general approach to all such matters is perhaps best indicated by some of his past estimates of other individuals and organizations. He has called President Kennedy "a pathological liar" and United Nations Under Secretary Ralph J. Bunche "a Communist sympathizer," and he has urged that the United States quit the U.N. because the world body is "a tool of Communism." On that basis his credentials as a book and television critic can safely be dismissed as nil; his credentials as a legislator cannot be examined with equal safety without the immunity the Congressional Record provides.

This editorial, in making its point, also exemplifies several different forms of verbal weaponry. What are they?

Avoiding the issue is sometimes confused with *begging the question*—assuming that the question raised has been proved. When two famous scholars go after one another—one claiming *certainty* and *facts* of literary history and the other in favor of literary criticism, or the study of literature as an art—they will be most conscientious to avoid being accused of *begging the question,* as is F. R. Leavis herein:

> Any history that deals in influences is committed to criticism—as Mr. Bateson, in his own way, is committed. This general proposition will surprise Mr. Bateson—or rather, he will feel, and perhaps rightly, that it justified his ascribing to me the more general proposition. It brings me, at any rate, to my essential point against him: the radical distinction he invokes, the distinction that he reduces to the difference between fact and opinion, seems to me extraordinarily uncritical (I hope he won't think this begging the question). What is this "fact" of "the dependence of Dryden's poetry on Waller's"? I should like to see by what "sober evidence-weighing" Mr. Bateson would set out to establish it. The only evidence he specifies is "that provided by parallel passages"—by which, indeed, Dryden can be proved to have read Waller just as he can be proved to have read Cowley and Milton.

The loaded question may not be a fallacy, but it leads to responses compounding the errors of any flaw in reasoning. Archetype of all such threatening inquiries is the one we referred to in the discussion of political devices used in mass persuasion: "Answer yes or no—Are you still beating your wife?" It has its multitude of variants: "Mr. Mayor, are you going to announce your candidacy for governor soon?" "Are you going to be a renegade all your life?" Anyone seeking to embarrass his opponent may fire a "challenge" at him in the form of a complex question, which, if answered directly, can only offend one group or another of supporters, as this one: "Senator, in all your speeches and articles on this topic of *featherbedding* and the unions, you keep telling the union leaders the same thing—'Take a good realistic look at the tremendous technological advances being made in your plants and factories.' Now tell us the truth, Senator. Don't you still really think that the fight of any union to keep its members employed on unnecessary jobs is *featherbedding?*" That this question is a booby trap is clear. But then, the wily senator may turn about and ignore the issue by looking properly indignant and counter attacking with the cry, "Let's look at the record and see what the real facts are!"

When the reader is offered only two alternatives, two choices of action or decision, and both are highly displeasing to him, he is said to

be *on the horns of the dilemma.* It is often most difficult to find a third
alternative which may deliver one from both of the *horns.* In *The
Decline of the West,* Oswald Spengler posed a famous dilemma that
helped eventually to drive the German people onto the horn of Nazism.
When he wrote that every event was "the prelude of a future . . . with
which the history of West-European mankind will be definitely
closed," he proceeded to set before them two almost equally unbear-
able choices:

> He who does not understand that this outcome is obligatory and
> insusceptible of modification, that our choice is between will *this* and
> willing nothing at all, between cleaving to *this* destiny or despairing
> of the future and of life itself; he who cannot feel that there is
> grandeur also in the realizations of powerful intelligences, in the
> energy and discipline of metal-hard natures, in battles fought with
> the coldest and most abstract means; he who is obsessed with the
> idealism of a provincial and would pursue the ways of life of past
> ages—must forego all desire to comprehend history, to live through
> history or to make history.

Does it seem possible that a nation of readers would accept such
meager choices? It is strange that a country that had produced great
philosophers could not come up with more suitable alternatives than the
ones of despair and callous destruction offered them by Spengler and
then by Adolph Hitler. Had readers ceased to be critical and become
wholly permissive?

Making an unhappy choice usually leads to *rationalization.* One
who rationalizes finds "good" reasons to justify making errors in judgment and action. It may take on the form of *sour grapes* thinking found
expressed in the attitude: "Aw, who wanted it anyway?" If not given
what he considers his due, he sulks and blames everyone but himself
without giving up any of his sense of superiority. Dostoyevsky has
made a powerful novel of the rationalizations of an "underground"
character. Here is the tormented man at a bachelor dinner party which
he knew he should never have insisted on being invited to:

> They forgot about me, and I sat there crushed and humiliated.
> "Good God, what kind of company are they for me!" I thought.
> "What a stupid light I've shown myself in! And I've let Ferfichkin

get away with too much. These lumps think they're doing me a great honor, allowing me to sit down to dinner with them, whereas it's I who condescend to dine with them! So I've grown thin and my clothes are shabby? Ah, the damned trousers! Zverkov probably noticed the yellow stain on the knee right away. Ah, why bother! I ought to get up right away, take my hat, and leave without saying a word. And tomorrow, I could challenge any of them to a duel. The miserable pigs! I don't have to stick it out to get my seven rubles' worth of food. They might think, though,—damn it all! To hell with the seven rubles; I'm leaving right now!"

It goes without saying that I didn't leave.

Perhaps the most vicious kind of self-justification through self-deception appears in the language of the "poison pen" writer or speaker. He demands that the silence of the one accused or slandered be interpreted as proof of guilt. His repeated theme is: "If he's not what I say he is, why doesn't he defend himself? What's keeping him from talking up, the way an honest man would do? He doesn't dare. That's why. If what I say isn't gospel fact, he can take me to court, can't he? But no, he keeps still, hoping you'll forget all about this business until after the election." In such a case, whatever denials are issued by the aggrieved party go unheard by the accuser. Unless constrained by court order, he continues making the same charges to different audiences even long after the claims have been proved false.

Post hoc ergo propter hoc—literally, "after this, therefore on account of this"—is the common error of attributing a cause-effect relationship where there is only one of time. If a family go on a long vacation without notifying their newspaper boy to discontinue delivery of the daily newspaper, they can expect to find a stack of yellowing papers behind the screen door or littering the yard. Here there is a causal relation between events. A sudden fall in barometric pressure will warn of a change in the weather, but the barometer reading itself is not the cause of that change. During the seventy-two-year reign of Louis XIV, many "glories and disasters" came to France, but they were not caused merely by the fact that Louis occupied the throne. He does not deserve either the credit or the blame for many of them, any more than President Herbert Hoover was the cause of the Great Depression which began during his term of office. What comes first may not be at all the cause of what follows subsequently.

CRITICAL FOCUS

Fallacies in reasoning and errors in facts can come from an ignorant writer or from a deceitful one.
They can do the unwary reader equal harm.
Fallacies to beware of:

hasty generalization	asking the loaded question
false assumption	horns of the dilemma
ignoring the issue	rationalization
attack on character	*post hoc ergo, propter hoc*
begging the question	

Exercise 18   Written assignment. Identify the kinds of fallacious reasoning, if any, evident in the following.

1. Why shouldn't universities sponsor symphony orchestras that employ professional, paid musicians? If college football is a professional rather than an amateur sport and is considered essential for public relations, why not a university symphony orchestra to accomplish the same purposes?

2. If parents and school boards no longer can be depended on to choose *values* for their children, says a psychologist, then, "The psychologist has *as much* right to posit values as anyone else, in some respects more. It is time to dispel the shopworn bromide that the humanist (or moralist or philosopher) has a corner on pronouncements about values, while the psychologist (or sociologist or scientist generally) must restrict himself to facts."

3. " 'Upon my word,' I muttered with admiration, rereading the note, 'there's even a certain aristocratic lightness to it! And all that because I'm a highly developed, civilized man! Another in my place wouldn't have known how to get out of it, but I've disentangled myself and will continue to enjoy myself precisely because I'm a well-educated, sophisticated man of my time. And the more I think of it, the more I believe that it really was my drinking that was at the root of it all. . . . Well, not really. . . . In reality, I didn't have any vodka or anything else while I was waiting for them. I just made that up, for Simonov, and now it makes me feel ashamed. . . . Ah, I still don't give a damn! What counts is that I've got out of it.' "

4. Today the emotionalists and the alarmists are arousing people in this country about the Monroe Doctrine. So it is fair to ask: "What Monroe Doctrine are you talking about? First, what do you understand the Monroe Doctrine to be? What was the Monroe Doctrine

in 1823; and is it the same Doctrine in 1962?" Accept all of the Monroe Doctrine and we would have to get out of Berlin, NATO, and close all bases abroad.

5. "Every divine and happy sentiment that we feel within our conscience is a revelation." *Lord Herbert*

Exercise 19   Report assignment. Since the dilemma offers only limited choices, persuaders of all kinds seek to impale audiences upon its *horns.* Describe instances of the dilemma at work in TV commercials, magazine and newspaper advertisements, reports of political speeches or comments, and cartoons. Point out other alternatives that would enable escape from the choices which are posed by the dilemma.

Exercise 20   Essay assignment. For the substance of your essay, note, identify, and classify the most common fallacies that you encounter daily in campus-life conversations and situations. In your essay, state and amplify your conclusions regarding them.

Exercise 21   Written analysis. *Congressional Digest* features pro-and-con arguments on current political matters up for congressional action. Study and discuss the quality of logic and persuasive argument found in one such debate.

Exercise 22   Written analysis. Explain in detail the kind of evidence and reasoning necessary for a person to convince himself that he was justified in doing one of the following. Provide some dramatic or real situation for the analysis.

Example: You have been angry with a friend and have just told your girl friend that the friend has mononucleosis, whereas he really has the "flu." Now you want to justify yourself even though you know the girl will spread the story.

1. Postponing study for a final examination
2. Having told a "white lie" that will have consequences
3. Having spent more than could be afforded
4. Breaking a promise
5. Damaging a borrowed article
6. Hurting, injuring someone
7. Having repeated gossip that was not true
8. Belittling another's success

9. Excusing a friend's meanness
10. Continuing to smoke cigarettes

Exercise 23   Identify the following arguments as to type, and apply the issues that would be necessary to prove the proposition of each.

1. Increasing commercial and free entertainment is the reason why only a few children grow up with the right books around them.
2. "Writing self-consciously as a woman, the Victorian woman of genius thought relatively little of her special feminine sensibility, but a great deal of a social fact: that women were an oppressed minority."
3. It's about time that people ended the mad space program, this research in germ warfare, and the income tax that supports all this bureaucracy.
4. Running the government is like running a big business. There is budget making, development planning, keeping the payroll down, efficient plant operation, and general sharp management.
5. High school reading lists for seniors should include books such as Salinger's *The Catcher in the Rye.*

Exercise 24   Identify the following statements by giving the proper term to each, e.g., *assumption, proposition, hasty generalization,* or any of the fallacies.

1. We've had "The Blackboard Jungle," "The Asphalt Jungle," "The Stained Glass Jungle"—life, I guess, is just one big jungle.
2. Nobody can know more than I do about what I really know from experience.
3. Businessmen are the big taxpayers for the schools, so they ought to have the most to say about them.
4. You can't tell your folks anything.
5. Athletics teaches you good sportsmanship and how to play the game of life.
6. You're nine years old. The jacket of the book says it's for children eleven to fourteen. So that book is not for you.
7. The search for self was the main theme in the fiction of the 1940s.
8. "The message of Cuba, of Laos, of the rising din of Communist voices in Asia and Latin America—these messages are all the same. The complacent, the self-indulgent, the soft societies are about to be swept away with the debris of history."

9. All psychotherapy makes use of the power of suggestion, but hypnosis makes the most direct and efficient use of it.

10. "When it comes to communications, scientists are naturally more interested in the means of conveying messages than in the messages themselves, even if spectacularly bounced off the moon or exchanged between astronauts; and it is here that the width of of the gap separating science from the humanities shows most comically."

11. "Benjamin Britten has emerged as England's greatest composer since Henry Purcell and, among this generation's composers, the only active peer of Dimitry Shostakovich."

12. "For every Ph.D. that it fails to educate the U.S. may soon pay the price of 100 or more unemployed people."

13. Who needs a lot of education? Look at Stanley Kubrick. He was a high school creep who flunked English and had such poor grades he couldn't get into any college. Now who can beat him in making antiformula movies like "Lolita" and "Dr. Strangelove"?

14. "General Motors is people . . . making better things for you."

15. "I would suggest to him that the popular culture—as represented, for example, on television and in comic books and in movies—is based on fantasies created by very ill people, and he must be aware that these are fantasies that have nothing to do with reality."

16. The trial of Sacco and Vanzetti in Dedham, Massachusetts, was a travesty of justice. It was established that the district attorney introduced perjured evidence against the defendants, that the foreman of the jury (before he heard a word of testimony) said of the defendants: "Damn them, they ought to hang anyway!" and that the trial judge, who was venomously prejudiced against the defendants, declared to friends that he would "get those guys [the defendants] hanged!"

17. "Nature has placed mankind under the governance of two sovereign masters, *pain* and *pleasure*." *Jeremy Bentham*

18. "It is the greatest happiness of the greatest number that is the measure of right and wrong." *Jeremy Bentham*

Exercise 25 Written report. (*a*) Read and summarize a controversial article appearing in a magazine or journal. Take care to sum up the proposition and the main issues without distorting the author's viewpoint and purpose. (Be objective.) (*b*) Identify the articles as to type of argument: fact, change of policy, analogy.

(*c*) State the argument in one hundred words or less. If you can reduce it to a syllogism or a series of related syllogisms, so much the better! (*d*) Point out and summarize any fallacies or appeals that may be present in the article.

Exercise 26   Essay assignment. On the basis of experience, we sometimes arrive at conclusions that, although not logical, do influence our behavior. Write an essay on your experiences with one of the following subjects, and state the conclusion you reached regarding them. Follow *inductive* order, so that the essay thesis or theme appears at the end.

parental advice	social conventions
cars	regulations
science	meaning of college
dormitory	meaning of religion
summer jobs	meaning of patriotism
friends	meaning of reading
library habits	professional athletics

chapter 6

READING IMAGINATIVE EXPRESSION

DICTION AND LOGIC IN POETRY

From the vantage point of logic, we have been able to reappraise the workings of language in advertising, politics, and journalism as they affect our daily lives. We have also seen how denotation and connotation are related to clear and orderly thinking. Now we can apply all that we have learned so far to the critical reading of language as art, as literature.

Through analysis of the diction and thought of several poems and passages of literary types of prose, we shall try to arrive at some general methods of evaluating the quality of any creative expression. With this knowledge the reader may sharpen his perceptions and his judgment of all that he reads. He may also discover how he can further apply those standards to the improvement of his own writing.

You may have worked through a few poems in earlier exercises and in doing so perhaps asked yourself: "Why doesn't a poet just put down in plain words what he has to say and be done with it? Why does he have to make a poem look and read the way poems do? Why can't a poem be read as easily as prose is?"

The obvious reply is that both poetry and prose are literary genres, but that each makes different demands upon the reader. A writer of prose knows that he must be understood at even a hurried reading; poets, however, have always desired and even required repeated readings of their poems. Their meanings are more concentrated, and their rhythmic word patterns plead for a more attentive ear and eye. Yet poetry and prose are close companions in language, as we shall see. Aside from possibly the rhythm and the usual appearance of the poem on a page, a passage of prose may possess all of the attributes usually considered the distinction of good poetry—qualities such as these:

imagination	insight, vision
emotional thought	figurative language
connotative meanings	economy of words
rhythm	structure and form

Both poems and prose can explain, argue, describe, and narrate; both equally have tone and theme as well as all such necessities of rhetoric as parallelism, antithesis, paradox, definition, analysis, comparison, and contrast. There is no difference between the language of poetry and prose in the sense of separate, distinct vocabularies, as was true of, earlier poetry.

A poem, as Gertrude Stein would say in definition, is a poem. Since every major poet has his own definition of *poem,* a Stein definition is not so flippant as it may sound. Perhaps as we learn how to recognize a good poem when we see one, we can work out a satisfactory definition of our own. To begin with, it seems reasonable, we need some methods of reading a poem and interpreting it.

The search for such methods leads us into *literary criticism,* which can be defined as the study of literature as art. It is a formidable field even for scholars, and as we enter it, we shall travel only well-defined paths. It may well be true, as literary critic R. S. Crane has said, "We can see in poetry or in individual poems . . . only what our critical language permits us to see." This critical language often becomes highly technical in that it attempts to define and explain what great poetry does and is. If there is dissension in theories of literature, it rises from the mysterious nature of poetry, and from the fact that language must be employed to talk *about* language.

As in many other matters, Western criticism begins with Aristotle, who wrote the book that has charted discussions of poetry— *The Poetics.* Throughout the centuries, down to the present, critics, and scholars have been adapting Aristotle's terms to their own purposes: terms such as *imitation, tragedy, pity, fear,* and *comedy.* To these, as time passed, others have been added, such as *classic, neoclassic, romantic, decorum, fancy, imagination, the sublime, intuition, high seriousness, imagery, irony,* and *epiphany.* And in recent times the new concern with the words themselves of a poem has brought into prominence these terms: *metaphor, symbol, myth, ambiguity, theme, tone, tension, objective correlative,* and our own two favorites in this book—*denotation* and *connotation.* In addition, the "new" sciences of cultural anthropology and psychology, as well as linguistics and the philosophy of science, have made their contributions to the sum of critical terminology devoted to the study of literature.

Most poems can nevertheless be enjoyed without conscious application of the kind of analysis implicit in these many terms. It is only when we wish to speak or write of what a poem means that we need critical terms. As concepts of or insights into what poets try to do, the terms are illuminating. Since also many of the best-known critics are likewise well-known poets, and have followers who themselves write poetry, their work can be understood fully only by the particular standards they have set for their work. Taken out of context, some of their definitions of poetry are puzzling, as, for example, this one: a poem "is a loose logical structure with an irrelevant local texture." Such expert distinctions are the province of the professional critic who is also a scholar. Our approach to understanding and analysis must be less technical.

Let us try now to read a famous poem and work our way through it. The title and the poet's name can wait.

> We are as clouds that veil the midnight moon;
>> How restlessly they speed, and gleam, and quiver,
> Streaking the darkness radiantly!—yet soon
>> Night closes round, and they are lost forever:
>
> Or like forgotten lyres, whose dissonant strings
>> Give various response to each varying blast,
> To whose frail frame no second motion brings
>> One mood or modulation like the last.
>
> We rest.—A dream has power to poison sleep;
>> We rise.—One wandering thought pollutes the day;
> We feel, conceive or reason, laugh or weep;
>> Embrace fond woe, or cast our cares away:

It is the same!—For, be it joy or sorrow,
   The path of its departure still is free:
Man's yesterday may ne'er be like his morrow;
   Nought may endure but Mutability.

With the very first words we know—"hear"—that someone is speaking to us: *We are as clouds,* he begins, and tells us which clouds and what happens to them: *Night closes round, and they are lost forever.* Note the colon that punctuates the end of the first stanza which, like the rest, has four lines. There follows another stanza, opening with the important conjunction *Or.* We are told that we are also *like forgotten lyres,* small harplike instruments hung in the open air to respond to any winds that may stir their strings, but the strings of these lyres vary in pitch, and never twice does a blast of wind produce the same sound.

Again the voice—it is the poet's—addresses us in the third stanza: *We rest.* But a dream can *poison sleep,* and when we rise in the morning one foul thought can *pollute* the whole day. Our lives are made up of contraries: feel—reason, laugh—weep, mourn—enjoy. And then the concluding stanza opens with the poet's assuring us that neither joy nor sorrow lasts, that nothing remains the same, and for man the experiences and meanings of a yesterday will not be the same as those of a tomorrow. He ends by saying that nothing remains unchanged but *Mutability,* which is, of course, another term for changeability.

Such is the general meaning of the poem, with each denotation given its significance according to the context. Without considering the many connotative meanings that give the poem its charm, we can paraphrase or summarize it briefly: A poet tells the reader that man has no certainty in life; each person reacts to everything differently from day to day. He suffers from bad dreams and bad thoughts, and it makes really no difference whether he weeps or laughs, for new troubles and joys will come and go to make his life one of constant change, and change is all the certainty he can know.

Reduced to one sentence, this summary of the meanings can be stated thus as the *theme* of the poem: "In all the varied acts of his life, man knows only that he is a creature of change." You will surely agree that the *tone* of this poem is not a joyous one. We infer that the author's attitude toward both the reader and the subject matter is a melancholy one. Yet there appears to be something courageous in confronting the "facts" of life as the poet sees them. He keeps his gaze fixed on them without self-pity and expresses his insight in direct and forceful terms.

The *tone* of the poem, therefore, is highly complex as it reveals from stanza to stanza the poet's resolving of his attitudes toward his vision and his audience. Its tone is suggested by the highly connotative language. Let us take a closer look at some of those words and terms that arouse emotional response.

One of the conventions of poetry, as also of poetic prose, is the presence of figurative language. The first stanza has two immediately noticeable figures of speech that are rich in connotative meaning: *simile* and *personification*. Both figures involve comparison: the simile—*as clouds that veil the midnight moon*—is identified by the word *as*, which indicates a comparison. The personification—*Night closes round*—compares by giving human traits to abstract or inanimate things. The second stanza begins with another simile, *Or like forgotten lyres*. As further described in that stanza, the *lyres* are seen to be a possible symbol of man's physical and emotional frailty—*frail frame* open to *each varying blast* of nature.

Almost every word or phrase has associations: *speed, gleam, quiver, to poison sleep, pollutes the day, yesterday,* and *Mutability*. They and the several personifications arouse images befitting the tone of the poem. It must be obvious also that all the pictorial images are of beautiful things, and the quick changes in what we identify ordinarily as *beautiful* have contributed to the poet's imagery as well as to his melancholy.

Parallelism (repetition of sentence pattern) adds its rhetorical force, notably in the first three lines of the third stanza: *We rest, We rise, We feel*. In the following parallelism of syntax (word order) we also find *antithesis*, which consists of pairing opposites side by side, as in these lines:

> We feel, conceive or reason, laugh or weep;
>   Embrace fond woe, or cast our cares away.

This concise ordering of ideas indicates full control over the thought and emotion making up the poem.

Note also that the attractive design made by the poem in its appearance on the printed page bespeaks the same kind of order and mastery. So do the measured rhythm and pattern of lines with their end rhymes. Logic is at work in every line. The poet moves inductively from one point of evidence to the other, from minor conclusions to the final major conclusion with which the poem ends.

Study of this poem for its syntactic meaning, that is, for the significance of its sentence patterns and their word-order meanings as shown partly by the punctuation, must wait until we have opportunity to take up syntactic meaning in more detail in Chapter 9.

You may well have other and additional comments to make as to the denotative and connotative meanings to be found in this poem. How it exemplifies patterns of imagery, typical themes, and attitudes found frequently in other works by the same poet, Percy Bysshe Shelley, will be found in the scholarly studies on him. Ours has been only a quick reading and outlining of some noteworthy aspects.

What was the poem meant to do to the reader, you may ask: Was it written just to tell us that life does not make much sense? Every reader will have to find his own answers to such inquiries. We can hardly know what complex of thoughts and feelings and memorable experience made Shelley write this poem or others much like it. We do know he once wrote to a friend: "I always seek in what I see the manifestation of something beyond the present and tangible object." He found—or sought—happiness in such a pursuit and surely intended to give the reader pleasure in writing of it even though it brought both poet and reader some melancholy. We can presume that like all artists whose work shows the striving to express some ineluctable vision only faintly glimpsed from time to time in visible objects, Shelley *enjoyed* creating this poem. The constant effort of a Rembrandt, a Cezanne, a Van Gogh, or a Picasso to give form in line and color on canvas to their own individual insights corresponds to the unremitting work in language of a Shelley.

Biographical research is not essential for the enjoyment of this poem, nor does the reader have to agree with its conclusions. Everyone who has ever been drawn late at night to watch dark clouds passing over a full moon will feel the vividness of the pictorial images here move him to recollecting such moments. By imagination he can experience *empathy* with the scenes: he can *project* himself into their world. This allowing of a part of our consciousness to share and mingle with that which we imagine on being told a little about it is the pleasurable experience of *empathy*.

But how is the pleasure a poem such as this gives us related to the *theme* or *message* of the poem? The best answer to this key question is to ask and answer a closely related one: "Was Shelley preaching in this poem?" It is true, as the whole plan of this brief work reveals, that Shelley had something to say, and it was an important discovery to him. Again it is the *tone* of the language, the shades of meaning of the connotative terms, that will show that he was not writing the poem to drive home a moral lesson or a philosophical observation. He was not being mainly *didactic.* Rather, he wanted to have his audience share his beautiful, if melancholy, vision with him and to contemplate the wonder—perhaps a very sad one!—of what it is to be a human being. In this respect, we can look at the poem as the record of a passing moment of insight recorded forever in rhythmic, connotative language.

Now we come to another possible reaction that you may have had to this particular poem. "So what?" some of you may have said and shrugged off all further consideration after the first perfunctory reading. "I don't go for that kind of poetry," some may have added. Here we come to the question of taste as well as the question of values. If it is the poet's declaration of values herein that some find objectionable, they are perhaps justified in their rejection of the poem. But if the distaste arises out of a lack of comprehension of almost all of the diction, the reaction is based only on ignorance and indifference. Illiteracy of the reader is hardly a basis for judging the worth of a literary work.

But Percy Bysshe Shelley alone does not suggest the range of poetry. Here is a very modern poem by May Swenson. In reading it, try to look for the same kinds of things we found in Shelley's "Mutability," except perhaps the attitude.

The Surface

First I saw the surface,
then I saw it flow,
then I saw the underneath.

In gradual light below
I saw a kind of room,
the ceiling was a veil,

a shape swam there
slow, opaque and pale.
I saw enter by a shifting corridor

other blunt bodies
that sank toward the floor.
I tried to follow deeper

with my avid eye.
Something changed the focus:
I saw the sky,

a glass between inverted trees.
Then I saw my face.
I looked until a cloud

flowed over that place.
Now I saw the surface
broad to its rim,

here gleaming, there opaque,
far out, flat and dim.
Then I saw it was an Eye:

I saw the Wink that slid
from underneath the rushes
before it closed its lid.

Let yourself see through the poet's eyes, and feel as your own the tension of peering deep, deep below the surface of the water. If you can succeed in identifying yourself with the poet and seeing and feeling at least somewhat what the words say the poet does, you not only have empathy but are also reading correctly her simple denotative words, which are also somewhat connotative:

First I saw the surface,
then I saw it flow,
then I saw the underneath.

In these lines what is *surface, flow, the underneath?* They are literal enough meanings to one who has gazed into evidently sun-lit stream or lake waters. But in lines five and six the language becomes figurative: *I saw a kind of room,/the ceiling was a veil.* This last is a *metaphor,* a comparison stating a literal identity between two things which have only a likeness between them. If one could make out or imagine he saw a *chamber* below the surface of a stream, he might very well also see that the ceiling of that chamber just below the surface was like a *veil.*

But to say *the ceiling was a veil* can hit the reader almost as a hard surprise. Another metaphor brilliant in its accuracy of suggestion is the one for the sky, suddenly perceived as being reflected: *a glass between inverted trees.*

This poem also develops according to design: it goes from the seen surface to the reflection on that surface of the *Eye* which is doing the looking into and beyond that surface. It concludes with the highly connotative *Wink* of that eye, as the eyelashes close over it and appear in the reflecting surface as *rushes* that grow under the water. *Rushes* for *eyelashes* is a perfect word choice and makes an exact metaphor, for rushes are plants with cylindrical stems that do grow in water. The poem also follows a spatial order of description; the eye shifts in order to at least ten different objects: *surface, the underneath, room, corridor, deeper depths, sky, face, cloud, eye,* and *wink.*

In appearance on the page the lines give pleasure also through their orderly design of three-line stanzas. May Swenson takes great pains in what might be called "page architecture." Parallelism and the repetition in ten places of I *saw* add to the charm-magic pattern.

Does "The Surface" have a theme? No philosophical observation bluntly asserts itself as does the one in "Mutability." Here apparently is only the record of an intense experience, ending with the closing of the eye of the side-turned head. One might be tempted to say: "The theme of this poem is this: These are exactly the things I saw in peering at the surface of the water." Yet the total connotation of the poem and the poet's emphasis upon the title word suggest something more as a theme. It is possible that "The Surface" may be a symbol of man's desperate efforts to name and define all that exists outside of himself— all that shows only its surfaces. Such interpretation indicates how "private" the meaning of a poem can be for different readers, without departing from the denotations of the context or doing violence to the connotations.

For one more poem and an analysis, let us settle on one of William Shakespeare's sonnets. He makes the same demands and pays back in pleasurable meanings, if he is carefully read. He requires occasional consulting of the *Oxford Dictionary* for terms that once had other meanings than they do now. The sonnet quoted here expresses the appreciation of a friendship. See whether, after the other two poems, you have learned what to look for in your reading of poetry.

So am I as the rich whose blessed key   1
Can bring him to his sweet up-lockéd treasure,
The which he will not ev'ry hour survey,
For blunting the fine point of seldom pleasure.
Therefore are feasts so solemn and so rare,   5
Since, seldom coming, in the long year set,
Like stones of worth they thinly placéd are,
Or captain jewels in the carcanet.
So is the time that keeps you as my chest,
Or as the wardrobe which the robe doth hide,   10
To make some special instant special blest
By new unfolding his imprisoned pride.
   Blessed are you, whose worthiness gives scope,
   Being had, to triumph, being lacked, to hope.

Shakespeare must have enjoyed writing this sonnet, for an active mind delights in seeing relationships between things as different from one another as the proverbial night and day. It is even hard to resist trying to envision what strange similarities he did see in friendship. First, in four lines he saw it as a treasure kept locked away: a wonder which its owner rarely permits himself to view, so as not to dull the keen pleasure he takes in seeing it. In the fifth and sixth lines, he links their friendship with feasts which, coming but rarely, are eagerly anticipated. As such they resemble stones so precious that they are placed at some distance apart on an ornament, or in a necklace or headband become the single great jewel among lesser stones.

Line 9 offers some difficulty. If line 1—*So am I as the rich*—suggests that the poet is rich in this friendship, then line 9's beginning, *So is the time,* seems to mean that time is rich because it keeps the friend as the rich keep the jewel in the chest and the ceremonial costume is put away to be worn only on the rarest of occasions. And in the last two lines the friend is reverently praised as one whose presence gives true luster to a triumph, or if there is no triumph, at least sustains hope. All of these comparisons express flattering respect for a friend and patron in typical renaissance style.

There are five similes in this sonnet, and each one names and suggests wealth and magnificence: *as the rich, like stones of worth, or captain jewels, as my chest,* and *or as the wardrobe.* One excellent metaphor deserves special attention in that it has become through timeworn repetition almost a *dead metaphor,* one that no longer suggest its original comparison: *blunting the fine point of seldom pleasure.* It was especially appropriate in Shakespeare's day when a fork was a rarity at table, and when knives with sharp blades and tips were used to cut, spear, and skewer joints of fowl and beef. A dull knife would spoil the pleasure of eating; so any pleasure that had been marred could rightly be said to be "blunted."

The English sonnet form as Shakespeare developed it is a model of careful reasoning. As every literary handbook will show, the three quatrains and the concluding couplet that make up the fourteen lines demand a tight and logical relationship of parts to the whole; the summary of this particular one has shown that harmony exists here. It reveals also the perfect unity and coherence expected of a fine essay employing the rhetorical development of comparison. Taken together, the language, theme, tone, and logic beautifully enhance the symmetry inherent in the sonnet form itself.

In three poems of different cultural eras in England and in America, we have found almost identical features that distinguish creative expression. In the exercises that follow, you will have an opportunity to try finding some of those same features at work in other poems. We shall then move on to consider prose as literature in a further attempt to arrive at some basic standards of judgment in reading prose and poetry.

CRITICAL FOCUS

Poetry, like all the arts, makes demands upon our critical intelligence as well as upon our emotional resources. A good poem is a balanced complex of diction, figures of speech, theme, tone, logic, rhetorical devices, design, and rhythm.

Exercise 1   Written analysis. Give the following poem by Browning several careful readings, line by line, phrase by phrase. Then in much the same manner as was done with the three poems discussed in this chapter, write your analysis and your appraisal of the poem.

Meeting at Night

The gray sea and the long black land;
And the yellow half-moon large and low;
And the startled little waves that leap

In fiery ringlets from their sleep,
As I gain the cove with pushing prow,
And quench its speed i' the slushy sand.

Then a mile of warm sea-scented beach;
Three fields to cross till a farm appears;
A tap at the pane, the quick sharp scratch
And blue spurt of a lighted match,
And a voice less loud; through its joys and fears,
Than the two hearts beating each to each!

Exercise 2   Written analysis. Here is a famous sonnet by William Wordsworth. Apply the focus points suggested in the Critical Focus as these have been exemplified so far in this chapter.

Composed upon Westminster Bridge

Earth has not anything to show more fair:
Dull would he be of soul who could pass by
A sight so touching in its majesty;
This City now doth, like a garment, wear
The beauty of the morning; silent, bare,
Ships, towers, domes, theaters, and temples lie
Open unto the fields, and to the sky;
All bright and glittering in the smokeless air.
Never did sun more beautifully steep
In his first splendor, valley, rock, or hill;
Ne'er saw I, never felt, a calm so deep!
The river glideth at his own sweet will;
Dear God! the very houses seem asleep;
And all that mighty heart is lying still!

Exercise 3   Analysis essay. The poet William Stafford has encouraged an interesting experiment with one of his short poems, "Locality," which appears in this exercise. Please follow carefully these directions. (*a*) Give "Locality" sufficient readings and thought so that you can fairly appraise it. (*b*) Make notes for your essay on its diction, theme, tone, etc. (*c*) Read the several student interpretations of this same poem and weigh them in the light of your own views. (*d*) Consider William Stafford's own comments on his poem. (*e*) Write your critical essay. You will be doing three things in this essay: analyzing the poem for yourself, judging the student views, and weighing the poet's own words on his work.

Locality

Rivers have rivers in them,
and the shore is more of a shore
where the cliff is. In a crowd
are gangs of men, and when we sing
a voice is trying to find us.

There are days your attention spills
all over the world; you forget
about names, but instead—river
with river—you go like water
to find with your hand every course
on the way from snow to the sea,
and your knuckles belong to the land between.

If someone says, "Where are you going?"
—such a local question!—
you drop your attention on them:
the great fog of Andromeda
reaches out and whiffs them away.

Student One: Special, separate things are seen as irrelevant, too small, too restricted for your soul's dwelling place or for your soul's destination. The fog of Andromeda is the boundless universe made up of the special worlds that are localities. The whole is your house and your destination. Even to consider the question, "Where are you going?" you must descend from the whole to the special, the contingent. The great erases the locality.

Student Two: Identification is a problem in life. We are ourselves, yet we belong to all on earth and in the heavens. We are single men in the groups of the crowd, and often our voices are not what we project from the mind. Every man concerned with the problems of the what, why, and where of his existence finds himself floating swiftly down the river. When the "great fog of Andromeda" whiffs all of us away, what do we care of the river's course and how defined the shore? It is the motion and its awareness that are important. We belong to a pile of dust that can be blown away by a galactic shift. We are too small to have a right to live importantly and stand against death. We all die.

Rivers have rivers, and the shore is only briefly touched upon while we take time to be born, to live, and to die, and to be washed back into the river once again. He is lonely, this poet, and is seeking a union with something, a goal somewhere.

The man who dares to ask such a prosaic question as "Where are you going?" must needs be prepared then for a Godlike attention: "you drop your attention on them," for only God, if He exists, knows.

Student Three: I think the argument of the poem is generally that we have names and ideas about things, places, or localities. Our habitual consciousness is pervaded by the ideas of things in stasis. It does not realize that all things that are, exist in a locality of time or space and are dependent upon something much vaster, deeper, more encompassing. All things are in continuum.

The poem is carefully balanced. The first stanza catalogs the finite things as we name them and tells of the fluid, changing but continuous substratum of those things. The second stanza describes the experience of moving out from your more limited focus and attention upon things. It describes how your consciousness expands to the source and the destiny of things. The final stanza is divided. The first half recalls the first stanza. The second half shows what effect the experience of the second stanza observations can have upon one's sense of locality—that is the finiteness of things: a deeper echo of "you go like water." It is a fine poem.

William Stafford: "Locality" lives in my mind—and grew to this state of being there—by virtue of several converging ideas. One idea is that things we ordinarily identify in a general way are really manifestations which exist more or less, here and there, variably. When we say "river" we identify something as a whole, but it is its parts, and even the parts exist or fade, or perhaps live by implication, as do the braided currents which make up the whole river. The shore, too, is variable, and I play with the idea that where it amounts to more (with a cliff) it is more of a shore.

Ordinarily we say something is here, or there; but we might say it *is* more than something else, or that its own existence is a state which varies. Once you have this idea, another one looms in the poem: your attention makes of things more than just names. By identifying with what is around you, you merge and exist with it. Names are not at all adequate. Then a person from outside these earlier considerations asks a simple question. It is too simple. "Where are you going?" deals with locality, but it is in terms of the foregoing a tremendous topic; and the readiness on the part of the questioner for a simple answer is paralyzing. You drop your expanded, more or less, intermittent attention on him, on such people; the vastest locality which occurs to you—the dispersed but discernible stellar system Andromeda—simply takes over, appropriates such a local and trivial way of thinking.

Exercise 4   Discussion assignment. Consider the diction, logic, theme, emotion, and figurative language in "A Complaint." What is Wordsworth's "Complaint"? What have *fountain, well,* and *the waters* to do with that complaint? Why is he *poor?*

A Complaint

There is a change—and I am poor;
Your love hath been, nor long ago,
A fountain at my fond heart's door,
Whose only business was to flow;
And flow it did; not taking heed
Of its own bounty, or my need.

What happy moments did I count!
Blest was I then all bliss above!
Now, for that consecrated fount
Of murmuring, sparkling, living love,
What have I? shall I dare to tell?
A comfortless and hidden well.

A well of love—it may be deep—
I trust it is,—and never dry:
What matter? if the waters sleep
In silence and obscurity.
—Such change, and at the very door
Of my fond heart, hath made me poor.

DICTION AND LOGIC IN CREATIVE PROSE

As people have everywhere, the North American Indians delighted in story sessions. Their storytellers related tales and myths of men who became great hunters, fishermen, and even gamblers because they had found magical spirit companions. Through these stories and their themes, generation after generation learned and perpetuated tribal ideals and customs. They shuddered also at the cruelty of "cannibal women" and "Grizzly men," who through magic could transform themselves into animals, but who were always eventually defeated by someone quick and clever. For the Indians as for us, acceptance of fictional accounts depended upon their being grounded in everyday reality, at least in part.

Indians responded to their world of make-believe, as we do to that of our short stories, novels, and dramas; for the language they heard was for them, as ours is for us, rich in connotation and symbol. Story, whether told in form of poetry or prose, appeals to the imagination and memory to create in hearer or reader that delicious state of identification with the characters and world being narrated. As noted in our discussion of poetry, *empathy* is the name given to this projection of oneself into the scenes and actions described; it applies also to those states of feeling and imagination wherein we "lose" ourselves in our surroundings through projecting our sympathies.

Like the poet, the author of prose narrative creates a world of illusion, and he employs all the same resources of language found in poetry: connotative diction, figures of speech, symbol, rhetorical forms, theme, and tone. Chekhov's famous short story "Heartache" serves well as an example of how these language features can build a plaintively sad world, which is acceptable to the reader because it has *verisimilitude:* it resembles real life. It is a typical Chekhov story in that it has little *plot*, no complex interweaving of characters and actions. It simply relates how Iona Potapov, a horse-cab driver, tries to tell several unfeeling passengers that his only son has recently died. Potapov finally ends up pouring out both his story and grief to the only one who will not interrupt him—his horse eating hay in the stable.

The speech of the old man is lifelike and highly connotative:

"You chewing?" Iona asks his mare seeing her shining eyes. "There, chew away, chew away. . . . If we haven't earned enough for oats, we'll eat hay. . . . Yes. . . . I've grown too old to drive. My son had ought to be driving, not me. . . . He was a real cabby. . . . He had ought to have lived. . . ."

Anyone who has ever watched a horse munch hay will be able to supply the sounds of tongue and teeth, the creak and rub of leather halter and rope, the stamping of foot, swish of tail. Feel and smell, too, the comradely warmth of the stabled animal, enjoying its long awaited hay, though perhaps restlessly sniffing the fragrance of oats remaining from other, more profitable days. When Iona says, *There, chew away, chew away*, he will be patting the bony, bobbing head. And how close his need for companionship has driven him to the animal is shown in his familiar identification with it: *If we haven't earned enough for oats, we'll eat hay.*

Thus the identification which Chekhov skillfully suggested at the opening of the story is completed. It begins with both driver and horse shown humped motionless under a heavy fall of wet snow in wintery twilight, and it ends properly here in the companionable warmth of the stall in the livery stable.

Our imagination welcomes the worlds that words can create—when patterned by artists. Thomas Wolfe in the autobiographical novel of his youth, *Look Homeward, Angel*, has many passages wherein the imagery is no different from that of poetry. What follows is the scene in which Eugene Gant returns home from college for the Christmas holidays, home to an hysteric mother whose life *expressed itself through a series of deceptions—of symbols: her dislikes, affections, grievances, brandishing every cause but the real one.* He comes home to a father dying of cancer, and to brothers and a sister who have their own share of troubles. On Christmas eve, alone in that house, Eugene is described in a state wherein alcohol has brought momentary self-clarity:

> He got up, and reeled out of the alien presences of light and warmth in the kitchen; he went out into the hall where a dim light burned and the high walls gave back their grave-damp chill. This, he thought, is the house.
>
> He sat down upon the hard mission settle, and listened to the cold drip of silence. This is the house in which I have been an exile. There is a stranger in the house, and there's a stranger in me.
>
> O house of Admetus, in whom (although I was a god) I have endured so many things. Now, house, I am not afraid. No ghost need

fear come by me. If there's a door in silence, let it open. My silence can be greater than your own. And you who are in me, and who I am, come forth beyond this quiet shell of flesh that makes no posture to deny you. There is none to look at us: O come, my brother and my lord, with unbent face. If I had 40,000 years, I should give all but ninety last to silence. I should grow to the earth like a hill or a rock. Unweave the fabric of nights and days; unwind my life back to my birth; subtract me into nakedness again, and build me back with all the sums I have not counted. Or let me look upon the living face of darkness; let me hear the terrible sentence of your voice.

There was nothing but the living silence of the house: no doors were opened.

This passage can be called *dramatic;* its language rings with an intense emotion, which is revealed in the many pictorial images and the highly rhythmic utterance of poetic drama. But it is hardly more dramatic, for example, than either of the briefer but equally intense poems of May Swenson and Percy Bysshe Shelley, although the pitch of Thomas Wolfe's voice may sound more shrill and unrestrained than do the quiet voices of the poets. And like the poems, the language of this prose is compressed into figurative images that contribute to the impact of the passage—images such as these:

Concrete, Connotative Terms	Metaphors	Personifications
light and warmth	reeled out	alien presences of light
dim light burned	grave-damp chill	and warmth
high walls	cold drip of silence	living face of darkness
stranger	door in silence	
ghost	quiet shell of flesh	
come forth	unbent face	
	grow to earth	
	unweave the fabric	
	of nights and days	
	unwind my life	
	subtract me into	
	nakedness	
	build me back	

There is only one simile—*like a hill.* Each of these pictorial images adds to the total context of the impassioned speech by one daring to invite what god there is in him, what inheritance, what *stranger* of consciousness that his intuition made him feel existed within him.

Impassioned speech often takes on the rhythms and similarity of word patterns that make up parallelism. There are six consecutive commands or desperate entreaties couched in the same sentence patterns:

1. Unweave the fabric of nights and days
2. Unwind my life back to my birth
3. Subtract me into nakedness again
4. Build me back with all the sums I have not counted
5. Let me look upon the living face of darkness
6. Let me hear the terrible sentence of your voice

Notice the two sets of rhythms among these six incantations: (1) *Unweave, unwind, subtract;* (2) *build me back, let me look, let me hear.* This same rhythm and parallelism give movement and intensity to the first two paragraphs of this passage. Notice how they correspond in their openings:

1. He got up, and reeled out . . .
2. He sat down upon the hard mission settle . . .

His speech, which begins with an invocation to Admetus, the shadowy god whose house he feels this one is, has a rhythm that scans like iambic verse.

Thomas Wolfe obviously wanted this scene to be highly dramatic in *tone* as well as in *theme,* for he employs the devices of dramatic speech such as incantation and the apostrophe (address to an invisible being, idea, or thing). The youth's appeal to Admetus is most appropriate, for Admetus is the fabled Argonaut whose wife Alcestis sacrificed herself to prolong his days, and in the house of Wolfe's novel, a powerful father, dying of cancer, is being cared for by his wife. On the whole, this passage has thus a definite rhetorical structure, consisting of one paragraph of movement, leading to one of unspoken thoughts, and a third of speech: all point to the final brief paragraph of conclusion which states the result of this almost melodramatic passage.

We have observed that prose fiction can become highly dramatic in striving for poetical effect. Many critics in fact consider Wolfe

as being too often melodramatic; they feel he emphasizes the sensa-
tional merely to create effect. But besides fiction there are other forms
of rhetorical prose that share the language of poetry. Description is one.

Literary artists such as Lawrence Durrell and his brother
Gerald, Osbert Lancaster, Christopher Isherwood, and the brothers Sir
Osbert and Sacheverell Sitwell write excellent travel description, as do
many other English authors. But one of the most compassionate record-
ers of a foreign scene has been a young American, Kevin Andrews. His
The Flight of Ikaros describes his four years of travel through Greece
as an archaeologist during the troublesome times at the end of World
War II. Here is how he describes an unusual bus ride and a representative incident of peasant life:

> In the square where the bus was leaving—I was well on time for
> once—the other passengers were getting on: dark-browed Maniate
> peasants and two women in black, one old, one young. When the bus
> was filled, the driver said I could ride on top. I pulled myself up the
> ladder at the back and the driver's boy, a lad of eighteen, climbed
> up after me on to the bulky, stiff tarpaulin tied down over baskets and
> bundles with ropes lashed back and forth between two thin wooden
> rails on either side. We braced ourselves among them as the bus
> started forward.
>
> Beyond the low houses of Kalamata and the ancient olive yards of
> the plain the road wound and climbed. Underneath us, jolting on its
> springs from side to side like a rickety cube, the little bus crawled
> along hot valley walls deeper and deeper into Taygetos. We were
> going too slowly to feel any breeze or move forward out of the
> towering dust off the road where ten years' rains had washed away
> the asphalt. The mountains were all the time growing higher ahead
> of us, but the road began to drop into a vast ravine. As the vehicle
> hung out over the first turn I saw the rest of the road falling in long,
> thick loops down to a bridge that crossed the gorge in a single span.
> One moment, roaring in low gear, we would pass it—far below—on
> the left; the next, heading out into the empty air, I saw it move be-
> hind us on the right as I clung to the tarpaulin. We reached the head
> of the bridge and halted. Heat rippled off the engine. Under the
> bridge the narrow sides of the ravine converged in a dry bed of white
> stones plunging from far above to the deeper valleys down the
> mountainside. People were getting off, and I saw again the two black
> women—the younger, with her face covered, standing at a distance
> with her back to the rocks, while the older one came to the corner

of the bus. Piercing eyes stared up at us under the kerchief drawn tight round her hooked nose and bristly chin, while the boy dislodged from the bundles a spade and mattock and threw them clanging on to the road. Then he flung down a burlap sack, calling, "Take this too." The women lifted the tools and the sack on to their shoulders; the other passengers got back into the bus and we started forward again.

Next to me the boy was talking, but I had difficulty hearing him above the noise of the motor: ". . . and he was coming back to his village, for he had given himself up during the amnesty, but the others were waiting for him and they were all on this same bus together, travelling to Zarnata. They began to say things to each other, he and they, and they got into an argument—you know the way it happens. Then he made some remark, and they shot him as the bus was crossing the bridge. They threw his body into the gorge. Now, a year later, his wife and mother go to gather up the bones and take them back to—"

"I can't hear," I shouted. "What did you say?"

We were across the gorge now, mounting, turning, doubling on our tracks until the road lay in all its loops beneath us. The women had vanished.

"They're hiding down there under the bridge," the boy said. "Eh, they do well to wait till we are out of sight, not to give us the Evil Eye."

We were nearly at the top when I looked back and saw them, two black specks moving far down the wall of the ravine in that windless heat still echoing to the roar of the engine climbing slowly up towards the sun.

This bus ride and its revealing incident, you may have noted, are described from the same point of view throughout: from the observer's perch on top of the little bus. The *tone* is consistently objective and unsentimental but hinting at the observer's respect and sympathy for the people of this hard land and life. He conveys the feeling of the wild ride in terms of the climbs and falls of the road as they appear to him in his precarious position. Then in contrast to the wild ride he relates the halt at the bridge in the tomblike ravine. But he does not give us the full import of that stop until the bus is again in motion and "We were . . . mounting, turning, doubling on our tracks. . . ."

Description of scenes in motion such as this require great writing skill in order to maintain a unity of impression—herein of speed over a dangerous mountain road in a country where the *Evil Eye* symbolizes all of the accidental and malicious violence that can befall mankind. In contrast to the Thomas Wolfe passage, you will observe the deliberate objectivity of the narrator. This bus ride becomes almost a symbol of the risks, hardships, courage, and acceptance of the peasants and their country, just as the *Evil Eye* is their own universally accepted symbol or portent of misfortune.

In diction, this Kevin Andrews passage also differs somewhat from that of Thomas Wolfe's, although both, as dramatic description, call for concrete, connotative terms and figures to create pictorial images. Here are typical expressions in the Andrews quotation: *dark-browed Maniate peasants, pulled myself up, bulky, stiff tarpaulin, ropes lashed back and forth, thin wooden rails, we braced ourselves, hot valley walls, the empty air, dry bed of white stones, hooked nose and bristly chin, windless heat.* There are some "dead" metaphors: *road wound and climbed, road falling, climbing . . . towards the sun, ten years rain had washed away the asphalt.* Both writers included only one simile.

In this writing we cannot fail to observe the care for unity and orderly development of purpose. There is no confusion of ill assorted details or haphazard arrangement of incidents. At work is some implicit logic of cause and effect, particularly in the Andrews passage. Yet despite this obvious self-discipline on the part of the authors, neither work shows undue strain—unless you agree with the critics who object to Wolfe's "lack of restraint." At least, both passages reveal the old fundamentals of all good writing: unity, coherence, and emphasis—which give the works their fine symmetry and feeling of right proportion.

CRITICAL FOCUS

1. *Literary prose is a companion to poetry.*
2. *Its diction or language is essentially the same as that of poetry.*
3. *Both have the same inner logic and rhetorical features as well as tone, theme, figures, symbol, and rhythm.*
4. *Both create worlds inviting reader empathy.*

Exercise 5   Creative essay. Choose some place or scene familiar to the rest of the class—local malt shop, bar, grill, campus Union, drug store—and try to describe it in images evocative of the sight, sound, smell, and perhaps even the taste and feeling. Do not identify the place by name. Let the class enjoy the *shock of recognition*. Pay attention to unity, order, and proportion of details. As with other essays, try to allow time for laying it aside and rereading aloud to find weak spots and errors in diction as well as in composition.

Exercise 6   Essay assignment. Describe in the objective but compassionate manner of Kevin Andrews a scene and an incident typical of that scene and the people who make it their home. You may choose a city, farm, small town, mountain, beach, park, campus, home-town block, or any other locale wherein you have had an experience that reveals the character of the place and its people.

Exercise 7   Discussion assignment. On the basis of the de-scriptive passages and poetry read and discussed in this chapter, what is your opinion of the following two prose passages? Be prepared to discuss their appropriateness of language or its lack. Do the passages have any discernible inner logic that gives them order? If so, what kind? Is there consistency of tone and theme? Explain.

1. To dream of logged off, scarped reaches, where candelabra of firs burn black in cold moonlight, and their amber pitch runnels gleam on the bark like crystal snail-trails; to hear in the night silence lambs nibbling grass-fists in the high rain pastures, while pale moths flutter mad in the fragrance calls of the moon-held air; to follow the road spiralled into darkest hills, while catching, too, the frosty echo-ings of fluted emptiness, like the nearings of galaxies caught in the glass tunneled to stars on Palomar—Who the hearer? Who the cry? Is it desire—the froth of blood whipped by the wind of your passing? Oh, feeler of feeling-bereft, oh yielder of unyielders, oh wind-willow weaver in the night! What of metamorphosis means this worm crawl, cat purr, dream turn?

2. Then was completed the passion of the mighty fugue. The golden tubes of the organ, which as yet had but muttered at intervals—gleaming amongst clouds and surges of incense—threw up, as from fountains unfathomable, columns of heart-shattering music. Choir and anti-choir were filling fast with unknown voices. Thou also, Dying Trumpeter, with thy love that was victorious, and thy an-

guish that was finishing, didst enter the tumult; trumpet and echo—farewell love, and farewell anguish—rang through the dreadful sanctus. Oh, darkness of the grave! that from the crimson altar and from the fiery font wert visited and searched by the effulgence in the angel's eyes—were these indeed thy children? Pomps of life, that, from the burials of centuries, rose again to the voice of perfect joy, did ye indeed mingle with the festivals of Death? Lo! as I looked back from seventy leagues through the mighty cathedral, I saw the quick and the dead that sang together to God, together that sang to the generations of man.

Exercise 8   Written assignment. Describe the tone, theme, and structural development of this poem by William Blake by showing the quality of the diction.

The Lamb

Little Lamb, who made thee?
Dost thou know who made thee?
Gave thee life, and bid thee feed
By the stream and o'er the mead;
Gave thee clothing of delight,
Softest clothing, woolly, bright;
Gave thee such a tender voice,
Making all the vales rejoice?
    Little Lamb, who made thee?
    Dost thou know who made thee?

    Little Lamb, I'll tell thee,
    Little Lamb, I'll tell thee:
He is called by thy name,
For he calls himself a Lamb.
He is meek, and he is mild;
He became a little child.
I a child, and thou a lamb,
We are called by his name.
    Little Lamb, God bless thee!
    Little Lamb, God bless thee!

Exercise 9   Analysis assignment. Appraise the structure and logic of the following sonnet by a famous poet, its choice of diction as related to tone and theme. Explain also in some detail your feelings about the poem as a poem.

Poverty

Once I beheld thee, a lithe mountain maid,
Embrowned by wholesome toils in lusty air;
Whose clear blood, nurtured by strong, primitive cheer,
Through Amazonian veins, flowed unafraid.
Broad-breasted, pearly-teethed, thy pure breath strayed,
Sweet as deep-uddered kine's curled in the rare
Bright spaces of thy lofty atmosphere.
O'er some rude cottage in a fir-grown glade.
O poverty! I behold thee as thou art,
A ruthless hag, the image of woeful dearth
Or brute despair, gnawing its own starved heart,
Thou raving, wretch! fierce-eyed and monster-lipped,
Why scourge forevermore God's beauteous earth?

DICTION AND LOGIC IN THE SHORT STORY

Reserving discussion of the short story's *structure* for a later chapter on that subject, we shall discuss here how language and reason function in short fiction. As indicated in the introductory reference to Chekhov's "Heartsick," the short story, like all other creative prose, seeks to give the reader pleasure on various levels, and does so especially through its resolving a *tension*.

It is usually concerned with a significant situation of tension or conflict as one main person deals with that situation and brings it to some conclusion. This main character remains throughout in some tension of feeling, and his efforts to free himself of it by various actions create the reader interest known as *suspense*. Since the main character is often the most important concern of the story, we may do well to inquire how language works to present him. Here are two famous story personages. What kind of diction delineates them?

1. Thus musing, he took his stand at the entrance of the gate and waited until the personage so singularly announced should make his appearance. After an instant or two he beheld the figure of a lean man, of unwholesome look, with glittering eyes and long black hair, who seemed to imitate the motion of a snake; for, instead of walking straight forward with open front, he undulated along the pavement in a curved line. It may be too fanciful to say that something, either in his moral or material aspect, suggested the idea that a

miracle had been wrought by transforming a serpent into a man, but so imperfectly that the snaky nature was yet hidden, and scarcely hidden, under the mere outward guise of humanity. Herkimer remarked that his complexion had a greenish tinge over its sickly white, reminding him of a species of marble out of which he had once wrought a head of Envy, with her snaky locks.

The wretched being approached the gate, but, instead of entering, stopped short and fixed the glitter of his eye full upon the compassionate yet steady countenance of the sculptor.

"It gnaws me! It gnaws me!" he exclaimed.

And then there was an audible hiss but whether it came from the apparent lunatic's own lips, or was the real hiss of a serpent, might admit of a discussion. At all events, it made Herkimer shudder to his heart's core.

2. "Precisely," said Kennedy. "She is very passive. It's enough to look at the red hands hanging at the end of those short arms, at those slow, prominent brown eyes, to know the inertness of her mind—an inertness that one would think made it everlastingly safe from all the surprises of imagination. And yet which of us is safe? At any rate, such as you see her, she had enough imagination to fall in love. She's the daughter of one Isaac Foster, who from a small farmer has sunk into a shepherd; the beginning of his misfortunes dating from his runaway marriage with the cook of his widowed father—a well-to-do, apoplectic grazier, who passionately struck his name off his will, and had been heard to utter threats against his life.

In the first we have a brief portrait of Roderick Elliston, the main character in Nathaniel Hawthorne's "Egotism: Or, the Bosom's Serpent." The second is the general description of Amy Foster in Joseph Conrad's story of the same name. Hawthorne has chosen only the connotative terms that will suggest a fantastic image of a man as a snake. The figure, look, eyes, hair, walk, and whole general appearance of the man suggest his *serpent* nature: *glittering eye, he undulated, his complexion . . . a greenish tinge over its sickly white.*

And where does this monstrous being live? We learn his mansion is shut off from the street by an iron gate, and the only servant is an old man, clad appropriately in black. No wonder the caller, George Herkimer, is appalled by what he sees has become of the old friend, whom he has not seen in the five years since Elliston's marriage failed.

Hawthorne has here achieved what Edgar Allan Poe later was to describe as the essential quality of a short story: *unity of effect.*

Without a flaw in diction, Hawthorne suggests Elliston's reptilian life in a city that is equally strange. The serpent-man has gone about stopping various people, and after fixing his serpent's eyes upon them and seeing by his "evil faculty of recognizing whatever was ugliest in man's heart," he has asked them: "How is the snake today?"

Hawthorne ends the story with a *happy ending* by arranging for the estranged wife to appear in the garden of the hateful mansion. She forgives, and Elliston redeems himself by asking forgiveness and thus frees himself from *the serpent.* At that moment, the sculptor friend "beheld a wavering motion through the grass, and heard a tinkling sound, as if something had plunged into the fountain."

The serpent gnawing at the vital life of the human heart is a *symbol,* as the theme of the story insists, of Elliston's egotism. Hawthorne repeatedly points out that even though it may destroy his life, a man will cherish his particular vice or fault; the wretch egotistically thinks it sets him off from the rest of the world. Much in the same manner as Albert Camus has done in *The Fall,* Hawthorne creates, with the kind of connotations suggested here, a world of moral evil.

This world operates strictly on a cause-effect basis. Sin, error, fault—self-nurtured or inherited weakness—inevitably produce disorder in one's life. Free yourself from the evil stain or *serpent,* and you can know love and life as a human being should.

It is this artistic blending of logic, human traits, painful situations, and believable settings that distinguishes good fiction. In a somewhat different combination, Joseph Conrad tells the story of Amy Foster.

Again with Conrad the language is the clue to his magic as a storyteller. This master of our language, who was brought up in Poland and did not learn how to speak and write English until a grown man, held high ideals of novel writing as an art. In his Preface to *The Nigger of the Narcissus,* he has described that art. A brief quotation from it will prepare us for a study of the language that reveals the character of Amy Foster.

> And art itself may be defined as a single-minded attempt to render the highest kind of justice to the visible universe, by bringing to light

the truth, manifold and one, underlying its every aspect. It is an attempt to find in its forms, in its colors, in its light, in its shadows, in the aspects of matter and in the facts of life, what of each is fundamental, what is enduring and essential—their one illuminating and convincing quality—the very truth of their existence. The artist, then, like the thinker or the scientist, seeks the truth and makes his appeal. . . . His appeal is made to our less obvious capacities: to that part of our nature which, because of the warlike conditions of existence, is necessarily kept out of sight within the more resisting and hard qualities—like the vulnerable body within a steel armor. . . . He speaks to our capacity for delight and wonder, to the sense of mystery surrounding our lives; to our sense of pity, and beauty, and pain; to the latent feeling of fellowship with all creation—to the subtle but invincible conviction of solidarity that knits together the loneliness of innumerable hearts, to the solidarity in dreams, in joy, in sorrow, in aspirations, in illusions, in hope, in fear, which binds men to each other, which binds together all humanity—the dead to the living and the living to the unborn.

We can observe this art at work even in the brief description of Amy by Kennedy, the country doctor. We also learn through his speech what a fine, humane man this doctor is, and through what eyes of wonder and kinship he beholds such tragedies of everyday life as this one he narrates in "Amy Foster." (Some critics prefer to call the long narrative a *short novel* or a *novella.*)

This simple, *very passive* country woman—the details of her appearance confirm this summary of her character—by chance became involved in the situation of conflict and tension that ended in tragedy for the good man she married. She had, as the doctor remarked, enough imagination to fall in love with a castaway, poor emigrant from Central Europe. The fact that Conrad hangs the tragedy of this story on the wife's failure to understand anything at all of her husband's foreign tongue or mannerisms is significant to our studies in this book of the workings of language as related to culture.

After her marriage and the birth of their son, Amy objected to his holding the child and "crooning" to it an old mountain lullaby in his native tongue. And she forbade his trying to teach the child a prayer in that same language which "sounded so disturbing, so passionate, and so bizarre." In her ignorance she felt he was somehow harming the child, and her distrust of him grew. When he was mortally ill with fever, she fled from the house because he called out to her in a cry that frightened her with its strange intensity. The doctor hurrying to the house found the man dying on the path outside and learned what the poor foreigner had called out: "I had only asked for water—only for a little water. . . ." Because of the guttural sound of the emotion-laden voice, Amy Foster had fled, and later easily forgot the strange man who was the father of her son: "the father, cast out mysteriously by the sea to perish in the supreme disaster of loneliness and despair." Here in the final sentence we find also the theme of this story. It is another cause-effect logic at work in the lives of people.

After having noted some of the means whereby fine writers work their language magic, perhaps now we can try to draw up the standards we spoke of at the beginning of this chapter. At best, however, any such listing can be only a very general guide, and any suggestions of rules or means for evaluating creative expression are worthless, unless we also bring to them much of the understanding that Joseph Conrad would have us bring to works of literary art.

CRITICAL FOCUS

A Critical Method for Reading
and Evaluating Creative Expression

1. Read first for pleasure but with awareness of *theme.*
2. Expect to find the same kind of *connotative* and *figurative language* in both poetry and imaginative prose.
3. Judge the *quality* of the language by its power to suggest the meanings and images making up the author's vision.
4. Determine with what right economy, or—as found in the works of some *experimental* writers—with what deliberate profuseness, the *diction* fulfills its intended purpose.
5. Find the *purpose* underlying the work by searching out the *theme.* (See pages 262 to 264 for additional discussion.)
6. Read for *tone:* the author's attitudes toward his work and his readers.
7. Search for the *logic* that gives the work its backbone of reasoned thinking, no matter how emotional the thought may appear; it may be a highly implicit logic.
8. Be hesitant to accept imaginative, emotional language that has no perceptible underlying sense or reasoning. It may be empty sentimentalism, yet again it may be a very legitimate *dream poem* such as "Kubla Khan."

9. Along with care for the logic, develop awareness of the *structure:* the relation between the whole and its parts. (See Chapter 8.)
10. Note as clues to word-pattern meaning all of the rhetorical forms, such as *parallelism, antithesis, comparison,* and *contrast.*
11. Watch for the rhetorical attributes of *unity, coherence,* and *emphasis,* and learn whether the author you are reading has been schooled in them: his work will tell.
12. Build foundations of *critical judgment* upon your own analysis of works of competent literary masters. Read the works before reading the criticism.

Exercise 10   Essay assignment. Here is a portion of *The Rubáiyát* of Omar Khayyám. Read the poem in its entirety and determine how the following stanzas are representative of the tone and theme of that famous work as translated by Edward FitzGerald. Remember *tone* reveals the underlying attitude or feeling of the author toward his work and the reader. What does the poet want the reader to think and feel? How does the language suggest it?

13

Some for the Glories of This World; and some
Sigh for the Prophet's Paradise to come;
  Ah, take the Cash, and let the Credit go,
Nor heed the rumble of a distant Drum!

22

For some we loved, the loveliest and the best
That from his Vintage rolling Time hath pressed,
  Have drunk their Cup a Round or two before,
And one by one crept silently to rest.

34

Then of the THEE IN ME who works behind
The Veil, I lifted up my hands to find
  A lamp amid the Darkness; and I heard,
As from Without—"THE ME WITHIN THEE BLIND!"

Exercise 11   Discussion assignment. Can any critical method be applied to this brief poem by Alfred, Lord Tennyson? Explain.

Flower in the Crannied Wall

Flower in the crannied wall,
I pluck you out of the crannies,
I hold you here, root and all, in my hand,
Little flower—but *if* I could understand
What you are, root and all, and all in all,
I should know what God and man is.

Exercise 12   Report assignment. Apply to a short story by Edgar Allan Poe as many of the points of A Critical Method (page 8) that you find applicable. Write a report which follows some logical order of classification. Remember to quote very sparingly and to summarize as much as possible. Place the major emphasis upon diction and whatever logic you discern in the story.

chapter 7

READING SPECIALIZED LANGUAGES

THE LANGUAGE OF SCIENCE

That logical thinking underlies even poetry and creative prose may have surprised readers who expect literature to express only soaring imagination and emotion. But as analysis of even a few literary works has shown, skilled authors owe much of the significance of their themes and unifying tone to their powers of reasoning, however indirectly those powers may function. If a good writer is one who has "something to say," he has found his basic understanding, his "vision," through the same processes as are found in systematic reasoning: processes such as analysis, definition, cause and effect, and comparison. He may never have deliberately worked through intellectual problems in the manner of a trained logician; yet, in his hours of meditation and composition, his thinking has followed those same inductive and deductive routes that the logician has charted.

This prevalence of logic is understandable. We learn its rudiments as children, along with our language and experiences with our environment. Through repeated warnings such as "Stay away, it's hot!" we soon acquire a sense of cause and effect, especially if we have once been burned. Thus, as the understanding of objective cause and effect replaces superstitious attitudes of early childhood, when chronological order alone sufficed to explain magically whatever occurred, a child forms the basis for all future development in logical thinking. All the academic and professional areas of learning rely on the formal processes of logic. Let us examine a few, beginning with those most spectacular exemplifiers of applied logic, the physical scientists.

It is true that the universal language of physical scientists is the symbolic one of mathematics, and that also in the other sciences symbolic logic is proving a useful substitute for words and terms that in varying contexts may undergo shifts in denotation. According to symbolic logic, for example, equations may be set up wherein four rats in cage number 1 will be represented by some such figure as Y_1, thereby eliminating the need to refer to "those four rats in cage number one." This substitution is an effort to give the denotation of a referent even in nonmathematical sciences the same kind of objectivity and convenience seen, for instance, in

$$T_f = \tfrac{9}{5}T_c + 32$$

the formula for changing centigrade temperature scale readings into Fahrenheit temperatures.

Still, scientists must fall back on words to express what can be said only in terms of language. And since, because of its tremendous expansion, science now enters all fields of learning, including those especially of the arts, it is important for us to inquire how its writers communicate their findings in our highly connotative English.

At the outset it must be said that throughout history, experimental scientists have, in their writing, had great influence on philosophy, religion, and literature. This influence is understandable. From the alchemists to Galileo and Newton, experimental scientists have interpreted the world of fact. They have laid down rules for judging the validity of what is experienced through the senses, in part by attacking the reliability of man's senses themselves as sources of knowledge. In doing so, they have questioned the reliability of man's reasoning and his capacity for obtaining a correct *world picture*. They thereby enter into a field once traditionally considered the exclusive sphere of those philosophers who dealt with *epistemology*, the study of the methods and grounds for obtaining knowledge. Any theories in such matters are bound to have serious repercussions among religious thinkers or theologians.

The poet, imaginative prose writer, and philosopher, in turn, may exert an influence on science through their critical analysis of the language and meaning used by scientists. Writers such as Thomas Hobbes and Francis Bacon are foremost among such philosophers of science.

Thus, there are two kinds of writers in the field of science: one writes to express the empirical facts of his findings and their inferences; the other speaks as a philosopher of science. The critical reader should be careful to distinguish between the two. Some, such as Julian Huxley, manage to do both kinds of writing, but the reader can easily discern which is which. The scope of the announced purpose and the methods of presentation make each type identifiable.

The practicing scientist regards himself primarily as a decision maker or problem solver. He is an expert in investigative procedures and in the technological equipment his work requires. He may work in either *pure* or *applied* science. One who engages in pure science carries out experiments that are designed to add knowledge to some field of interest or to satisfy a curiosity. In applied science, experiments are conducted to solve a specific problem or to facilitate a specific decision. The report of the pure scientist, of course, is expected to be as accurate in its presentation as is that of the physicist reporting on the success or failure of a specific problem-solving attempt—for example, reduction of the city-disturbing noise of the sonic boom caused by jet airplanes.

Especially today, it is more reasonable to consider the physical scientist a decision maker rather than an observer. In many experiments, such as those on atomic particles, the role of the scientist as observer and experimenter has changed enormously from what it once was. Instead of checking a process with his own senses, he now must rely on electronic eyes and ears, as well as on computers, as the testers of assumptions. The human senses cannot register what takes place in a cyclotron. Yet the scientist does remain the decision maker.

When the scientist puts pen to paper to communicate his findings, what qualifications must he have for acceptable scientific writing? Any student who has taken a required laboratory science course can supply some of the answers if he will think of the reports he has completed when filling out laboratory manual sheets. Science textbooks and manuals are actually introductions to attitudes regarding the handling of empirical facts under observation as much as they are introductions to the principles and methods themselves. They stress the basic techniques and habits of mind required of the reliable researcher. Such efficient ways of thinking may not by themselves have brought the discovery of penicillin or the invention of nylon, but they have contributed to their development as usable products. We shall try to consider both attitudes and methods, but let us begin with the routine outlook and the mode of its written expression.

Scientific method is largely based on deductive reasoning. It may be said that a chief goal of science is to construct what has been called a *deductive system.* To understand this concept, let us look, first of all, at the statements that form the basis of scientific writing. At the risk of oversimplifying, we may classify statements as follows:

General—*All Olympic winners receive medals.*
Particular—*Bill is an Olympic winner.*
Qualitative—*Bill is a great athlete.*
Quantitative—*Bill has won two medals.*

To be properly scientific, words in a *qualitative* statement must have a strictly defined denotation. For example, the word *great* as applied to an athlete needs to meet rules set up to determine just what feats and qualities of performance constitute greatness in athletics. Such qualitative scientific terms as *tensile, infinite, crystalline,* and *parasitical* likewise require consistent and unequivocal denotations.

Our example of a *quantitative* statement—*Bill has won two medals*—represents the expression of measurement (counting, in this case). The *particular* statement, which classifies, puts Bill (whose medals we have counted) into a class—that of all Olympic winners. Let us note in passing that the quantitative and the qualitative statements are both also particular statements.

We come finally to the *general* statement, which as we have seen in our study of syllogisms is indispensable to deductive reasoning. (See the rules governing *distributed* terms, page 100.) In science, a *general* statement is what in logic is called a *distributed* statement, one which includes a term that treats all members of a class. Its importance in the deductive system of science requires that certain distinctions be made regarding it.

First of all, what is the chief characteristic of a *general* statement? Let us begin by comparing our general statement example—*All Olympic winners receive medals*—with another but somewhat different example, but one which also attributes something to all members of a class:

It rained every day last week.

You will readily detect basic differences between these two general statements. The second one affords few and trivial deductions and restricts the scope of the "general" to only seven days. The first general statement, on the other hand, does not narrowly limit the deductions that can be drawn from it. There have been many Olympic contests and many winners in them; each competitive sport and every winning contestant could possibly be involved in deductions from the general statement. The fact that in its early history Olympic game winners were awarded laurel wreathes instead of medals need not invalidate the principle implicit in our general statement.

Our Olympic statement, furthermore, illustrates the feature necessary to make a statement in science a *law*. This essential characteristic required of a *law* can be stated thus: Theoretically, the statement must permit an unlimited number of deductions to be made from it. Not all of the deductions, of course, can ever be tested. If you think for a moment of even the most familiar of scientific laws—for example, the temperature at which water freezes or boils—you can make deductions from them that may never be tested. Tomorrow, let us say, the proverbial watched pot may never boil (although the temperature of the water reaches 212°F). Or perhaps despite the laws of Galileo, Kepler, Newton, and the poet Longfellow, an arrow shot into the air may never come to earth. These are whimsical conjectures, but they serve to illustrate the point that there can always be more particular instances of a *law* than can ever be observed.

Particular statements are those which express facts: The water in *this* kettle boiled at 212°F; Bill, an Olympic winner, has won two medals. Science attempts to "explain" facts as instances of a law. One scientist may have induced a law from numerous observed facts; but after he has formulated the law, other scientists can make it serve as the major premise of their syllogisms and arrive at a potentially infinite number of deductions. The *particular* statement pinning down the fact remains, however, the starting point and test of all the other three kinds of statements.

We have so far touched upon the concepts, types of statements, and characteristics of facts and law that distinguish scientific thought. We come now to the most elevated and significant feature of the deductive system that we set out to examine: *theories.* The scientist does not regard his vast body of knowledge as a hodgepodge of seemingly unrelated laws. As the philosopher does in his field, the scientist seeks *theories*—statements having a level of generalization higher than that of laws. He regards theory as the apex of the complete deductive system, which has for its aim the construction of integrating theories offering the possible deduction of new laws. Here is the structure of such systematic thought as stated by one scientist:

> In a deductive system there are (1) a set of undefined and defined concepts [words and parts of statements], (2) a set of assumptions (axioms and postulates, or formation and transformation rules) [theory], (3) a set of deduced theorems [laws], and (4) instances of the theorems [facts]. The assumptions constitute the theory, the theorems constitute laws, and the instances of the theorems are the facts.

For the scientist, the instances of theorems are facts, and a complete deductive system consists of various levels of generalizations expressed as statements of fact, of law, or of theory. Russel Ackoff, the author of the passage just quoted, has nicely summed up this range of generality:

> The less general a statement, the more *fact-like* it is: the more general a statement, the more *law-like* it is. Hence, facts and laws represent ranges along the scale of generality. There is no well-defined point of separation between these ranges.

Although we may thus admit some relativity in the use of the terms *law* and *fact*, we should be careful to distinguish between them in any particular usage. The term *theory*, on the other hand, must be restricted to the highest order of generalization, to integration of related laws or theorems—as in the examples of Einstein's theories of relativity or the theories of electricity or matter.

Any example of a scientific deductive system, then, would take us necessarily into a discussion too highly technical to be fair to the metatheory involved. Let us try to illustrate certain levels of the system as developed by observation and scientific testing, however, by considering that exotic animal the camel.

The problem that we as scientists shall set out to solve is how the camel survives for several days in the desert with little or no water. To exercise our new vocabulary, we may say that the camel was not properly defined in an operational sense: There was disagreement as to how much it drank at one time and how many days it could survive without drinking—details that made for legend. For a long time, an untested law maintained that the camel stored water in its stomach or hump. Cursory observation may have mistaken the digestive juices for stored water, but more careful scientific examination showed that, being a ruminant, the camel has a stomach consisting of chambers for regurgitation and chewing of the cud. The hump, moreover, was found to consist of solid fat. The original law was discarded as a result of these scientific observations, and a new explanation was sought.

It was inferred that the camel might be able to convert its hump of fat into water by some form of internal combustion. Assuming this to be true, tests were devised, and it was shown that the hump can indeed yield between 20 and 30 pounds of water. Further observation clearly showed that the camel finds a certain amount of water in the spiny desert vegetation that it eats. Finally, the most careful observation to date indicates that eight days is the limit of this animal's ability to go without a big drink. Until such time, then, as the facts alter drastically—camels become unable to survive without water, for example, or they endure for much longer periods of time—or until some thorough examination can disprove the present findings, a new law has been established: Camels can survive for up to eight days without water because of the vegetation they feed on and the combustible fat of their humps.

Hopefully, this discussion has illustrated the basic scientific way of thinking, which we stressed at the outset as being so important. In whatever we read in science, we need to remember that such is the vast rate of increase of knowledge in every field that no one expert can hope to keep up with that spate of new knowledge. Here is how a geneticist explained his predicament:

> If I could spend, as I am told many Russian scientists today indeed spend, one-half of my working hours reading and studying the literature—and if I had no teaching or other duties to perform—I could probably cover 2000 articles annually, but this total must be reduced by the time consumed in the literature search and in the reading of books and longer reviews. In actuality, I could rarely spend more than two hours a day reading the literature; and this would not suffice even to read all the articles sent to me in reprint form by my colleagues throughout the world. Abstracts and sum-

maries alone I find very dull and uninviting to read unless followed up by the account of the work, the presentation of the actual data, the discussion of the significance of the findings.

This problem is now a concern of the National Science Foundation as an accumulating and classifying agency for all this new knowledge.

The language of science, like that of politics and journalism, has its share of *jargon*, technical terms or shop talk, along with a high ratio of abstractions. Ritchie Calder, a widely recognized science reporter, calls this jargon *Babelology* and, in noting that there is too little communication between the sciences and hardly any between the sciences and the humanities, speaks as follows on this breakdown of communication:

> One of the major difficulties is the terminology—the jargon of science. The scientists in the various branches and disciplines of science have invented their own language of convenience. Where once the terms were descriptive, they are now cryptic—sometimes one feels that like code names for military operations, they have been deliberately invented to mislead and, like the sign language of the medieval crafts, designed to preserve the inner mysteries for the few.
>
> Sometimes—like "barn" in nuclear physics or "hardware" in the jargon of the electronic engineer—they are survivals of common-room jokes. Sometimes they are borrowed, like the confiscation of the word "plasma" by the physicist from the biologist.

Philosophers of science seldom lapse into such language. Thinkers such as Charles Darwin, Thomas Henry Huxley, A. N. Whitehead, Homer W. Smith, George Gaylord Simpson, Julian Huxley, and Rachel Carson communicate scientific knowledge in models of good diction. They may even become poetic in envisioning how the new knowledge of their specialties can change the *world picture* for mankind.

Inductive reasoning, perhaps, best embodies this "poetic" nature of intuition. Without any conscious awareness of having reasoned, great scientists have made famous discoveries under circumstances resembling those from which come poems. A dream, a fantastic notion, a sudden realization may usher in the brilliant concept. In *The Act of Creation*, Arthur Koestler has described many such surprising discoveries; he is so impressed by their frequency that he has attempted to make claims for them that some critics consider hardly tenable.

This same creative process has led Sir Charles P. Snow, novelist and student of science, to maintain that there are now two cultures prevalent, and that they are at far poles from each other: the one a scientific culture, operating within the confines of observation, logic, and verifiable evidence; and the other, a literary culture concerned largely with emotion, imagination, and intuition. Since the appearance of his book *The Two Cultures,* numerous symposia and articles have dealt with the similarities and differences between the nature of scientific and literary thought processes.

From such discussions emerges the conclusion that both the scientist and the literary artist rely upon observation, imagination, feeling, and even intuition—"hunch"—as well as on careful induction and deduction. But the scientific tradition of caution makes the scientist restrict his findings to relationships that are verifiable by repeated experiment. Snow, after a severe attack by the literary critic F. R. Leavis, has appeared with a new book on the subject: *The Two Cultures: And a Second Look.* According to one British authority, Snow has redefined the two cultures:

> [Snow] argues that if two cultural camps are to be identified, they are those of creative artists and the scientists on one hand and the purely verbal scholars on the other. . . . For although he reiterates firmly his defence of the intellectual, aesthetic and moral values inherent in the pursuit of science, he equally repeats that neither the scientific system of mental development, nor the traditional system, is adequate for our potentialities, for the work we have in front of us, for the world in which we ought to begin to live.

CRITICAL FOCUS

Some Critical Questions for Reading Science

1. Is it a report of an experiment or an item in philosophy of science?
2. If it is a report, does the author show scholarly competence in the problem of his report?
3. Is it recent scholarship? (In some subjects one-year-old information is already "ancient history.")
4. Does it have coherent organization?
5. Is the diction burdened with jargon?
6. Has each step of the deductive or inductive reasoning been supported by conclusive evidence?
7. Is the reasoning valid throughout?

Suggestion: The *Journal of Chemical Education* recommends to freshmen these paperbacks for background in the language of science: (1) Glen T. Seaborg's *Man-made Transuranium Elements,* in the Prentice-Hall *Foundations of Modern General Chemistry Series;* (2) O. T. Benfey (ed.), *Classics in the Theory of Chemical Combination,* in the Dover *Classics of Science Series.*

Exercise 1   Written assignment. In scientific publications a definition given for a term in a statement should be in accord with the general scientific usage of that term and should also be appropriate to the objectives of the researcher who has written the article. (*a*) Find and read a scientific article that has a definition. (*b*) Copy out the definition. (*c*) Compare it with the definition given for that term in a dictionary of science. (*d*) Show how the author's definition fits the context of the article. Suggested sources for such articles: *Discovery, Science, Sky & Telescope, Nature, Scientific American, Isis,* or any professional journal of science.

Exercise 2   Written assignment. Define these terms commonly found in scientific terminology that general readers should know. Use each in the context of a sentence.

a priori	ratio	properties
a posteriori	sampling	deviation
extrapolation	positivism	formulate
interpolate	efficiency	risk
bias	fact	equation
variability	function	hypothesis

Exercise 3   Discussion assignment. Formulate the assumptions in the following letter to an editor, trace them through as premises leading to conclusions, and then discuss the logic and diction of the argument.

In regard to Joan W.'s letter, I must state my conviction that the people and organizations she has listed as endorsing fluoridation of public water reflect an appallingly low degree of intelligence when there are sensible alternative means of individual dosing, some of which are available at much lower cost to the taxpayers. Smallpox vaccinations and other vaccines certainly are not administered by public water supply but by individual prescription or treatment.

We are not against fluorides in an absolute sense, for we do not object to individual dosing. In fact we are just as much concerned about tooth decay problems as anyone, but we see no intelligence whatsoever in wasting 599 out of 600 parts of treated water used for other than human consumption, nor imposing it also on people who cannot utilize it or are adversely affected by it.

Regardless of so-called authorities' documentations of "safety," it is obvious that all human beings have not been duly examined for after-effects over a human life span. The ignoring of numerous individual complaints does not prove nonexistence of ill effect. . . . It is true that some individuals may forget their daily doses, but if Johnny forgets to treat his Coca Cola that most certainly does not snatch Susie's dose from her milk across the street.

We "ignorant cranks," "crackpots," and "know-nothings" believe we are fair in not objecting to sensible means of individual dosing for those who want or need it. But we consider public fluoridation of our water an assault on our person, and some of us shall fight it as if lives depended on our efforts.

Exercise 4   Discussion assignment. Computers perform all manner of research calculations. The following mailing piece from a university press describes the results of a *word count* study made of the poetry of William Butler Yeats. Explain your answers to these questions about the advertisement in detail and with good logic:

1. According to the mailing piece, what is a *concordance,* and what are the unique features of this particular one?
2. What does this advertisement of the book suggest to you of the workings of the poet's mind? Can such scientific tallying serve as a verifiable experiment? Can it be said to be conclusive about the nature of the language of poetry?
3. What kind of diction do you think a poet having a *mythopoetic* imagination would prefer?
4. Are there symbols or mythopoetic expressions in the quoted lines?
5. Does the piece suggest that the poet's intuitions might resemble those of a scientist?

A Concordance to the Poems of W. B. Yeats

The *unpurged* images of day *recede;*
The *Emperor's* drunken soldiery are abed;
Night *resonance recedes, night-walkers'* song
After great *cathedral* gong;

A starlit or a moonlit dome *disdains*
All that man is,
All mere *complexities*,
The fury and the mire of human veins.

The italicized forms in the opening stanza of "Byzantium" above occur nowhere in Yeats outside this poem; moreover, "abed," "soldiery," "gong," and "dome" show up elsewhere only once or twice. Such facts were discovered by an electronic computer that recorded the frequencies of all words in Yeats's poems.

The computer discovered that "old" is the second most commonly used word in Yeats, and that "heart," "love," "men," and "man" are also among the dozen most common words. An appendix in this concordance lists all indexed words in order of frequency and gives the frequencies. In addition, the frequencies are given for even those words in Yeats's poetry omitted from the index—the common prepositions, conjunctions, pronouns, and the like.

The body of this volume is an alphabetical index of all significant words in Yeats's poems, each word shown in its context, that is, in the line or lines of verse in which it occurs. Opposite each line is given the line number, abbreviated title of the poem, and the number of the page on which the line occurs in the variorum text of Yeats, edited by Colonel Russell K. Alspach and Peter Allt. Basing the concordance on the variorum edition makes it possible to include all variants that occur in printed versions of Yeats's poems.

Since the publication of the first Cornell Concordance, *A Concordance to the Poems of Matthew Arnold,* the technique of computer concordances has advanced so that this volume is able to include punctuation and give cross references for the second parts of hyphenated words. Also, it was possible to edit out and discriminate certain troublesome homographs ("art," "might," and "will" were listed when they occurred as nouns, not as verbs; "rose" was listed separately as a noun and a verb).

In the Editor's Preface, Dr. Stephen Maxfield Parish, Associate Professor of English at Cornell University, sets forth editorial principles, lists the omitted words, gives a table of title abbreviations, and discusses Yeats's poetic vocabulary. James Allan Painter, Development Mathematician at the International Business Machines Corporation in Poughkeepsie, N.Y., provides the Programmer's Preface, in which he describes for the layman the techniques used to produce both this concordance and the Arnold one using an electronic computer, the IBM 704 Data Processing Machine.

This first concordance of a symbolist poet undertaken makes it possible to trace in a systematic way the language patterns of a symbolist and mythopoetic imagination. Although one may be uneasy at invoking the aid of an electronic computer to map Yeats's private worlds of myth, symbol, and Irish legend, one may find in this book information never before readily accessible. It will be a valuable aid for the study of one of the greatest poets who have written in the English language.

Exercise 5   Essay assignment. Develop the topic given below into a full-length essay. Define terms where necessary, amplify with detail and example, comparison or contrast all important points. You may discuss the topic with others, but make the essay as completely your own in viewpoint and development as possible. Read the first draft aloud to yourself; look for faulty diction and weak reasoning.

Topic: What differences are there between these two statements: "God is the Creator of all"; "The universe is in a process of continuous creation"?

Exercise 6   Report assignment. In one of the journals suggested in Exercise 1, select and read an article that discusses a *deductive system,* as considered on pages 175 and 178. Write a brief report on whatever content of a *deductive system* you find in your article. Your analytic report of the article is to show that you understand the various steps beginning with concepts and ending up, possibly, with a proposed theory. In your article you probably will find, however, only experimental data and a conclusive general statement.

Exercise 7   Report assignment. Write a report on the diction and logic of one of the philosophers of science listed on page 179 as found in a chapter of one of his books.

Exercise 8   Written assignment. If you are taking a laboratory science course, report on your attempts to follow the deductive system in one of your assigned experiments. The experiment most likely had for its purpose the duplication of the steps taken by some pioneer in the field to arrive at the conclusion you are asked to reach.

LANGUAGE OF THE SOCIAL SCIENCES

Although still comparatively new fields of organized study, the social sciences have produced a vast library of volumes. In the effort to find principles, forces, and patterns in human social organizations, they have developed a highly varied language, as may be seen in these terms culled from a book review:

antirational, inverted nationalism	typology
totalitarian socialism	disorientation
sophisticated reactionary	technocrats
reactionary romanticism	pragmatic morality
inner alienation	gerontocracy
a hollow society	integrative function
cartoon-strip rationale	charismatic leader
ruling elite	ideology

As may be expected, some writers in the disciplines of sociology, anthropology, political science, and other social sciences are more effective writers than are some of their colleagues. Too many seem to be tempted to flaunt the highly conceptualized terms of their special language and to write jargon. In deriding this tendency, a prominent educator recently suggested how a group of jargon-minded social scientists might rewrite the first lines of the 23d psalm:

> The Lord is my external, internal, integrated mechanism. I shall not be deprived of gratifications for my visceral generic hungers or my need dispositions. He motivates me to orient myself towards a non-social objective with affective significance. (That's the green pastures.) He positions me in a non-decisional situation. (Besides the still waters.) He maximizes my adjustment.

This is not to say, of course, that new, useful terms cannot be introduced, if contextually defined, to pithily express a social phenomenon. Suppose an academic reader encounters the term *empty nesters,* for example, in an article on suburban housing. Obviously it is a neologism, aptly coined to describe some housing phenomenon; try finding its sense in this well-written passage:

> Each year, an increasing number of suburban husbands and wives, mainly the so-called "empty nesters"—couples whose children have flown off to college or to build their own nests—are feeling the new urban urge. They are leaving the commuting trains and the lawn mowers behind to return to the rediscovered delights of the big city. As one remarked, "I've served my time. Now, I'm back in town."

Comparison of one of Machiavelli's statements with a political science textbook analysis of the same political theory is enlightening. Machiavelli is so brutally clear that many readers misunderstand him:

> Some students of history have been puzzled by the ease with which Agathocles and one or two other of the same kidney were able in spite of the most appalling cruelty and treachery, to live long in security in their own dominions, to defend themselves against external enemies, and never be menaced by conspiracy; while many others have not by these methods succeeded even in maintaining their positions in time of peace, let alone in war.
>
> I think the answer is that it depends on whether brutality is well or badly handled. Well-handled brutalities (if one may use the phrase about evil things) are those which are all applied sharply and simultaneously to ensure control and not repeated, but succeeded by consideration for the welfare of the subjects. Badly applied cruelty is that which starts mildly but gives the impression of increasing rather than diminishing with the passage of time.
>
> Tyrants following the first rule may, through the short memories of God and man, secure their dominion. . . . The prince must so order his conduct that it will not vary from good times to bad. In a dangerous emergency it is usually too late for ferocious repression, and benevolence will be deemed to be forced by circumstances and will not earn gratitude.

What is plainly said in this passage may either fail to register with some readers or be completely misinterpreted. The subject is repugnant: how to get by as a cruel tyrant. The advice seems tinged with cynicism, but twentieth-century experience with tyrants leads observers to agree with this analysis.

Consider next a textbook analysis of and comment on dictatorship:

> It is now easy to see why some individuals seek to increase their influence by gaining control over the State. For when an actor controls the State, he can enforce his decisions with the help of the State. More concretely, he can use the State's monopoly over physical coercion to try to secure compliance with his policies. But one can seek compliance not only through punishment but also through rewards; and control over the State generally provides resources that can be used to create large benefits as well as severe punishment. In

short, the State is a peculiarly important source of *power*. Let us examine this point more closely.

Two kinds of influence are sometimes singled out for particular attention:

1. *Coercive influence:* influence based on the threat or expectation of extremely severe penalties or great losses, particularly physical punishment, torture, imprisonment, and death.

2. *Reliable influence:* influence in which the probability of compliance is very high.

Before comparing the two passages, we must observe that the subject matter itself is somewhat different because of the contrasting approaches of the two authors. Machiavelli does not even consider here the question of why one desires power. He seeks merely to explain why some rulers have succeeded in attaining broad goals by using extreme cruelty, whereas the cruelty of other rulers has proved totally ineffective. The textbook, on the other hand, starts out by answering the question of why one hopes to increase his influence by becoming a ruler: to be able to enforce compliance more effectively by drawing upon the state's tremendous resources of power.

At this point, the textbook sets out to define power, first substituting the euphemism *influence*, then proceeding to divide influence into two categories: that based on threat of punishment, and that which, apparently, requires no coercion because it is only "used" to "enforce compliance" where compliance is already very probable. There is certainly some confusion introduced here: The terms *coercive influence* and *reliable influence* seem to be parallel, to express two types of influence. Actually, however, the two terms are not at all parallel. One refers to a *means* of enforcing compliance (coercion); the other, to an undefined kind of influence used in a defined *situation*, i.e., a situation in which one might expect compliance to begin with. Let us also note that the very first sentence of the passage seemed to use the word *influence* in a different sense! *Influence,* we were told, is the achievement of compliance and is sought through *power,* which is now defined as two types of *influence!*

In short, the textbook discussion leaves us with many unanswered questions: What is the definition of *power,* of *influence;* does coercive influence work, and if so, when and how; in what sense is reliable influence truly influence if compliance is already probable, and what means should be used to ensure total compliance? In evaluating the clarity of the passages, we must say that the textbook has taxed us with two new terms not well enough defined for us to use. Machiavelli's phrases certainly present a contrast. At no time does he resort to jargon; even when he uses words in a surprising way—*well-applied cruelty*—he defines their meaning very carefully.

Besides jargon, there is another stumbling block in reading social science material. The critical reader must expect to encounter different schools of thought in each of the major fields, and each proponent of a different school may use certain words in a different way. Anthropology, for instance, generally deals only with verifiable data at hand in the form of cultural artifacts, but it also offers several different *private* interpretations of its subject matter: the history and culture of mankind. Anthropologists, like the other social scientists, form schools of opinion, such as Christian, rationalist, Freudian, Marxian, and data gatherers. Each of these may give special significance to terms held in common by the others in the same general area of study. For it is obvious that a Marxist, who interprets social man as a figure in emergent class wars, will not accept the meaning of a Freudian, who sees all as evidence of another kind of "war." And the data gatherer may shrug his shoulders at the conflicting notions of man at war with himself and his environment, as those views are fiercely disputed by the Christian and the rationalist.

Perhaps a principal reason for lack of clarity in social science writing lies in the recent origins of these academic disciplines. Many people feel that in attempting to say, scientifically, something about man in society, the sociologists have not yet found a scientific form in which to consider and express their findings. Too often they express their data by analogy, a form particularly suspect in contemporary philosophy of language. If an analogy is perfect, no new insight is gained; if it is not close enough, the data are forced into an inappropriate structure and come out distorted. One social scientist has expressed this problem well in discussing the sociologist's attempt to express himself on the basic subject of communication, a subject which this author considers "as basic to man's nature as food and sex":

> We have also elaborated biological, physical, mechanical, and, more recently, electronic analogies of communications into models, or "designs," for exercises in research techniques. . . . Symbols are the directly observable data of sociation, and, since it is impossible to

use symbols without using them in some kind of structure or form, we cannot discourse about society with any degree of precision unless we discourse about the form social relationships assume in communication. . . . As matters now stand in American social thought, the study of forms of communication is suspect, or tolerated only until social scientists achieve an "intellectual clarity" which science, and usually science based on quantification is supposed to produce. . . . Man as a social being exists in and through communication; communication is as basic to man's nature as food and sex.

Finally, a basic goal of social science writing is the clear statement of objectives of each particular academic field. Clear distinctions need to be made to avoid needless controversy. Through analysis of diction, by showing points of similarity and of difference in specific instances, we can test distinctions for clarity. Many may be distinctions without differences, but generally by means of clear defining and classifying, writers can make effective differentiations, as does this one in distinguishing between three kinds of *truth*—truth of science, truth of faith, and truth of history:

The distinction between the truth of faith and the truth of science leads to a warning, directed to theologians, not to use recent scientific discoveries to confirm the truth of faith. Microphysicists have undercut some scientific hypotheses concerning the calculability of the universe. The theory of quantum and the principle of indeterminacy have had this effect. Immediately religious writers use these insights for the confirmation of their own ideas of human freedom, divine creativity, and miracles. But there is no justification for such a procedure at all, neither from the point of view of physics nor from the point of view of religion. The physical theories referred to have no direct relation to the infinitely complex phenomenon of human freedom, and the emission of power in quantums has no direct relation to the meaning of miracles. Theology, in using physical theories in this way, confuses the dimension of science with the dimension of faith. The truth of faith cannot be confirmed by latest physical or biological or psychological discoveries—it cannot be denied by them.

Historical truth has a character quite different from that of scientific truth. History reports unique events, not repetitive processes which can be tested again and again. Historical events are not subject to experiment. The only analogy in history to a physical experiment is the comparison of documents. . . . History describes, explains, and understands. And understanding presupposes participation. This is the difference between historical and scientific truth. In historical truth the interpreting subject is involved; in scientific truth it is detached. . . . Faith cannot guarantee factual truth. But faith can and must interpret the meaning of fact from the point of view of man's ultimate concern. . . . Neither scientific nor historical truth can affirm or negate the truth of faith. The truth of faith can neither affirm nor negate scientific or historical truth.

These careful distinctions between the objectives of the various disciplines, as compared by a churchman, illustrate the work of the social sciences in discovering, classifying, and interpreting all aspects of man as a social being.

CRITICAL FOCUS

The language of the social sciences reflects the methodology and reasoning of science as applied to human behavior in the physical and social environment. It reflects also the objective, questioning attitude of science. The critical reader must determine for himself, always judging the merits of the particular case, where technical language is validly employed and where it is merely jargon resulting from the desire to appear scientific.

Exercise 9   Written assignment. Here are two samples of social science language couched in jargon. Using the dictionary whenever necessary, rewrite both pieces in good, clear English without sacrificing distinctions made in the quotations. Consider, as well, whether the second passage is guilty of what we have called "mistaking the map for the territory."

Analysis of the data supports the hypothesis that the size of the shift toward background opinion and away from private opinion increases with increases in discrepancy of background reports from modal responses. We have now to consider why a more discrepant background had a greater weight in shifting attitudes than backgrounds closer to the modal position since this is not true with all types of material. The task involved expressions of attitudes with regard to verbal materials. By comparison with highly structured cognitive materials such as easy arithmetic problems or judging number of metronome clicks, the attitudes evoked in this study represent internalized norms or frames of reference developed from social inter-action and electively incorporated in cognitive-emotional frames of reference.

A person becomes delinquent because of an excess of definitions favorable to violation of law over definitions unfavorable to violation of law.

Exercise 10 Written assignment. To show that you under-stand the various implications of the author of the following observa-tions, rewrite his statement. You are to expand it by giving concrete, specific instances of concepts he states as abstractions; for example, where he speaks of *unexpected causes of lasting discord,* you might list quarrels over money, bills, etc.

> I know not . . . whether marriage be more than one of the innumera-ble modes of human misery. When I see and reckon the various forms of connubial infelicity, unexpected causes of lasting discord, the diversities of temper, the oppositions of opinion, the rude collisions of contrary desire where both are urged by violent impulses, the obstinate contests of disagreeable virtues where both are supported by consciousness of good intention, I am sometimes disposed to think, with the severer casuists of most nations, that marriage is rather per-mitted than approved, and that none, but by the instigation of passion too much indulged, entangle themselves with indissoluble compacts.

Exercise 11 Written assignment. In the quoted material of this social science section of the chapter, find and list as many examples as you can find of these four types of statements. Then identify which ones were employed as theories, laws, or facts:

General
Particular
Quantitative
Qualitative

Exercise 12 Essay assignment. Explain your opinion of what changes would occur if modern readers took to heart what Henry David Thoreau recommends in The Conclusion of *Walden.* He speaks as a social critic, so you will want to determine exactly what his views are, how their adoption would affect life as we know it now, and how you feel about them. Do not write only generalities, but support every point you make with concrete examples and solid, supporting detail. You may wish to use comparison and contrast to show what results his ideas would have in our modern society. Somewhere in your essay, you may wish to make clear your opinion of his sense of values, since his book is full of value judgments.

chapter 8

READING FOR STRUCTURE

COMPOSITION STRUCTURES AND THEIR PARAGRAPHS

In every kind of expression we have found language and logic fused together within a context which usually had some distinct form or organization that we referred to as *structure*. It is high time that this third important element for the critical reader and writer be given its proper emphasis. For language requires a structure of composition as much as it does logic. In fact, man's ability to reason led also to the formation of needed systems of organized composition. The Greeks, who first sketched the scope of literary and forensic art, included diction, logic, and structure in the study of rhetoric.

Rhetoric was defined by Aristotle as "the power to see the possible ways of persuading people about any given subject." He saw nothing wrong in the efforts of a speaker or dramatist to employ all suitable means to persuade his audience of the truth and acceptability of his views. But Aristotle did distinguish between the sincere person and those *sophists* who, with little regard for principle, might try every device and strategy of language in order to win an audience. *Sincerity* is a much abused term, but it still denotes the quality of utterance that gains our respect. As Herbert Read has said: "The only thing that is indispensable for the possession of a good style is personal sincerity. . . . Those who would persuade us of the truth of a statement must rely, not on an air of conviction or a show of reason, but on the compelling force of an emotional attitude."

Persuasion, in the rhetorical sense, thus remains a fundamental purpose in all the four types of composition: exposition, argumentation, description, and narration. The writer wants to be believed when he explains, argues, describes, or tells a story. We have seen that in order to gain such acceptance, he can fashion diction and logic into most attractive unions. To the same degree he depends on a structure suitable to his purposes and intents. We hope to end this examination of those structures with some means or criteria whereby the critical reader can formulate sound judgment on the writer's means of organizing his expression.

In determining what he wants to say and how he feels about it, a good writer determines also his general structure. If he is too deeply stirred with conviction or excitement about his subject, he may begin writing, and trust to some *intuitive arrangement* to emerge as he hurries along. He starts off with lively opening sentences, and words and phrases spring into sentences and paragraphs as if he were only a kind of transmitting medium. But we can be sure that such apparently effortless good writing is a result of inbuilt habits of organization. He knows almost intuitively that the essay must have an interesting introduction, a developed body, and a strong conclusion. Somewhere in his years of training, he has taught himself certain fundamentals of coherent, unified organization. But this same writer generally will consider it necessary to lay out his plan before starting to write.

His subject matter will suggest to him several possibilities of *tone*. His first task is to decide what and how he feels about his subject and also what kind of audience he wants to accept his purpose. He will have to decide whether he should explain clearly, argue, describe, or say what he has to say in the form of a story. His previous training may limit his choice; he may also make a bad decision. There have been many published stories that would have made better essays or sermons than they did narratives. We can presume, however, that the authors whom we deal with here have been judicious enough to find a suitable form and structure.

Exposition provides a system of organization basic to all writing structures. To state and amplify an idea of any complexity, one may have to write paragraphs that in whole, or in part, do one of these:

1. Identify   5. Illustrate or exemplify
2. Define   6. Compare or contrast
3. Classify   7. Analyze
4. Show cause

Any one of these methods of exposition may serve either alone or in combination with the others to give an essay its organizational structure.

The Foreword to *The Territory Ahead* by Wright Morris is a model of expository structure. Let us examine it by paragraph with analytical summaries in the margin:

Foreword

Dramatic opening sentence followed by thesis of book and Foreward. Clear, direct language.
Tone: *candid, restrained statement to highly literate audience.*
Main expository methods: *informal definition, example, and cause.*

From Hawthorne to Faulkner the mythic past has generated what is memorable in our literature—but what is not so memorable, what is often crippling, we have conspired to overlook. This is the tendency, long prevailing, to start well then peter out. For the contemporary, both the writer and the reader, this pattern of failure may be more instructive than the singular achievements of the past. The writer's genius, as a rule, is unique, but in his tendency to fail he shares a common tradition. This blight has been the subject of many inquiries, and the prevailing opinion has been that an unresponsive and Philistine culture has, as a rule, corrupted the writer's promise. Such an exception as Henry James, the exile, would merely seem to prove the rule. He succeeded or he failed—depending on the point of view—by becoming a non-American.

Fine transition leading to restatement of topic sentence in sentence 3 and its development by example, cause, and repetition for emphasis.

"Mr. Henry James, great artist and faithful historian," Joseph Conrad observes, "never attempts the impossible." This would seem to be the opposite, however, of accepted American practice. Failure, not success, is the measure of an artist's achievement. Mr. Faulkner has given this notion fresh currency in a recent statement concerning Thomas Wolfe: Wolfe was the greatest of them all, Faulkner said, because he tried to do the impossible. This is tantamount to saying that the dilettante is superior to the master craftsman, since the master craftsman achieves what he sets out to do. Failure, not achievement, is the hallmark of success. The romantic origins of this statement are less pertinent to this discussion than the prevailing tendency to find in such a statement a profound truth. The great writer *must* fail. In this way we shall know that he is great. In such a writer's failure the public sees a moral victory: what does his failure prove but how sublime and grand the country is? This point of view has so much to recommend it that to call it into question smacks of un-Americanism. It calls, that is, for a shrinking of the national consciousness.

Formal restatement of purpose of book and thesis of Foreward, for clarity and reassurance of possibly hostile readers.
Method to be followed explained by means of analogy. Tone again made clear: purpose and attitude toward subject and readers.

It is the purpose of this book to inquire if this climate of failure is not linked, in a logical fashion, with the prevailing tendency of the American mind to take to the woods. Literally, like Thoreau, or figuratively, like Faulkner, our writers of genius face backward while their countrymen resolutely march forward. It is little wonder, faced with this fact, that we lead such notably schizoid lives.

Reappraisal is repossession, and this book is an act of reappraisal. In such a fashion I seek to make my own what I have inherited as clichés. To make new we must reconstruct, as well as resurrect. The destructive element in this reconstruction is to remove from the object the encrusted cliché. Time itself, in architecture and sculpture, does this in terms of what it leaves us. The fragment means more to us—since it demands more of us—than the whole. The mutilations are what we find the most provocative and beautiful. Since we cannot, in any case, possess the original—which exists in one time and serves one purpose—our reappraisal is an act of re-creation in which the work of art is the raw material. Short of this we are dealing with the bones of a fossil, the remains of a form that has served its purpose.

More reassurance for readers possibly critical of his analytical method. Definition of character of art.

Such an attitude questions, of course, one of the sentiments most congenial to our nature—the uniqueness and inviolability of art. Art is indeed unique and inviolable—but its uniqueness may lie where we do not choose to look: in the creative response it generates in the participant; in the need he feels to repossess it in his own terms. The creative act itself is self-sufficient, having served the artist's purpose, but it lives on only in those minds with the audacity to transform it. The classic, from such a point of view, is that characteristic statement that finds in each age an echoing response—echoing, but not the same. Hemingway's Huck Finn is not Mark Twain's, nor is my Huck Finn Hemingway's. Nor do I mean to suggest that art itself is atomized in an infinite series of personal impressions—but that it survives, archetypally, in and through an endless series of transformations. Through the Huck Finns, that is—through each age's reappraisal—the young heart is reassured and the consciousness expands.

Tone again of candor and independence.

This book has grown out of an essay written at the suggestion of Granville Hicks, and is an act of synthesis rather than analysis, a personal inquiry in the sense that it grows from my experience as a reader and a writer. No effort has been made to be inclusive, and I do not imply that other evaluations, from other points of view, are not equally useful. This is how it looks to me.

Restatement of thesis with additional detail to show scope of book.

In the nineteenth century the writer took to the woods or the high seas, literally as well as figuratively. In the present century the same flight is achieved through nostalgia, rage, or some such ruling passion from which the idea of the present, the opposing idea, has been excluded. In the American writer of genius the ability to function has been retained—with the exception of James—by depreciating the intelligence.

Dramatic conclusion. Thesis restated in form of paradox.

For more than a century the territory ahead has been the world that lies somewhere behind us, a world that has become, in the last few decades, a nostalgic myth. On the evidence, which is impressive, it is the myth that now cripples the imagination, rather than the dark and brooding immensity of the continent. It is the territory behind that defeats our writers of genius, not America.

Analysis for structure of this essay, or any other, can be quickly made by drawing up a topic sentence outline of every paragraph. At a glance, then, the essential points stand out ready for classification into general outline headings to show the organizational structure. This analysis also asks two revealing questions concerning the author: (1) Does his skill, or lack of it, in orderly development suggest his competence both as writer and coherent thinker? (2) What do his tone and style reveal of his attitudes toward his subject and his readers?

Such an analysis, paragraph by paragraph, of Morris's Foreword produces this result:

Topic Sentence Outline

1. American literary geniuses start well and then peter out.
2. *Failure, not success, is the measure of the artist's achievement.*
3. The American literary mind tends *to take to the woods* and to look back.
4. . . . *This book is an act of reappraisal.*
5. The uniqueness of art does not preclude such reappraisal.
6. *This is how it looks to me.*
7. The American writer of genius apparently can function only *by depreciating the intelligence.*
8. The writers are defeated not by America, but by a tendency to look back.

Outline

Thesis: In America, *failure, not success, is the measure of an artist's achievement.*

1. The American literary genius tends to fail (paragraphs 1, 2, 3).
   a. It starts well but peters out.
   b. It looks back to the past.
2. Reappraisal of American authors is a reliable method (paragraphs 4, 5, 6).
   a. Art is unique.
   b. Its uniqueness, however, may be in the participant's creative reappraisal.
3. American writers are not defeated by their environment, but by their flight therefrom (paragraphs 7, 8).
   a. Former authors fled, literally, away in space.
   b. Now their flight is backward, in time.

It can be said, then, of the Foreword that it shows Wright Morris as restrained and candid in his attitude toward what he considers a tragic tendency in America's great writers. He shows a fine appreciation and insight into the nature of art. His Foreword, as a short essay, reveals a unified, coherent structure and has a style strong in candor and conviction.

Most paragraphs of competent authors seem to have been designed to be little essays complete in themselves. As such, their topic sentence becomes the *thesis*, and the sentences may take on the emphasis of paragraphs because of their distinctive diction. The following one-paragraph "essay" by Sir Winston Churchill is a memorable example:

> Even though large tracts of Europe and many old and famous States have fallen or may fall into the grip of the Gestapo and all the odious apparatus of Nazi rule, we shall not flag or fail. We shall go on to the end. We shall fight in France, we shall fight in the seas and oceans, we shall fight with growing confidence and growing strength in the air; we shall defend our Island, whatever the cost may be. We shall fight on the beaches, we shall fight on the landing-grounds, we shall fight in the fields and in the streets, we shall fight in the hills; we shall never surrender; and even if, which I do not for a moment believe, this Island or a large part of it were subjugated and starving, then our Empire beyond the seas, armed and guarded by the British Fleet, would carry on the struggle, until, in God's good time, the New World with all its power and might, steps forth to the rescue and the liberation of the Old.

If we apply our two tests to it, we are struck first by Sir Winston's magnificent skill in developing his idea, and, second, by his tone of stirring conviction that Britain will yet win the war and that the people of the British Empire are the bravest, finest, most loyal in the world. His parallelism of sentence structure adds dramatic emphasis to his highly connotative diction. Every term is emotion-arousing for the bomb-seared audience to whom the speech was addressed. The pronoun *we* serves as a *key word* giving coherence of repetition, and aiding in keeping the same point of view throughout.

Here is another one-paragraph "essay," written by an old master, William Hazlitt. It is, for him, a comparatively short paragraph, since many of his approximate 1,000 words in length—such was the leisurely generation of readers for whom he wrote. It affords an excellent means for analysis to show what a paragraph traditionally does as a unit of structure.

Another error is to spend one's life in procrastination and preparations for the future. Persons of this turn of mind stop at the threshold of art, and accumulate the means of improvement, till they obstruct their progress to the end. They are always putting off the evil day, and excuse themselves for doing nothing by commencing some new and indispensable course of study. Their projects are magnificent, but remote, and require years to complete or to put them in execution. Fame is seen in the horizon, and flies before them. Like the recreant Boastful knight in Spenser, they turn their backs on their competitors, to make a great career, but never return to the charge. They make themselves masters of anatomy, of drawing, of perspective; they collect prints, casts, medallions, make studies of heads, of hands, of the bones, the muscles; copy pictures; visit Italy, Greece, and return as they went. They fulfill the proverb, "When you are at Rome, you must do as those at Rome do." This circuitous, erratic pursuit of art can come to no good. It is only an apology for idleness and vanity. Foreign travel especially makes men pedants, not artists. What we seek, we must find at home or nowhere. The way to do great things is to set about something, and he who cannot find resources in himself or in his own painting-room, will perform the Grand Tour, or go through the circle of the arts and sciences, and end just where he began!

Analysis: In structure this paragraph consists of thirteen sentences closely related in thought and mood. It begins with the topic statement, which by means of its opening words—*Another error*—at the same time relates it in transition to what has already been said on the general essay subject: "On Application to Study." It further adds to the particular attack on all those persons, earlier described, "whose minds seem to move in an element of littleness, or rather, that are entangled in trifling difficulties, and incapable of extricating themselves from them." And as the second to last paragraph of the essay, it prepares for the concluding one, which applies all that has been said also to business with the advice: "Give a man a motive to work, and he will work." So this paragraph has excellent unity as well as coherence in relation to the essay as a whole. And as a unit of composition, it has the same qualities. By use of the *key word—they—*and the related pronouns, which are found in one sentence after the other, Hazlitt makes it easy for the reader to follow the amplifying thoughts. The author gives the final-sentence idea *emphasis* by being dramatic and forceful through specific reference.

The implications of the topic sentence are brought out by most of the customary means of developing a paragraph statement, as can be seen by this outline:

1. Definition (sentence 2)
2. Details of identification (sentences 3, 4, 5, 8, 9, 10, 12)
3. Comparison (sentence 6)
4. Example (sentences 7, 13)
5. Analogy (sentence 11)

CRITICAL FOCUS

Four Questions for Determining Structure in Exposition
1. **What is the thesis or central purpose?**
2. **How is the thesis developed? By what expository means, paragraph by paragraph, is the idea amplified?**
3. **What rhetorical devices, such as parallelism, key word, repetition, and figurative language, give the essay coherence and emphasis?**
4. **What does the tone tell of the author?**

Exercise 1 Discussion assignment. Analyze this one-paragraph essay for its structural organization, sentence by sentence, in terms of the expository methods of development each exemplifies: identification, definition, etc. How does the diction set the tone? What is the tone? What purpose does the opening clause serve?

If the Frankish rulers of Athens are to-day unrepresented by a single monument, the Turks who succeeded them and maintained their sway for almost four hundred years, during which they accomplished far more in the way of destruction, produced little that now bears witness to their long sojourn. A couple of mosques, one of them the work of a Greek architect, a doorway hard by the Tower of the Winds bearing a carved Kufic inscription, a few place-names, and that is all. Of all nations the least creative, forever borrowing and never producing, the Turks are represented in the long roll of Athenian monuments by gaps rather than additions; innumerable masterpieces vanished beneath their tender care, and thanks to their lighthearted disposal of ammunition dumps combined with an unexpected accuracy of aim on the part of a Hanoverian gunner in the Venetian service, the Parthenon was, in the late seventeenth century, reduced to a ruin. There do exist, it is true, even in Athens a few so-called

"Turkish houses," but these, like the "Turkish bridges" one finds all over Greece, have, as one's Greek friends are tireless in pointing out, no connection with the Turks save that they were built during the period of their rule.

Exercise 2   Written assignment. Here is another one-paragraph essay. Show particularly how tone and structural organization are fused with diction. (Apply the four questions given in the last Critical Focus.)

They followed the fog all the way across the county line at Elk-head. When it began to lift and burn off they were on the main road in the rich alder-bottoms along Mud River, traveling between miles of dark-green arbors hung with long bunches of pale-green flowers. Hop-driers stuck out every few miles, great barnlike structures four stories high, with a blind belfry on top. They came to places where the arbors had been torn down and ripped to pieces, the strings cut and the poles lying on the ground, and places where there were tents and wickyups and blanket lean-tos and corrals of parked wagons. People were eating breakfast on the ground; women were cooking and hanging out clothes on the wild-lilac bushes and hauling water from the creek; men were cutting wood and currying teams and sloshing cold water on themselves; children were yelling and scuffling and putting their clothes on or running around the camps without any. There were no people in sight except the campers. Nobody was supervising them, nobody was there to inquire who they were or where they came from or anything about them. This was the hop-fields, where all the homeless and jobless and worthless people in the country were camped to pick hops at a cent and a half a pound, and as long as the hops needed picking nobody cared whether the pickers belonged anywhere or amounted to anything or not. If all the people in that country had been solid and respectable, there would have been nobody to get the hops picked.

Exercise 3   Discussion assignment. Compare the following two paragraphs on the basis of the four questions in the last Critical Focus.

Consider the face of a blond woman in a film shot; the color of hair and complexion approximate to each other as a curious pale white— even the blue eyes appear whitish; the velvety black bow of the mouth and the sharp dark pencil lines of the eyebrows are in marked contrast. How strange such a face is, how much more intense—because unconventional—is the expression, how much more attention it attracts to itself and to its expression. How much more readily one observes whether the line with which a dense black braid of hair frames a white face is beautiful and suitable. Anyone who has noticed how unreal most film faces appear, how unearthly, how beautiful, how they often give the impression of not being so much a natural phenomenon as an artistic creation—toward which, of course, the art of make-up helps considerably—will get the same pleasure from a good film face as from a good lithograph or woodcut. Anyone who is in the habit of going to film premieres knows how painfully pink the faces of the film actors appear in real life when they come on stage and make their bows after the performance. The stylized, expressive giant masks on the screen do not fit beings of flesh and blood; they are visual material, the stuff of which art is made.

But stars don't always run to avoid the bright lights. Some of them can't do without them, stay for years and try not to grow old. Among them: Cary Grant, Robert Cummings, Marlene Dietrich, Loretta Young, Gloria Swanson, and Robert Taylor. Their publicity people claim that the seemingly eternal youth of their clients is the product of an "inner radiance." But all those who know better, realize that flesh can "radiate" just so long. After that, it must be coddled, caressed, and surgically manipulated.

Exercise 4   Written assignment. Outline this NBC advertisement appearing in *The New Yorker,* and appraise its structure according to the four questions in the last Critical Focus.

Big-Daddy of Waters

In Mark Twain's loving eyes it was "the great Mississippi . . . the majestic, the magnificent Mississippi."
    A visiting Charles Dickens, on the other hand, said he couldn't find words ugly enough to describe "this enormous ditch . . . running liquid mud at six miles an hour."

Point of View

Both men were right, of course, and their diverging assessments would be just as valid today; for the Mississippi, over its 2,348 miles, has as many faces as it has bends. Life along the river's course is a study in contrasts. And it's this world—from the rice marshes of Minnesota to the Louisiana bayous—that David Brinkley will be exploring Sunday night, February 2, in NBC News' full-hour color special, "Our Man on the Mississippi."

No travelogue, this. (There'll be no steamboat slowly sinking in the west at fadeout.) Instead, viewers will be shown how life along the Mississippi has changed. The great shipyards, elegant mansions and luxury boats have all but disappeared. Today, power craft and water-skiers zip past ancient, shore-bound paddle-wheelers. River rats have given way to beatniks. Even the raging floods (which once gushed regularly and madly across newsreel screens) have—thankfully—been corseted into obedience.

Yet, in many ways, the people of the river country are as colorful as ever. Brinkley interviewed one Southern politico who lights his cigars with a lighter that plays "Dixie." And even Mark Twain never had the good fortune to bump into a character who earns part of his livelihood by trapping grasshoppers he later sells as bait.

This last chap, as the special will show, has attached a trough-like contraption to the front bumper of his ancient Ford. In a 15-minute romp through a weedy field, the car can collect as many as 2,000 of the insects, few of whom ever dreamed there was a Ford in their future.

There is, to be sure, more money in Southern cotton than in grass-hoppers, as will be evidenced in Brinkley's visit to the Arkansas' vast Wilson fields, across the river and about 40 miles from Memphis. Famed as America's largest family-owned plantation, the 30,000 acres are serviced by some 1,100 employes.

Despite the existence of such enterprises, the economy of the Mississippi valley is not nearly what it was. Today the river's strongest commodity is nostalgia. The February 2 special, produced by Ted Yates and Stuart Schulberg, will be evoking much of that nostalgia.

Yesterday's Giant

Brinkley will be examining a waterway that once meant boom towns, fur companies, showboats, rich timber lands, and noisy gambling casinos. Its very name continues to conjure up a uniquely American era.

In actuality, the Mississippi is something else again. As Coproducer Ted Yates puts it, "Most of the river's new things are ugly, including the drug store cowboys, the oil refineries and the housing developments. And the things that are old and beautiful are chipped and poor." Be that as it may, in terms of the American saga, the Mississippi is much more than a twisting meandering landmark. It is an endless stream of consciousness.

Exercise 5   Writing assignment. Select one of these topic sentences—rephrase it if you wish—and develop it into a substantial paragraph by giving examples, reasons, details, definition, and comparison or contrast, as you deem most suitable. If possible, let the first version lie for at least several hours, and then read it aloud to yourself, keeping alert for sentences or phrases that do not contribute what they should to the topic, or that are in faulty and clumsy order or position. For improvement of coherence, try using a *key word* and its pronouns as principal parts of sentences. Rewrite, keeping in mind the particular readers whom you wish to interest and impress.

1. I know what it means to drive in heavy traffic.
2. From neighbors I have learned at least one thing.
3. Living away from home does something to you.
4. The artist's life is not an easy one.
5. You learn about human nature from the other side of the counter.
6. There is a certain protocol involved in having and riding a bicycle.
7. Marriage is something of a handicap in getting a college degree.
8. Jets take you there in a hurry, but then. . . .
9. Some things are more a question of taste than of morality.
10. It is said that hands frequently reveal the personality as much as the face does.
11. The tourist folder says, *See the magic of the Taj Mahal at the time of the full moon,* but there is more to see in India than the Taj Mahal.
12. Folders describing student tours of Europe omit some significant facts.
13. The neighborhood could not be called wholesome or attractive.
14. In a hard-played game, the team having the best leader wins.
15. Some people seem to hate even themselves.
16. It's possible to experience claustrophobia in a supermarket.
17. No campus organization is "normal" without at least one.
18. It takes more than skill to become an Olympic winner.
19. A drama read is not the same play as that seen on a stage.
20. A parking lot is a circus all of its own.

Exercise 6   Written assignment. To show their structure, outline two articles in any issue of a "quality" magazine. Summarize the tone of each as shown by its diction. What can you say of the style of each when judged for conviction or sincerity?

Exercise 7   Discussion assignment. Below an almost full-page magazine picture of a lone cowboy standing beside a campfire appears the following caption and message. Discuss the structure in the light of the four questions in the last Critical Focus.

An American Hero

The true cowboy: living American symbol of independent man. Today there aren't as many true cowboys around. But the spirit they stand for is part of all that is America.

That spirit lives in the professions, businesses and industries that serve you today—enterprises built and run by free and independent people. Businesses owned by investors—by people like you and your neighbors—who still prize their freedom and their individuality.

Yet some other people think that our federal government—rather than individuals—should own certain businesses. Our investor-owned electric light and power companies are one of their chief targets. These are companies built, run, owned by and employing people who believe in individual effort. They have served you well, and you have made them strong by your support as a customer.

When you consider what our country has always stood for, can you see why anyone should want our federal government to do any job it doesn't have to do—such as owning and managing the electric light and power business? Isn't it best to leave that to individuals, like you, who believe individual effort is the quality that will always keep our nation strong?

Invester-owned Electric Light and
Power Companies . . . serving more than
140,000,000 people across the nation.

Exercise 8   Written assignment. Make an outline showing the organizational structure, paragraph by paragraph, of an article in a recent issue of a learned journal dealing with a subject matter in your field of interest. Discuss its tone, methods of expository development, and clarity of diction.

Exercise 9   Report assignment. Outline for structure a speech made by a President of the United States or by a candidate for the Presidency in recent years. Analyze its tone and diction in terms of the audience for whom it was intended.

INFORMAL EXPOSITORY STRUCTURE

Not all writers wish or find it appropriate to confine themselves to the formal, carefully planned structure. Montaigne and his English emulator, Francis Bacon, both personal essayists, discovered the ease and air of conversational intimacy that distinguish this form of writing.

It lacks a tightly coherent structure, and often consists of individual sentences held together only by their dealing with some such general topic as *friendship, reading, gardens,* or *nature.* Addison and Steele in the eighteenth century, among others, further developed this often whimsical form into the instrument admirably suited to a Charles Lamb, a Ralph Waldo Emerson, or a Henry David Thoreau. In this century, it has become the mainstay of newspaper and magazine columnists as well as of advertising and public relations agencies.

One of the most lively sources of the traditional informal essay is the *The New Yorker* feature, The Talk of the Town. Here is a representative sample of that "talk." What can you say of its tone and structural organization?*

Fun for All

One of the merriest places in town last week was the vast and rather chilly stage of the Metropolitan Opera House, where rehearsals of Gian Carlo Menotti's "The Last Savage" were under way. The work, which had its world première in Paris last October and had its American première here January 23rd, is an *opera buffa,* in the comic tradition of Mozart and Rossini, and the gaiety of the music, the exuberance of the sets and costumes, and the outrageous improbability of the plot—a rich lady anthropologist captures what she believes is the last primitive caveman and carries him off to her penthouse in Chicago—had combined to produce a state of euphoria not often encountered in rehearsals, especially rehearsals of operas, and still more especially rehearsals of operas at the Metropolitan. "The fact is we've never seen anything like it," a Met factotum told us as he led the way to the front row of the darkened auditorium. "The chorus breaks up regularly at some of the lines, the orchestra obviously

* "Fun for All," © 1964 The New Yorker Magazine, Inc.

loves Menotti's parody of a twelve-tone composition, the principals are as happy as children working out various bits of stage business, and even Mr. Bing has been smiling for days." Sure enough, as our eyes grew accustomed to the dim light, the first figure we spied was the slender Mr. Bing, a scarf wrapped tightly about his throat and a broad smile on his face. "This is the seduction scene," our guide whispered. "Roberta Peters, playing the anthropologist, who's from Vassar, is teaching George London, the savage, all about civilized love. Pretty racy for the Met."

Miss Peters, looking not at all anthropological in a long red dress, was cracking a whip at Mr. London, who, his hair shaggy and his nakedness covered only by a leopardskin, might have leaped, beating his chest, straight out of a *very* old Tarzan movie. Standing at a short distance from the bizarre couple was Mr. Menotti, who likes to direct as well as compose. "Too slow with the whip, Roberta," he said, in a quiet voice. "Remember, you're taming a dangerous man. You should turn back and pick up the whip quickly, like this." Menotti pivoted on his heel, snatched up the whip, and cracked it several times, each time raising a puffball of white dust from the stage floor. Miss Peters nodded, and then sang, in a high, clear soprano, "First we sit upon a sofa . . . then, more whiskey." The scene ended, a few minutes later, in a passionate embrace and a blackout, after which London, uncoiling from the couch and adjusting his rumpled leopardskin, suggested to Menotti that for the sake of sartorial modesty the blackout had better begin a good many bars earlier. Menotti appeared to agree with the suggestion, and went off to talk over lighting cues with the electricians, whereupon Miss Peters and Mr. London executed an impromptu tango around the couch and were applauded by an audience scattered at random through the auditorium.

Once the tango was finished, we had a chance for a word or two with Miss Peters and Mr. London.

"It's such *fun* to do this opera," Miss Peters said, jauntily brandishing a two-foot-long cigarette holder. "How do you like my prop? In real life, I don't smoke, and I hope I can be convincing onstage without actually inhaling, or anything. I'm also worried about my costume change after the love scene. Embracing me, George gets a lot of makeup on me, and I've exactly four minutes to rush back to my dressing room, take off this red dress, clean up, and climb into a lovely green party dress."

"*I* have to hop out of my leopardskin and into the damnedest double-breasted purple suit you ever saw," Mr. London said, not to be topped. "I'm enjoying this role immensely. It's a nice change from the sort of thing I usually do—Wotan and Boris, for example, where

I have to be dignified and tragic. Also, I find it easy to identify with Abdul, the savage—a decent man who gets trapped by the pleasant corruption of modern society."

"The music is marvellous," Miss Peters said. "I can't tell you how helpful it is to have the composer alive and on hand, so you can ask him to put an extra high E in the score if you want it."

As if "high E" had been his cue, Mr. Menotti strolled back onstage, eating a banana and conducting a debate, in both Italian and English, with a couple of his production assistants. Though he was nursing a bad cold, he seemed as highspirited as everyone else. "An *opera buffa* such as this requires a special clarity of style," he told us. "The music must express pure joy. In a Broadway musical comedy, you make an audience laugh with jokes; in *opera buffa*, it is the music that must laugh first and thus inspire the audience to do so. The plot of 'The Last Savage' is a gentle satire on contemporary life and gives me a chance to poke fun at quite a number of things— Action Painting, obscure poetry, the stabile at Lincoln Center, and so on. To some extent, the opera embodies my own somewhat schizophrenic nature. Half of me yearns for the solitude and peace of the cave, and the other half feels guilty over not proving useful enough to society. To seek happiness through solitude is a form of selfishness; even the man who becomes a hermit to achieve sainthood has to be selfish. However, my poor savage is defeated not because he feels bad about leading a simple, solitary life but because he finds that he cannot give up love. By accepting love from the young anthropologist, he betrays his savage ideals."

Menotti's secretary, a tall and pretty blonde, came up and reminded him of a couple of appointments, which he assured her he would be unable to keep, and then pressed upon him a Contac capsule, a container of hot tea, and a box of dates.

"While I'm working," Menotti said, "I survive, like my savage, on fruit."

In structure "Fun for All" is a chronological report of what the author saw and heard from the time he entered the opera house until he wound up the visit with the final interview, recording that humorous last remark. Before trying to describe the tone of this piece, why not first try to glimpse the writer as he appears between the lines? He is remarkably present for one who can almost totally absent himself. His voice appears in the opening sentence, the thesis, where in good journalistic fashion we are given the who-what-when-where facts. The second sentence is a very long one: exactly 100 words. It contains impersonal background information regarding the opera being rehearsed. There follows the first of the "tape recorder" kind of enthusiastic remarks that characterize all "Talk" essays and that fill the rest of this essay, except for the appropriately lively observations and sympathetic comments of the author.

The general tone, made up of all these items, suggests a person who enjoys watching enthusiastic behavior of competent people and listening to their ramblings. He seems secretly to know that all may be slightly exaggerated for his benefit as reporter. He appears to abash no one by his presence, as with a quiet smile he looks on and listens while meantime keeping his pencil busy. His tastes may be very catholic, but his willingness to enjoy all good fun in its essential good sense and grace tempers that broad and tolerant approval of the ironic antics of human beings seeking success in a great city.

CRITICAL FOCUS

It is often possible to recognize the familiar essay by the presence of these characteristics:

1. It has a warm, personal tone, one suggestive of a fine intelligence welcoming your equally warm attention.
2. Its structure may be loose and rambling; that is, the author may be widely discursive and rely upon his general tone and mood for his unity.
3. Its paragraph and sentence structure may be highly irregular, corresponding to a conversationalist's shifts and starts in talking.
4. It charms rather than convinces or demonstrates.
5. Its purpose is to give pleasure by creating in the reader a relaxed mood by means of beguiling wit.
6. Its diction is full of surprises and avoids the trite expression.
7. Throughout one hears the voice of the "speaker."
8. It glaringly reveals the shortcomings and defects of any unskilled amateur who attempts this deceptively simple essay form.

Exercise 10   Written assignment. *Time* is noted for its highly informal journalistic essays. In this one on a London newspaper columnist, show what kind of order gives it organizational structure. Is it cause and effect, analysis, chronological enumeration, series of illustrations, or a combination of these expository means? Show in detail by accounting for all the paragraphs how your reply fits the article. Just what features of tone and diction give this piece its informality?

How to Succeed as a Slut

She rewrites the marriage vows: "Dost thou, Algernon, promise to laugh at this woman's jokes, push the car until it starts and bring her sherry in the bath?" She loathes trading stamps: "If I want to buy a watch, I want to buy a watch; I don't want to buy 27,720 lbs. of self-raising flour and then get a watch free." She loves sluts, and enlists herself bravely in their cause.

In her 3½ years as fashion columnist for the London Observer, Katharine Whitehorn, 35, may have permanently revised the British notion of what a slut really is. To the uninitiated, a slut may remain a woman of easy virtue. But the dictionary's first definition is "a slovenly woman; a slattern," and that's the one the Observer's Whitehorn also likes. She asks: "Have you ever taken anything out the dirty-clothes basket because it had become, relatively, the cleaner thing? Changed stockings in a taxi? Could you try on clothes in any shop, any time, without worrying about your underclothes? How many things are in the wrong room—cups in the study, boots in the kitchen?" The right answers, says Whitehorn, make "you one of us: the miserable, optimistic, misunderstood race of sluts."

Far Afield. Defending untidiness may be a strange crusade for a fashion columnist. But Katharine Whitehorn is that kind of fashion columnist. The world of *haute couture* distresses her: " 'A useful little dress' means one with no distinguishing characteristics; 'romantic' means 'cleft to the waist.' " She regularly takes excursions far afield. Sometimes she drafts axioms that are applicable to the opposite sex: "No nice men are good at getting taxis." "If your wife looks like a sow's ear, try dipping into the silken purse." She excoriates local hairdressers: "I left the salon at 7:15, by 8 it was slipping, by 9 it was down, and it was not even that sort of evening."

The Observer's freewheeling columnist tacked into journalism in a typically roundabout feminine way. The offspring of a long line of Presbyterian ministers, she proved impervious to the polish of six secondary schools and Cambridge University, toured the U.S. working as a waitress and short-order cook, then returned to England and became a journalist.

"Feel Like a Blond." Along the course she picked up a husband—British Author and Journalist Gavin Lyall—and a berth on the Observer, one of London's seven Sunday papers. The Observer has sensibly refrained from fettering its most uninhibited and uninhibitable staffer, whether she is attacking the trade ("Any journalist may be exchanged for any other journalist without penalty") or rinse jobs

("I am not sure which is worse—to look like a blonde and feel like a journalist, or look like a lady and feel like a blond") or her own kin: "My aunt's problem was remembering to remove a moustache she could no longer see, and trying not to wander around the house with her mouth open." As for the sluts of England—they may still feel miserable and optimistic, but they know they are no longer misunderstood.

Exercise 11   Discussion assignment. What is the compositional structure of this informal, persuasive essay appearing as an advertisement? What contributes to its tone? Is it suitable to the thesis? (Note the location of the thesis. Why so located?)

How to Build a Boy

Liberally mix several old tin cans full of fun, with a mop of hair that *always* seems to need to be cut. Then blend in scuffed knuckles and knees, a missing tooth (optional).

Sprinkle in streaks of orneriness, pride, courage, envy and maybe even a little fear (lightning can *kill* you, you know, and everybody knows that empty house down the block is haunted).

And there: you've made a boy. Well, almost.

Boys, wonderfully, have a sweet sense of the bigness and beauty and mystery we hope they'll never lose.

Religion is an awfully big word to a little boy. But the *spirit* of it isn't. And it's the spirit of religion that can bring peace, comfort, security and goodness to a boy—his whole life through.

Hit-the-bat, pals, hide 'n' seek—they are as vital to a boy as peanut-butter sandwiches. So is the help of true religious faith. Your children should worship this week in your church or synagogue. And the best way to see to it is to be there with them yourself.

WORSHIP THIS WEEK

Exercise 12   Analysis assignment. Congressman Morris K. Udall recently read in Congress a letter that was never sent (reprinted in Exercise 13). It affords a fine example of structural arrangement expressing a courageous stand. Discuss the divisions of this letter and the interplay of its parts.

Exercise 13   Frame a letter of reply to Congressman Udall making it clear that you fully understand his perception of the irony of his political situation.

Letter to a Constituent

Dear Friend:

You have expressed alarm at the rate of federal spending, and asked me as your Congressman where I stand. I had not intended to discuss this controversial question at this particular time. However, I want you to know that I do not shun a controversy. On the contrary I will take a stand on any issue at any time no matter how fraught with controversy it may be. Here is exactly how I stand.

If, when you say "federal spending," you mean the billions of dollars wasted on outmoded naval shipyards and surplus airbases in Georgia, Texas and New York; if you mean the billions of dollars lavished at Cape Kennedy and Houston on "moondoggle" our nation cannot afford; if, sir, you mean the $2 billion wasted each year in wheat and corn price supports which rob Midwestern farmers of their freedoms and saddle taxpayers with outrageous costs of storage in already bulging warehouses; if you mean the $4 billion spent every year to operate veterans hospitals in other states in order to provide 20 million able-bodied veterans with care for civilian illness; if you mean such socialistic and porkbarrel projects as urban renewal, public housing and TVA which cynically seek votes while robbing our taxpayers and weakening the moral fiber of millions of citizens in our Eastern states; if you mean the bloated federal aid to education schemes calculated to press federal educational controls down upon students in this nation; if you mean the $2 billion misused annually by our Public Health Service and National Institutes of Health on activities designed to prostitute the medical profession and foist socialized medicine on every American; if, sir, you mean all these ill-advised, unnecessary federal activities which have destroyed state's rights, created a vast, ever-growing, empire-building bureaucracy regimenting a once free people by the illusory bait of cradle-to-grave security, and which indeed have taken us so far down the road to socialism that it may be, even at this hour, too late to retreat—then I am unyielding, bitter, and four square in my opposition, regardless of the personal or political consequences.

But, on the other hand, if when you say "federal spending" you mean those funds which maintain Davis-Monthan Air Force Base, Fort Huachuca and other Arizona defense installations so vital to our nation's security, and which every year pour hundreds of millions of dollars into our state's economy; if you mean the Truman-Eisenhower-Kennedy-Johnson mutual security program which bolsters our allies along the periphery of the Iron Curtain, enabling them to resist the diabolical onslaught of a Godless Communism and maintain their independence; if you mean those funds to send our brave astronauts voyaging, even as Columbus, into the unknown, in order to guarantee that no aggressor will ever threaten these great United States by nuclear blackmail from outer space; if you mean those sound farm programs which insure our hardy Arizona cotton farmers a fair price for their fiber, protect the sanctity of the family farm, ensure reasonable prices for consumers, and put to work for all the people of the world the miracle of American agricultural abundance; if you mean those VA programs which pay pensions to our brave soldiers crippled in mortal combat and discharge our debt of honor to their widows and orphans and which provide employment for thousands of Arizonans in our fine VA hospitals in Tucson, Phoenix and Prescott; if, sir, you refer to such federal programs as the Central Arizona Reclamation project which will, while repaying 95 percent of its cost with interest, provide our resourceful people with water to insure the growth and prosperity of our state; if you mean the federal educational funds which build desperately needed college classrooms and dormitories for our local universities, provide little children in our Arizona schools with hot lunches (often their only decent meal of the day), furnish vocational training for our high school youth, and pay $10 million in impact funds to relieve the hard-pressed Arizona school property taxpayers from the impossible demands created by the presence of large federal installations; if you mean the federal medical and health programs which have eradicated the curse of malaria, small-pox, scarlet fever and polio from our country, and which even now enable dedicated teams of scientists to close in mercilessly on man's age-old enemies of cancer, heart disease, muscular dystrophy, multiple sclerosis, and mental retardation that afflict our little children, senior citizens and men and women in the prime years of life; if you mean all these federal activities by which a free people in the spirit of Jefferson, Lincoln, Teddy Roosevelt, Wilson, and FDR, through a fair and progressive income tax, preserve domestic tranquillity and promote the general welfare while preserving all our cherished freedoms and our self-reliant national character, then I shall support them with all the vigor at my command.

That is my stand and I will not compromise.

THE STRUCTURE OF ARGUMENT AND PERSUASION

Controversy in every argument generally stems from disagreement over differences of views on certain key viewpoints. These basic points of difference on which the argument hinges, when formulated into questions or statements, are called the *issues*. In Reading for Logic, in Chapter 5, we chose the process of argument to illustrate the workings of deductive logic. We saw that by classifying an argument as to its type—change of policy, analogy, cause, fact, values—we could raise certain questions helpful in stating the issues for any argument.

The organizational structure of an argument usually centers on supporting the favored side of those issues, and each paragraph will contribute the evidence and reasoning needed for the support of the viewpoint taken. At the same time, the resourceful writer will attempt to win over or persuade the reader by his tone. Analysis of Bertrand Russell's argument on causal laws will show both this structure and persuasion.

Causal Laws

Tone of definition suggests law may be strong term.

A "causal law," as I shall use the term, may be defined as a general principle in virtue of which, given sufficient data about certain regions of space-time, it is possible to infer something about certain other regions of space-time. The inference may be only probable, but the probability must be considerably more than a half if the principle in question is to be considered worthy to be called a "causal law."

Examples, comparison, and four conditions that make laws only probabilities. Thesis or proposition of argument: causal laws . . . may be mistaken. Much evidence and reasoning.

I have purposely made the above definition very wide. In the first place, the region to which we infer need not be later than those from which we infer. There are, it is true, some laws—notably the second law of thermodynamics—which allow inferences forward more readily than backward, but this is not a general characteristic of causal laws. In geology, for example, the inferences are almost all backward. In the second place, we cannot lay down rules as to the number of data that may be involved in stating a law. If it should ever become possible to state the laws of embryology in terms of physics, enormously complex data would be required. In the third place, the inference may be only to some more or less general characteristic of the inferred event or events. In the days before Galileo it was known that unsupported heavy bodies fall, which was a causal law; but it was not known how fast they fall, so that when a weight was dropped it was impossible to say accurately where it would be after a given lapse of time. In the fourth place, if the law states a high degree of probability it may be almost as satisfactory as if it stated a certainty. I am not thinking of the probability of the law being true; causal laws, like the rest of our knowledge, may be mistaken. What I am thinking of is that some laws *state* probabilities, for example, the statistical laws of quantum theory. Such laws, supposing them completely true, make inferred events only probable, but this does not prevent them from counting as causal laws according to the above definition.

Comparing of those laws with common-sense generalities. Tone of broadmindedness and "sense."

One advantage of admitting laws which only confer probability is that it enables us to incorporate in science the crude generalizations from which common sense starts, such as "Fire burns," "Bread nourishes," "Dogs bark," or "Lions are fierce." All these are causal laws, and all are liable to exceptions, so that in a given case they confer only probability. The fire on a plum pudding does not burn you, poisoned bread does not nourish, some dogs are too lazy to bark, and some lions grow so fond of their keepers that they cease to be fierce. But in the great majority of cases the above generalizations will be a sound guide in action. There are a large number of such approximate regularities which are assumed in our everyday behavior, and it is from them that the conception of causal laws arose. Scientific laws, it is true, are no longer so simple; they have become complicated in the endeavor to give them a form in which they are not liable to exceptions. But the old simpler laws remain valid so long as they are only regarded as asserting probabilities.

Two types of causal laws and explanation by example of how old law was discredited. Knowledge of science is persuasive.

Causal laws are of two sorts, those concerned with persistence and those concerned with change. The former kind are often not regarded as causal, but this is a mistake. A good example of a law of persistence is the first law of motion. Another example is the persistence of matter. After the discovery of oxygen, when the process of combustion came to be understood, it was possible to regard all matter as indestructible. It has now become doubtful whether this is quite true, but it remains true for most practical purposes. What appears to be more exactly true is the persistence of energy. The gradual development of laws stating persistence started from the common-sense belief, based on pre-scientific experience, that most solid objects continue to exist until they crumble from old age or are destroyed by fire, and that, when this happens, it is possible to suppose that their small parts survive in a new arrangement. It was this pre-scientific point of view that gave rise to the belief in material substance.

Causal laws of change of Galileo and Newton; comparison with Einstein's shows modern concept. Air of solid facts and reasonable deductions; more real knowledge of science.

Causal laws concerned with change were found by Galileo and Newton to demand statement in terms of acceleration, i.e., change of velocity in magnitude or direction or both. The greatest triumph of this point of view was the law of gravitation, according to which every particle of matter causes in every other an acceleration directly proportional to the mass of the attracting particle and inversely proportional to the square of the distance between them. But Einstein's form of the law of gravitation made it more analogous to the law of inertia, and, in a sense, a law of persistence rather than a law of change. According to Einstein, space-time is full of what we may call hills; each hill grows steeper as you go up, and has a piece of matter at the top. The result is that the easiest route from place to place is one which winds round the hills. The law of gravitation consists in the fact that bodies always take the easiest route, which is what is called a "geodesic." There is a law of cosmic laziness called the "principle of least action," which states that when a body moves from one place to another it will choose the route involving least work. By means of this principle gravitation is absorbed into the geometry of space-time.

Work in physics on quantum theory shows limitations of knowledge of causal laws. More apparently

The essential laws of change in modern physics are those of quantum theory, which govern transitions from one form of energy to another. An atom can emit energy in the form of light, which then travels on unchanged until it meets another atom, which may absorb the energy of the light. Such interchanges are governed by certain rules, which do not suffice to say *convincing evidence.*

what will happen on a given occasion, but can predict, with a very high degree of probability, the statistical distribution of possible happenings among a very large number of interchanges. This is as near as physics can get at present to the ultimate character of causal laws.

Conclusion: justification of belief in causality is a question of theory of knowledge, which author will take up after showing how causality is considered in science. The thesis or proposition has been "proved." Maintains only that causality is a belief. Writer remains reasonable, cautious, well-informed, genuinely concerned with the issues he deals with and their bearing on human knowledge.

Everything that we believe ourselves to know about the physical world depends entirely upon the assumption that there are causal laws. Sensations, and what we optimistically call "perceptions," are events in us. We do not actually see physical objects, any more than we hear electromagnetic waves when we listen to the wireless. What we directly experience might be all that exists, if we did not have reason to believe that our sensations have external causes. It is important, therefore, to inquire into our belief in causation. Is it mere superstition, or has it a solid foundation?

The question of the justification of our belief in causality belongs to the theory of knowledge, and I shall therefore postpone it for the present. My purpose in this part is the interpretation of science, not an inquiry into the grounds for supposing science valid. Science assumes causality in some sense, and our present question is: In what sense is causality involved in scientific method?

Now we can look at the issues involved in this argument, which is one of fact. Russell's proposition can be stated thus: The laws of causality may be only probabilities based on belief. The argument stands or falls on the validity of its evidence and reasoning as examined by means of our issue questions:

1. Are the facts in evidence he introduces relevant and unquestionable?

2. Is Bertrand Russell reliable in character?
3. Is he competent to speak on causal laws?

Complete answers might require considerable research and restraint to keep from bringing in irrelevant issues.

An informal letter pursuing an argument may have a similar tight structure of logic and persuasion. What structure underlies these three hortatory paragraphs taken from a letter of an older poet to a young poet?

> There is perhaps no use of my going into your particular point now; for what I could say about your tendency to doubt or about your inability to bring into unison your outer and your inner life, or about all the other things that worry you—is always the same as I have already said: always the wish that you may find patience enough in yourself to endure, and simplicity enough to believe; that you may acquire more and more confidence in that which is difficult, and in your solitude among others. And for the rest, let life happen to you. Believe me: life is right, in any case.
>
> And about emotions: pure are all emotions that gather you together and lift you up; impure is that emotion which seizes only *one* side of your being and so distorts you. Everything that you can think in the face of your childhood, is right. Everything that makes *more* of you than you have heretofore in your best hours been, is right. Every enhancement is good if it is in your *whole* blood, if it is not intoxication, not turbidity, but joy, which one can see clear to the bottom. Do you understand what I mean?
>
> And your doubt may be a good quality if you *train* it. It must be *knowing*, it must be critical. Ask it, whenever it wants to spoil something for you, *why* something is ugly, demand proofs from it, test it, and you will perhaps find it perplexed and embarrassed, or perhaps up in arms. But don't give in, insist on arguments and act this way, watchful and consistent, every single time, and the day will arrive when from a destroyer it will become one of your best workers—perhaps the cleverest of all that are building your life.

Each paragraph rings with persuasive conviction, with deep belief that one who has the patience and strength to endure his doubts and to use them as tests will eventually find he has built a good life for himself. The first paragraph assures the worried youth that doubt and uncertainty are part of everyone's life, and must not be allowed to destroy one's confidence in the fact that "life is right." The diction, even in a somewhat rough translation from the German original, reveals a tone of genuine interest in the young man's concerns. The second paragraph affirms trust in joy and its conditions as a test as well as an emotion. In the third, the poet returns to the problem of doubt and reaffirms its importance. The tone of the letter seems to include the sympathetic reader in the poet's circle of friendship.

In structure and kind, we have here an argument of values as well as one of fact. Its logic is founded on intuition and inductive reasoning meant to be accepted by those readers who discover they feel as the poet does.

The *Old Testament* and the *New* abound with hortatory arguments that have their structural roots in the logic, direct and indirect, found also in poetry. They present vivid illustrations, comparison and contrast, definition, cause, and all the other structural forms of thought and composition.

CRITICAL FOCUS

Checkpoints for Structure in Persuasive Argument:
1. *Determine type of argument and its issues.*
2. *Look for the tonal attitudes, and weigh sincerity.*
3. *Take particular care in considering arguments of value.*

Exercise 14   Essay assignment. Imagine yourself, or someone you know well, in some such situation as one of those suggested below. Decide on what type of argument you are going to write, apply its issues to your situation, and prepare an outline showing your structure for the argument. Write it with a particular reader or audience in mind whom you would like to convince that your views are right.

1. The engagement is broken.
2. No money and twenty-six days to wait for the monthly check.
3. A promise has been broken twice.
4. Under the circumstances, can one be expected to keep on trying?
5. Still overweight! Nothing seems to take pounds off.
6. "Enough is enough," he has been told.
7. The kid brother and his stacks of comic books.
8. On receiving a begrudging apology.
9. Everyone has heard it a hundred times, so. . . .

10. Word of advice to one of these: a borrower, a gossip, a worrier, a drudge, a nuisance, a bore, a low-grading instructor, a deceased author, a remembered old friend, the brother or sister you never had, a car salesman, a coach, a shower singer, a party goer, a nasal talker, a yearbook editor, a bowler, a ski bum, an inquisitive relative, a blind date, a coffee house habitué, a high school teacher, a barber, a hairdresser, a campus policeman, the person you were when you wrote what you did in your diary some years ago.

Exercise 15 Apply the checkpoints of the Critical Focus (page 220) to this stanza from Lord Byron's "Don Juan."

There's doubtless something in domestic doings
  Which forms, in fact, true love's antithesis;
Romances paint at full length people's wooings,
  But only give a bust of marriages;
For no one cares for matrimonial cooings,
  There's nothing wrong in a connubial kiss;
Think you, if Laura had been Petrarch's wife,
He would have written sonnets all his life?

Exercise 16 Written assignment. Thomas Carlyle in his confessional book, *Sartor Resartus,* records his self-admonitions in arguing with himself over spiritual certainties. Here are two famous paragraphs from that book. Express in your own words what you think he is saying in one of them, and then apply the Critical Focus checkpoints to it.

But it is with man's Soul as it was with Nature: the beginning of Creation is—Light. Till the eye have vision, the whole members are in bonds. Divine moment, when over the tempest-tost Soul, as once over the wild-weltering Chaos, it is spoken: Let there be Light! Ever to the greatest that has felt such moment, is it not miraculous and God-announcing; even as, under simpler figures, to the simplest and least. The mad primeval Discord is hushed; the rudely-jumbled conflicting elements bind themselves into separate Firmaments: deep silent rock-foundations are built beneath; and the skyey vault with its everlasting Luminaries above: instead of a dark wasteful Chaos, we have a blooming, fertile, heaven-encompassed World.

I too could now say to myself: Be no longer a Chaos, but a World, or even Worldkin. Produce! Produce! Were it but the pitifullest infinitesimal fraction of a Product, produce it, in God's name! 'Tis the utmost thou hast in thee: out with it, then. Up, up! Whatsoever thy hand findeth to do, do it with thy whole might. Work it is called Today; for the Night cometh, wherein no man can work.

THE STRUCTURE OF NARRATION: THE SHORT STORY

Since description is now generally a part of narrative writing, its structure needs little more attention than it has already been given (see pages 207 to 209). Its pictorial images of places, sense impressions, and psychological states contribute much to all the forms of fiction: short story, novel, myth, tale, fable, parable, allegory, romance, epic, and drama. But our main concern now will be with the short story and its functional use of such images.

The short story shares with the novel these four elements of narrative structure: (1) the narrative substance, (2) the narrator, (3) the story form, and (4) the intended audience. It differs from the novel, however, not only in its length but also in the narrative pattern it shapes from these elements.

The *narrative substance* is the incident in nature, the act of a person, the imaginative fantasy, the half-buried memory, the sudden perception of person, place, or thing out of which a story can grow. It is that magical matter out of which the skilled writer can spin his spider's web of illusion, or depict the "imaginary garden with real toads" and real people in it. It rises out of the curiosity of a creative imagination as well as out of the compassion of a thoughtful observer. Whether it be treated as comedy, satire, tragedy, or some combination of these genres depends wholly upon the temperament and circumstances of the author.

The *narrator* is the character or voice who tells the story; he is the spokesman chosen by the author to present the narrative design created out of the basic narrative substance. Through the narrator we can detect the point from which the author views his fictional world, and from that *point of view* we can glimpse the hopes, fears, and insights that give the narrative its form and meaning. The narrator's voice speaks to the reader, relates the incidents, records the dialogue, and tells what the characters are thinking and feeling. He may be likened to a camera coming in for a close-up, recording a flare-up of tempers, and then withdrawing for perhaps a panoramic view of some distant quiet scene. Unlike earlier authors such as Henry Fielding and William Makepeace Thackeray, who entered into their stories with unabashed value judgments and comments on the lives of their fictional characters, making author and narrator so often one and the same, modern writers generally attempt to remain anonymous or *objective*.

The first-person narrator, the *I*, as in Ring Lardner's "Haircut," may be the kind of person the author himself does not like or admire at all. Again, the *I* doing the narrating may be a respected main character such as Marlow in Conrad's *Heart of Darkness*. In Henry James's short stories and novels, the narrator is a "central intelligence" who knows and tells all that a main character can think and do in a complex social scene. In "The Garden Party," Katherine Mansfield as author takes great pains to keep all traces of her presence out of the story, as does Hemingway, for example, in "The Killers" and all of his other fiction.

In the Mansfield story, we see and hear the young girl, Laura, at her mother's garden party on the beautiful lawn; we see and hear what she does when she learns of the accidental death during the party of the working man whose house is just below the party scene. We go with Laura on her visit with a basket of party leftovers to that house, where she discovers that the dead man was a human being: a husband and father whose family had none of the things Laura has. And while she fumbles to apologize for wearing the garden party hat to this house of grief, we watch her grow in understanding. But all the while, the invisible narrator who knows all, who has told us all and suggested even more, has kept from intruding.

The *story form* is the principle of organization that unifies the short story and gives it shape or design. It is unique in every fine story, for each has something individual and distinctive about its shaping art. Form includes these organizational features:

1. The theme that gives the story its significance
2. The parts of the story as they relate to each other and to the whole design
3. The tone that gives the writing its character and style
4. The integral symbols, motifs, ironies, myths that impart poetic strength and add to the beauty of symmetry
5. The point of view from which the story is told (already discussed)

With respect to *audience* the author may, depending on his temperament and circumstances, write to meet the demands of an editor who will accept only one kind of story, or the writer may work on in hopes that he will find his own proper audience someday, somewhere.

Theme corresponds somewhat to *thesis* in the essay. It is the unifying meaning permeating all aspects of the story; it is the *point* of the narrative, the reason for which it may have been written. It is not, as in an Aesop fable, a moral tag pinned to a story ending. It may not even be clearly discernible to the most cultivated of readers. Who, for example, can say for certain what Nathaniel Hawthorne intended to tell us in *romances* such as "Young Goodman Brown"? It is the story of the young Puritan husband who thought he left his wife, Faith, safe and sheltered in their Salem home, and then found her—or imagined that he found her—at a meeting of witches in the depths of the dark forest, into which he had been led by a guide who was the Devil. *Theme* is the sum of the meanings Hemingway leaves the reader to find in the Nick Adams stories, wherein Nick encounters the ugliness of adult life in terms of human weakness and failure in a world where violence can engulf even the innocent.

The *parts of a story* in some narratives make up the plot, that much abused term: the various stages in the hero's, or protagonist's conflict, leading to a climax and ending with a quickly following denouement or conclusion, wherein all tensions are resolved. The parts are the various self-defeating efforts of the tenderfoot in Jack London's "To Build a Fire," wherein every attempt to survive in the deadly temperatures fails. The parts may appear as the interesting but apparently at first not very significant incidents of an Irish family party, and the final preparing of one of the main guests to go to bed in a hotel room with his wife. That final incident as he stands looking out of the window into the night and thinking about his wife's first lover, now dead, gives weight and impact to all the earlier episodes. These are some of the *parts* that make up James Joyce's excellent short story, "The Dead."

The *tone* we recognize as the author's purpose and attitude to both audience and story matter. It generally resounds through the diction and is linked with any symbols, motifs, ironies, or myths in the story (see pages 143 to 168). Tone in story will also include the rhetorical balance, contrast, parallelism of language and situation that contribute to symmetry and drama.

Hemingway's "A Clean, Well Lighted Place," even in brief summary, suggests the art with which a writer of supreme technique can fuse into a wondrous whole all the elements of short story art and structure. Through dialog written without comment, we overhear two waiters late at night in a Spanish café, the younger one complaining about the one patron left, an old man, who does not hurry to leave. The older waiter defends the lone customer on the grounds that the café is a pleasant place to pass a few night hours. At last the younger waiter can hurry home to bed, wife, and family; the older waiter goes to his own lone room but cannot sleep until morning comes.

By reading between the lines, one finds the theme: lonely old men, whose lives are finished, need havens such as this cheerful café at night; life is hard on the old or the defeated. The narrative substance is a scene with the kind of people anyone might have seen numerous times in any city without giving it much thought. But Hemingway did. The narrator is *invisible* as the point of view from which the observing intelligence *tells* of the two waiters. The tone is one of conscious restraint, pleasure in this kind of café, tightly reined compassion for the old, and the irony of impatient youth that will itself grow old. The café is the most obvious symbol, but as with every other excellent story, space is required even to hint at its art.

Although consideration of the novel comes later (pages 259 to 264), let us take a glimpse at a well-known novel, *The Great Gatsby,* by F. Scott Fitzgerald, as an example of this skillful combining of story elements. In nine paragraphs, but in less than 300 words, Fitzgerald unites exposition, argument, description of place, of person, and state of mind, while at the same time creating suspense. It is the scene wherein Gatsby, the man with a past, waits with his neighbor, Nick— the narrator—for the arrival of Daisy, the woman whom in memory Gatsby has endowed with every rare perfection. Though he has not seen her in five years, he still thinks that the past can be repeated.

> The rain cooled about half-past three to a damp mist, through which occasional thin drops swam like dew. Gatsby looked with vacant eyes through a copy of Clay's *Economics,* starting at the Finnish tread that shook the kitchen floor, and peering toward the bleared windows from time to time as if a series of invisible but alarming happenings were taking place outside. Finally he got up and informed me, in an uncertain voice, that he was going home.
> "Why's that?"

"Nobody's coming to tea. It's too late!" He looked at his watch as if there was some pressing demand on his time elsewhere. "I can't wait all day."

"Don't be silly; it's just two minutes to four."

He sat down miserably, as if I had pushed him, and simultaneously there was the sound of a motor turning into my lane. We both jumped up, and, a little harrowed myself, I went out into the yard.

Under the dripping bare lilac-trees a large open car was coming up the drive. It stopped. Daisy's face, tipped sideways beneath a three-cornered lavender hat, looked out at me with a bright ecstatic smile.

"Is this absolutely where you live, my dearest one?"

The exhilarating ripple of her voice was a wild tonic in the rain. I had to follow the sound of it for a moment, up and down, with my ear alone, before any words came through. A damp streak of hair lay like a dash of blue paint across her cheek, and her hand was wet with glistening drops as I took it to help her from the car.

"Are you in love with me," she said low in my ear, "or why did I have to come alone?"

In paragraph 1, the rain and Gatsby's most uneasy state are described. In 2, 3, and 4, Gatsby's half-hearted argument is squashed, but he is on his feet with the action of 5. Movement of the car and Daisy are shown in 6. Her exciting voice and appearance—she is wet from riding in a chauffeur-driven car with the top down—affect the first-person narrator in 7, 8, and 9. But as the next passages show, he can hardly wait to see what will happen when she meets Gatsby in the living room. The poetic wonder which pervades the acts and characters of this ironicpathetic episode indicates another aspect of the author: he has a sense of poetry, humor, and pathos as well as an insight into the ironies that beset our lives.

CRITICAL FOCUS

The short story has characteristic structural features.
1. Its four elements are these:
   a. The narrative substance, or origin of the story
   b. The narrator whom the author has given a certain *point of view* and who tells the story
   c. The story form—its parts (plot), its development or movement in tension to a climax and conclusion
   d. The audience or readers

2. **The story form includes also the tone, theme, and whatever of symbol, irony, motif, or myth are fused in the work to give it symmetry and beauty.**

Exercise 17   Discussion assignment. What discernible tone, theme, narrator, and descriptive mood can you find in this passage from a Dylan Thomas short story?

"I don't want to be home, I don't want to sit by the fire. I've got nothing to do when I'm in and I don't want to go to bed. I like standing about like this with nothing to do, in the dark all by myself," I said.

And I did, too. I was a lonely night-walker and a steady stander-at-corners. I liked to walk through the wet town after midnight, when the streets were deserted and the window lights out, alone and alive on the glistening tram-lines in dead and empty High Street under the moon, gigantically sad in the damp streets by ghostly Ebenezer Chapel. And I never felt more a part of the remote and overpressing world, or more full of love and arrogance and pity and humility, not for myself alone, but for the living earth I suffered on and for the unfeeling systems in the upper air, Mars and Venus and Brazell and Skully, men in China and St. Thomas, scorning girls and ready girls, soldiers and bullies and policemen and sharp, suspicious buyers of second-hand books, bad, ragged women who'd pretend against the museum wall for a cup of tea, and perfect, unapproachable women out of the fashion magazines, seven feet high, sailing slowly in their flat, glazed creations through steel and glass and velvet. I leant against the wall of a derelict house in the residential areas or wandered in the empty rooms, stood terrified on the stairs or gazing through the smashed windows at the sea or at nothing, and the lights going out one by one in the avenues. Or I mooched in a half-built house, with the sky stuck in the roof and cats on the ladders and a wind shaking through the bare bones of the bedrooms.

Exercise 18   Written assignment. Analyze this passage from a Henry James narrative for its discernible tone, theme, narrator, and mood.

This spectacle had for him an eloquence, an authority, a felicity—he scarce knew by what strange name to call it—for which he said to himself that he had not consciously bargained. Her welcome, her frankness, sweetness, sadness, brightness, her disconcerting poetry, as he made shift at moments to call it, helped as it was by the beauty of her whole setting and by the perception, at the same time, on the observer's part, that this element gained from her, in a manner, for effect and harmony, as much as it gave—her whole attitude had, to his imagination, meanings that hung about it, waiting upon her, hovering, dropping and quavering forth again, like vague, faint snatches, mere ghosts of sound, of old-fashioned melancholy music. It was positively well for him, he had his times of reflecting, that he couldn't put it off on Kate and Mrs. Lowder, as a gentleman so conspicuously wouldn't, that—well, that he had been rather taken in by not having known in advance! There had been now five days of it without his risking even to Kate alone any hint of what he ought to have known and of what in particular therefore had taken him in. The truth was doubtless that really, when it came to any free handling and naming of things, they were living together, the five of them, in an air in which an ugly effect of "blurting out" might easily be produced. He came back with his friend on each occasion to the blessed miracle of renewed propinquity, which had a double virtue in that favouring air. He breathed on it as if he could scarcely believe it, yet the time had passed, in spite of this privilege, without his quite committing himself, for her ear, to any such comment on Milly's high style and state as would have corresponded with the amount of recognition it had produced in him. Behind everything, for him, was his renewed remembrance, which had fairly become a habit, that he had been the first to know her. . . .

Exercise 19   Written analysis. Select a short story by one of the authors referred to in this chapter or by any other author suggested by your instructor. Read and reread the story in terms of the Critical Focus story elements, taking notes as you go. Then write a critical analysis of that story. Don't make extensive quotations, and all quoted passages must be thoroughly discussed for the points that you wish to make with them. Try to classify and arrange similar features found throughout the story, such as instances of *tone, theme, narrator,* and the other story elements you can detect. (Consult the treatment of theme and symbol and myth in Chapter 9.)

STYLE, TONE,
AND THE SENTENCE

WHAT IS STYLE?

We have come to the unavoidable point where distinctions must be made between style and tone, both of which are based on the diction and the word patterns of the sentence. From what has been said and shown so far of tone, its relationship to diction, logic, and structure may be clear enough. But the meanings of *style* have been scanted. And for good reason: this term has a complicated history of denotations and connotations.

We could acknowledge this difficulty and drop the term after a few general remarks, or treat it as a simple, practical matter that can be taken care of by adopting a specific formula certain to give the writer a "good style" and the critical reader a rough rule-of-the-thumb set of criteria. But we must try to do better, for a sound critical approach to the sentence and its syntactic meaning depends on a careful distinction between style and tone.

Controversy over the meanings of *style* appears to have arisen historically from disagreements over what should be the "correct" attitude toward the poetic writer's use of language. In the seventeenth and eighteenth centuries, one school generally identified as the *neoclassic* held that "language is the 'dress' of thought, and figures are the 'ornaments' of language, for the sake of the pleasurable emotion which distinguishes a poetic from a merely didactic discourse." The neoclassicists held that the "rules" of taste and judgment formulated by Renaissance critics should dictate the kind of language a writer might adopt. Ben Jonson, Shakespeare's defeated rival as poet and dramatist, chided him for not following these precepts, by means of which the critics had explained the greatness of Latin and Greek authors. In England this neoclassicist view dominated most of the eighteenth century under the successive literary leadership of John Dryden, Alexander Pope, and Samuel Johnson. During this era certain standards of taste and style held sway.

Violent reaction to neoclassicism came at the beginning of the nineteenth century in the form of a movement vaguely called *romanticism*. The conflict raged over these two basic issues as stated by M. H. Abrams:

1. Should poetic literature (prose as well as verse) be *subjective*—personal, self-revealing, self-expressive, *romantic*—or should it be *objective*—impersonal and dealing only with universal traits and features considered *classical?*
2. Which should a writer trust in choosing diction and literary forms: *nature*—meaning his own private intuitions, visions, romantic emotions—or *art*—meaning neoclassical traditions and models?

William Wordsworth became the first spokesman for the romantic attitude toward language: "Words, a Poet's words more particularly, ought to be weighed in the balance of feeling. . . . For the Reader cannot be too often reminded that Poetry is passion: it is the history or science of feelings. . . ."

The winning side in this historic argument turned out to be that of the romantics, and their views on language and form have affected our present-day writers' choice of diction and, therefore, also influenced our prevailing concepts of what constitutes "good" style. Yet, as earlier chapters have suggested, views that can be identified as neoclassic continue to urge practices of "standard taste and decorum" in subject matter, attitude, and diction.

This battle of nature versus art involved another important issue: Do the works of a writer reveal the character of their author? Those who answered in the affirmative maintained that "Style is the man!" For centuries it was held that great literary works—those that posterity acclaimed as masterpieces—came only from great men. The book therefore mirrored the mind that produced it. The author's temperament as well as his virtues and weaknesses showed up in the finished work, and determined not only *what* he said but also *how* he said it. This view that "Behind the book stands the Man" found its most ardent defender in Walter Pater, the late-Victorian critic, who through his methods of "imaginative criticism" believed he could penetrate into the very heart and brain of the author, and discern his most carefully concealed motives and identity.

Along with this concept of style as the man, there developed the definition best stated by Herbert Read, the aesthetics critic, for "good" style: "The only thing that is indispensable for the possession of a good style is personal sincerity." In the sense of earnest conviction and truthful utterance, *sincerity* became a criterion of style. The term took its connotations from the post-Reformation use of *sincerity* to suggest deep religious conviction. So good style became synonymous with the expression of earnest conviction on any topic. Closely related to this religious notion of style is another descriptive term, *grace,* which means the indefinable excellence a piece of good writing has.

In summary, then, we can say that historically *style* has been thought of, and is still considered, as related to these four concepts:

1. Ornament
2. The man
3. Sincerity
4. Grace

It follows, therefore, that when we speak of *style* we must speak of tastes and admired models fashionable in other times and ours. At present it is reasonable to assume that a writer can develop a personal style, one which becomes identified with his name and consists of certain attitudes of tone and manner. In fact, every author now tries to develop a style suitable to his abilities and interests. But since the task of this book is to steer a middle course and to suggest methods of evaluating all levels of writing, we shall eventually examine some now widely accepted standards for judging style.

As the history of our language and literature reveals, we have borrowed from the ancient Latin and Greek and the modern European authors several standard levels of discourse as these flourished at various times. The styles can be shown in their relationships by this schema:

Formal
High or *grand* style for orations and formal documents; *mannered* style: an artificial style such as *euphuism*

Middle
Intellectual, academic style
Informal
Plain style: gentlemanly, conversational style; terse narrative style;
and *natural* style

All variations of these styles call for careful distinctions in the use of
language and vocabularies; they involve the same conflicts that raged
over *nature versus art.*

To understand what makes a word the right word for the right
place, we need to know something about these style levels. But before
analyzing some examples of them, we should take up the other two
basic concerns in this chapter, which together make up the nature of
any style: tone and sentence pattern.

CRITICAL FOCUS

Controversy over *style* stems from conflicting attitudes toward language
and ancient dispute of *nature versus art,* or *romanticism versus
neoclassicism.* Style has been thought of as ornament, the man,
sincerity, grace.

Exercise 1   Discussion assignment. Do you believe that "the
style is the man"? Do you think you can tell much about the character
of the author by studying his works? Does a poem, or a volume of
poetry, reveal the personal traits—tastes, beliefs, values, etc.—of the
poet who wrote them? Does a play? A novel? Does a "filthy" book come
from a "filthy" mind? A "noble" book from a "noble" mind? The
following quotation is a remark by Samuel Johnson on this topic. How
valid is his judgment?

> The biographer of Thomson has remarked, that an author's life is
> best read in his works: his observation was not well-timed. Savage,
> who lived much with Thomson, once told me, how he heard a lady
> remarking that she could gather from his works three parts of his
> character, that he was a "great lover, a great swimmer, and rigorously
> abstinent"; but, said Savage, he knows not any love but that of the
> sex; he was perhaps never in cold water in his life; and he indulges
> himself in all luxury that comes within his reach.

Exercise 2   Written report assignment. Read a biographical
sketch or a full-length biography of a famous author and report on the

following points: (*a*) Does the biographer rely on the famous author's works to show what kind of person the writer was? (*b*) If so, how sound and valid are those deductions and analogies? (*c*) Have the works that are said to "mirror the mind" been thoroughly examined by the biographer? (*d*) Of what importance is the reading of this author's biography for the understanding of his works? (See Chapter 10, pages 256 to 258.) Suggested authors: Shakespeare, Donne, Marlowe, Bunyan, Robert Burns, Coleridge, Shelley, Byron, Keats, Tennyson, Kipling, Whitman, Crane, Melville, and Dreiser.

STYLE AS RELATED TO TONE AND THE SENTENCE

Whether he writes a formal oration such as Churchill's distinguished Fulton, Missouri, speech, or fires off a witty satire such as Evelyn Waugh's *A Handful of Dust,* the effective author takes pains to give his work a proper tone. As has been seen, his tone reflects his attitude toward the subject matter and what he hopes it will do for his readers, as well as how he seems to feel about those readers. He may, for example, despise them but still plan to make himself loved by them. The tone may be ironic, angry, friendly, sarcastic, self-deprecating, bitter, tragic, humorous, or whatever other frame of mind he wishes to suggest.

For his tone with respect to his audience, the writer has three alternatives. First, he can elect to maintain a completely impersonal, objective point of view and present the subject for the sake of the topic alone, as in this description of Montaigne as essayist:

So, leisurely, page by page and day by day, after 1570, he wrote his *Essais.* He seems to have invented the term, almost the type; for though there had been *discorsi* and *discours,* they were formidably formal, not the informal, meandering conversations of Montaigne; and this easygoing, buttonholing style has tended to characterize the essay since his death, making it a predominantly modern genre. "I speak to paper," he said, "as I do to the first person I meet." The style is the man, natural, intimate, confidential: it is a comfort to be spoken to so familiarly by a seigneur of the mind. Open him at any page, and you are caught by the arm and swept along, never knowing, and seldom caring, where you will go. He wrote piecemeal, on any subject that struck his thought or matched his mood; and he diverged anarchically from the initial topic as he rambled on; so the essay "On Coaches" rattles off into ancient Rome and new America. Of the three volumes, three consist of digressions. Montaigne was lazy, and nothing is so arduous as producing and maintaining order in ideas or men. He confessed himself *divers et ondoyant*—wavering and diverse. He made no fetish of consistency; he changed his opinions with his years; only the final composite picture is Montaigne.

Though the tone here is objective in that each sentence contributes to a portrait of Montaigne as essayist, the authors, Will and Ariel Durant, without directly appealing to the reader or referring to themselves, have created a sympathetic image of Montaigne. Their tone toward him is one of respect, affection, and admiration. By taking the pains to assemble details and striking quotations, they show every desire to share their feelings with their readers. Their style is clearly one of gentlemanly conversation.

An author's second alternative regarding tone and audience is to include his readers deliberately in what he writes, and even to address them directly. Read Henry Fielding's *Tom Jones*, or almost any other eighteenth-century novel, and you will find the author chatting cosily with his readers. It is this intimate tone, though a more restrained one, that is found in a reflective passage from a letter of William James, the psychologist:

> It is obvious and palpable that our state of mind is never precisely the same. Every thought we have of a given fact is, strictly speaking, unique, and only bears a resemblance of kind with our other thoughts of the same fact. When the identical fact recurs, we must think of it in a fresh manner, see it under a somewhat different angle, apprehend it in different relations from those in which it last appeared. And the thought by which we cognize it is the thought of it-in-those-relations, a thought suffused with the consciousness of all that dim context. Often we are ourselves struck at the strange differences in our successive views of the same thing. We wonder how we ever could have opined as we did last month about a certain matter. We have outgrown the possibility of that state of mind, we know not how. From one year to another we see things in new lights. What was unreal has grown real, and what was exciting is insipid. The friends we used to care the world for are shrunken to shadows; the women, once so divine, the stars, the woods, and the waters, how now so dull and common! the young girls that brought an aura of infinity, at present hardly distinguishable existences; the pictures so empty; and

as for the books, what was there to find so mysteriously significant in Goethe, or in John Mill so full of weight? Instead of all this, more zestful than ever is the work, and fuller and deeper the import of common duties and of common goods.

The third alternative of tone for audience is the author's deciding that in his mood of openheartedness and confession, he will reveal himself to his readers; he will take them into his confidence, talk of his foibles, and perhaps even chuckle at them with his readers, as Charles Lamb does here in his intimate, conversational style:

> I have no ear. Mistake me not, reader—nor imagine that I am by nature destitute of those exterior twin appendages, hanging ornaments, and (architecturally speaking) handsome volutes to the human capital. Better my mother had never borne me. I am, I think, rather delicately than copiously provided with those conduits; and I feel no disposition to envy the mule for his plenty, or the mole for her exactness, in those ingenious labyrinthine inlets—those indispensable side-intelligences.

Lamb's diction is humorously pompous, that is, it delights in big words and ridiculous comparisons, such as *exterior twin appendages . . . handsome volutes to the human capital.* Consulting a dictionary helps one to appreciate the pun involved in this last phrase: *capital* is derived from the Latin for *head* and refers to the top or "head" of an Ionic column, which features a pair of volutes or spiral shell-shaped ornaments. Thus, the pun also functions as a metaphor since the head is the top of the column of the body and the ears are shell-shaped. It is evident that Lamb wanted informed, awake readers to chat with.

Were you puzzled by that third sentence in the Lamb paragraph? It reads: *Better my mother had never borne me.* It has the word pattern of an exclamation rather than the subject-verb-object order of a statement, and it is a humorous use of a most serious expression, meaning here that it would be better not to be born if one came into the world without ears. Following the humorous pun-metaphor in the previous sentence, this exclamation seems at first glance out of place. But as one recognizes its incongruity, its strangeness is no wilder than was the pun before it, and we can smile at that strangeness.

Henry David Thoreau, like Lamb, enjoyed puns and paradoxes when he wrote a sentence. They keep a reader awake, he said. He disliked "torpid words, wooden or lifeless words, such words as 'humanitary,' which have a paralysis in their tails." His concept of a good sentence was one so economical with words that it was "concentrated and nutty." "A sentence," he said, "should read as if the author, had he a plow instead of a pen, could have drawn a furrow deep and straight to the end." He spent five years of spare time polishing and perfecting the wonderful sentences of his *Walden*. It took that long to find a publisher for *Walden* after the failure of his first book.

Thoreau did not have to rely only on his ear to improve his sentences; he had studied Latin and Greek and knew grammar and syntax as well as he did rhetoric. It cannot be denied: A critical reader should know the differences between simple, compound, and compound-complex sentences; he should also be able to distinguish between balanced, loose, and periodic sentences. These are the possible structures of our sentences, determining the word order. Look the terms up in a handbook, if necessary; we shall be referring to them.

We begin now the fascinating business of analyzing paragraphs for style through sentences by turning to the old master of plain, idiomatic diction and style, Jonathan Swift:

> [1] Another general fault in conversation is, that of those who affect to talk of themselves. [2] Some, without any ceremony, will run over the history of their lives; will relate the animals of their diseases, with the several symptoms and circumstances of them; will enumerate the hardships and injustice they have suffered in court, in parliament, in love, or in law. [3] Others are more dexterous, and with praise. [4] They will call a witness to remember, they always foretold what would happen in such a case, but none would believe them; they advised such a man from the beginning, and told him the consequences, just as they happened; but he would have his own way. [5] Others make a vanity of telling their faults; they are the strangest men in the world; they cannot dissemble; they own it is a folly; they have lost abundance of advantages by it; but, if you would give them the world, they cannot help it; there is something in their nature that abhors insincerity and constraint; with many other insufferable topics of the same altitude.

The paragraph has five sentences; the first is the topic sentence, amplified by the remaining four. Each of the supporting four gives a special type or category of *those who affect to talk of themselves*. (The denotation of *affect* is here "are fond of.") Notice the coherent order gained by employing similar subjects for these four sentences: *Some,*

Others, They, Others. Each clause, which gives detail through parallel structure, features the same key word *they*. Each sentence contributes the strength of its own statement of type to the paragraph. Their arrangement is in the order of climax so that the *strangest* appears as the final classification. Sentence 2 achieves an elliptic, clipped tone through the use of *will run, will relate,* and *will enumerate.* Sentence 3 repeats *will* as does sentence 4, which offers a fine illustration of antithesis through the paired-off use of the conjunction *but.* Sentence 5 contains a direct reference to the audience by means of an indefinite *you—but, if you would give them the world.*

One can say, then, that Swift's diction, word order, and structure in the sentence contribute to the tone of his disapproval and impatience with conversational bores; the tone is couched, or voiced, in a plain, informal style of direct and emphatic conversational pitch. He obviously expects all sensible readers to agree with him. His avoidance of metaphor and other figures of speech is deliberate and characteristic of his style. He prefers the economy of simple, direct statement and clear denotative meanings. One can imagine what he would have thought of Charles Lamb's *exterior twin appendages.* (Yet this stern man could write his own special kind of "sweet talk" to the woman he loved.)

By way of contrast, let us turn to a lively contemporary writer, Kingsley Amis. What does each sentence contribute to the tone and style of this paragraph?

> Dixon was alive again. Consciousness was upon him before he could get out of the way; not for him the slow, gracious wandering from the halls of sleep, but a summary, forcible ejection. He lay sprawled, too wicked to move, spewed up like a broken spider crab on the tarry shingle of the morning. The light did him harm, but not as much as looking at things did; he resolved, having done it once, never to move his eyeballs again. A dusty pudding in his head made the scene before him beat like a pulse. His mouth had been used as a latrine by some small creature of the night, and then as its mausoleum. During the night, too, he'd somehow been on a cross-country run and then been expertly beaten up by secret police. He felt bad.

After all of the metaphors of tortured seeing, feeling, and tasting, the final sentence comes as a ludicrous understatement. The sudden letdown in rhythm and momentum, as well as in language, contributes to the humorous shock, and the abrupt incongruity of the sudden plain tone makes self-conscious hyperboles of the already ridiculous comparisons.

Eight sentences make up this paragraph of description, and the first analytical glance over them reveals that the six sentences between the first and the last—so far as the narrative is concerned—are descriptive details. All that the paragraph explicitly says is: *Dixon was alive again. . . . He felt bad.* Amis has six impressionistic sentences laden with figures and highly connotative diction to show why Dixon *felt bad.* The intended effect on the reader should be one of wry shock and laughter leading up to the ludicrous anticlimax of the final sentence. The author has us laughing at his hero, but the laughter is mixed with some recognition of the familiar by those readers who have once awakened in a similar state.

Now for a representative passage from one of our country's first famous novelists, James Fenimore Cooper:

> Deerslayer knew that his adversary must be employed in reloading, unless he had fled. The former proved to be the case, for the young man had no sooner placed himself behind a tree, than he caught a glimpse of the arm of the Indian, his body being concealed by an oak, in the very act of forcing the leathered bullet home. Nothing would have been easier than to spring forward, and decide the affair by a close assault on his unprepared foe; but every feeling of Deerslayer revolted at such a step, although his own life had just been attempted from a cover. He was yet unpractised in the ruthless expedients of savage warfare, of which he knew nothing except by tradition and theory, and it struck him as an unfair advantage to assail an unarmed foe.
>
> His color had heightened, his eye frowned, his lips were compressed, and all his energies were collected and ready; but, instead of advancing to fire, he dropped his rifle to the usual position of a sportsman in readiness to catch his aim, and muttered to himself, unconscious that he was speaking—"No, no—that may be red-skin warfare, but it's not a Christian's gifts. Let the miscreant charge, and then we'll take it out like men; for the canoe he *must* not, and *shall* not have. No, no; let him have time to load, and God will take care of the right!"

These seven sentences relate a young woodsman's first encounter with an Indian. Cooper's attitude toward the young hero is one of warm approval of moral, religious outlook, for he is not given to the kind of irony with which a modern reader might interpret the scene. Cooper knew his nineteenth-century audience would approve of the final *and God will take care of the right!* The tone is as dated as is much of the diction in the expressions: *close assault on his unprepared foe; let the miscreant charge.* Yet through the use of simple clauses and the frequent coordinate conjunctions *but* and *and,* Cooper laid the foundations for the American action story style, which reached its highest art with Ernest Hemingway.

In structure, Cooper's paragraph development is chronological, ending with the sentence of high moral speech. The style thus is fast-moving narrative, heavily moralistic in tone, but original in describing a scene that was to be copied countless times. The diction at times is forceful: *caught a glimpse of the arm,* and *forcing the leathered bullet home.* Present also are the future clichés of such narratives: *savage warfare* and *red-skin warfare.*

In 1921 E. M. Forster appeared with one of the first postwar novels showing the ironic incongruities and shortcomings of life in London among the better classes and of those who, like the young man shown here in his basement apartment, hoped to improve themselves enough to become worthy of advancement:

> As Leonard was kicking off his boots he jarred the three-legged table, and a photograph frame, honourably poised upon it, slid sideways, fell off into the fireplace, and smashed. He swore in a colourless sort of way, and picked the photograph up. It represented a young lady called Jacky, and had been taken at the time when young ladies called Jacky were often photographed with their mouths open. Teeth of dazzling whiteness extended along either of Jacky's jaws, and positively weighed her head sideways, so large were they and so numerous. Take my word for it, that smile was simply stunning, and it is only you and I who will be fastidious, and complain that true joy begins in the eyes, and that the eyes of Jacky did not accord with her smile, but were anxious and hungry.

The first two sentences relate an incident, and the remaining three in order of climax tell of its meaning: Leonard is no judge of character in women. The tone is representative of the highly marketable style of satire and brilliant wit we have come to expect of English writers. In the final sentence, wherein the author speaks directly to the reader, he flatters him by assuming they share the same fastidious judgment of girls who smile with their teeth but not with their eyes. He has some pity for Leonard, yet ridicules him for his lack of character and weakness. Those who find themselves caught up in that last sentence as realizing that they never have thought to judge a smile for what it was worth, may think for a moment that they are no better than poor Leonard. But they think so only for a moment. Forster kindly lets them laugh in superiority at this young man who even *swore in a colourless sort of way,* and who is shown in the next paragraph to own nothing but some books and *a draped mantelshelf bristling with cupids.*

On an empty stomach, Leonard is trying to *form his style* by reading a volume of John Ruskin, an incident which again reveals the Forster wit:

> "Seven miles to the north of Venice—"
> How perfectly the famous chapter opens! How supreme its command of admonition and of poetry! The rich man is speaking to us from his gondola.

Forster again speaks directly to his readers, and this time in a hoot of ridicule of what he has just been praising. He gives the impression that he has at that moment for the first time seen through the pretense of Ruskin's famous "purple passages." Even Leonard reaches the conclusion that the Ruskin style is not for him:

> Something told him that the modifications would not do; and that something, had he known it, was the spirit of English Prose. "My flat is dark as well as stuffy." Those were the words for him.
> And the voice in the gondola rolled on, piping melodiously of Effort and Self-Sacrifice, full of high purpose, full of beauty, full even of sympathy and the love of men, yet somehow eluding all that was actual and insistent in Leonard's life. For it was the voice of one who had never been dirty or hungry, and had not guessed successfully what dirt and hunger are.
> Leonard listened to it with reverence. He felt that he was being done good to, and that if he kept on with Ruskin, and the Queen's Hall Concerts, and some pictures by Watts, he would one day push his head out of the grey waters and see the universe. . . . He hoped to come to Culture suddenly, much as the Revivalist hopes to come to Jesus.

Forster presents Leonard's plight in alternating sentences of description and comment. At the same time he exactly defines the tone and style of Ruskin and implies that for both Ruskin and Leonard the style is the man. Ruskin is the rich man in the gondola: a man who could not even guess what it is like to be dirty and hungry. In choosing Ruskin as a guide in language style, the youthful clerk in a dingy basement apartment is deluding himself with false values. Through a startling analogy Forster drives home his attack on all such pretense.

It is easy enough to catalog the devices of irony, satire, burlesque, and rhetorical juxtaposition that make up the Forster tone, and to point out the kind of moral insight that enabled him to set up a clay pigeon like Leonard and to pop him down to the delight of all who can laugh at Leonard but not at the same attitudes within themselves. Yet no such listing of the devices of wit can encompass the Forster style.

What now can we call a good style? In the light of the analysis in this chapter and all the earlier ones, the following outline of positive and negative attributes may serve as a guide to style:

Positive	Negative
Economy and vivid concreteness	Stale imagery or cliché
A tone of conviction	Tautology—excess verbiage
Effective pattern and structure in sentence and paragraph	Obscurity of thought
	Haphazard structure
	Ambiguity

Following some exercises to give you practice in analyzing sentences and paragraphs for elements of style, we shall next consider *irony* as it relates to tone and style.

CRITICAL FOCUS

Suggestions for a Method of Appraising a Style

1. Choose a paragraph that has particularly impressed you as being representative of an author.
2. Study that paragraph thoroughly as follows:
   a. Try to sum up the impression that several very careful readings of it give you, e.g., humorous, sad, witty, matter of fact.
   b. Analyze what each sentence means and does as a whole unit and in its phrases and clauses.
   c. Go on the principle that every word either by its denotation or connotation is important.

   d. Determine how one sentence relates to the one going before it
and to the one coming after.

   e. Find the order of development: Is it from the less important to
the most important? chronological?

3. Now try to express the author's attitude toward his topic and his
audience—describe his tone.

4. What do his tone, his views, his paragraph and sentence design
and structure, his diction—taken all together—tell you
about his style?

5. Try to state your appraisal in some kind of definitive statement, and
then explain and illustrate the terms of your statement.

6. Always consider the context of the passage you are analyzing for
style. Be sure to read carefully the paragraphs coming before and
after.

     Exercise 3   Written assignment. As a preliminary to analysis
of style in a paragraph, test your skill in sentence analysis by classifying
these sentences as to grammatical and rhetorical types, and discuss the
tone and meaning of each.

   1. The youngest man on board (barring the second mate), and un-
tried as yet by a position of the fullest responsibility, I was willing
to take the adequacy of the others for granted.

   2. We are always in these days endeavoring to separate the two; we
want one man to be always thinking, and another to be always
working, and we call one a gentleman, and the other an operative;
whereas, the workman ought to be thinking, and the thinker often
to be working, and both should be gentlemen, in the best sense.

   3. Conscience was the last tie of New England to its past.

   4. I would rather sit on a pumpkin and have it all to myself than be
crowded on a velvet cushion.

   5. As the waves of the ocean are each different—having a different
form—yet are nevertheless one with it and inseparable from it, so
each melody, though individual, was one with the great art-work
of which it formed a part.

   6. In the glad old days, before the rise of modern morbidities, when
genial old Ibsen filled the world with wholesome joy, and the
kindly tales of the forgotten Emile Zola kept our firesides merry
and pure, it used to be thought a disadvantage to be misunderstood. (If necessary, consult an encyclopedia for these names.)

     Exercise 4   Written analysis. What is the sentence structure
of *one* of these poems? How do the phrases and clauses relate, and

what does each contribute to the sentence as a whole? What is the poet's tone? What is the total impression?

> But rather, when, aware of your mirth
> From full hearts still unsatisfied ye sigh,
> And, feeling kindly unto all the earth,
> Grudge every minute as it passes by,
> Made the more mindful that the sweet days die—
> Remember me a little then, I pray,
> The idle singer of an empty day.

> Out of the night that covers me,
>   Black as the Pit from pole to pole,
> I thank whatever gods may be
>   For my unconquerable soul.

> When I have fears that I may cease to be
>   Before my pen has gleaned my teeming brain,
> Before high-piled books, in charact'ry,
>   Hold like rich garners the full-ripened grain;
> When I behold, upon the night's starred face,
>   Huge cloudy symbols of a high romance,
> And think that I may never live to trace
>   Their shadows, with the magic hand of chance;
> And when I feel, fair creature of an hour,
>   That I shall never look upon thee more,
> Never have relish in the faery power
>   Of unreflecting love!—then on the shore
> Of the wide world I stand alone, and think
> Till love and Fame to nothingness do sink.

> They sailed to the Western Sea, they did—
>   To a land all covered with trees;
> And they bought an owl, and a useful cart,
> And a pound of rice, and a cranberry tart,
>   And a hive of silvery bees;
> And they bought a pig, and some green jackdaws,
> And a lovely monkey with lollipop paws,
> And seventeen bags of edelweiss tea,
> And forty bottles of ring-bo-ree
> And no end of Stilton cheese.

Exercise 5   Discussion assignment. Apply the Critical Focus six-point method of analysis for style to this paragraph. Could the paragraph have been improved? How?

In this world, involved in the material process of existing, we sometimes become lost in the furious pace of doing, and ignore what we are doing. Most of us live and work, aliens to our own personalities. In our efforts for easier survival we have a tendency to subdue our personalities to the ritual of existence, and unconsciously we begin revelling in, almost worshipping, that which is not *us,* but which is merely the means of our existence. We work eight hours a day, then spend our evening trying to ease the tension enough to be able to work another day. Our work is only to gain the money to afford the relaxation we need to survive the succeeding days of work. And so the years proceed, years without meaning. We yearn for greater things, but somehow our yearning becomes lost in the complexities of our physical desires. To this world, which sometimes seems meaningless, the artist brings meaning.

(This paragraph is taken from the editorial of a city college literary magazine on the occasion of its first issue.)

Exercise 6   Essay assignment. Using the excerpt on page 240 as basis for your essay, what are the implications of what E. M. Forster has to say about developing a personal style and its relation to "culture"?

Exercise 7   Written assignment. Analyze for tone, structure, and style the following sentences.

1. But immediately after seven, this clock sprung its alarm with the abruptness of an explosion, and within the second, Annixter had hurled the bed-clothes from him and flung himself up to a sitting posture on the edge of the bed, panting and gasping, blinking at the light, rubbing his head, dazed and bewildered, stupefied at the hideousness with which he had been wrenched from his sleep.
2. And as a pilgrim who goes by a way he has never traveled, who believes every house he sees afar off to be his inn, and not finding it to be so directs his belief to another, and so from house to house till he comes to the inn, so our soul forthwith on entering upon the

new and never-travelled road of this life directs its eyes to the goal of the highest good, and therefore believes whatever thing it sees that seems to have in it any good to be that.

3. We fancy we suffer from ingratitude, while in reality we suffer from self love.

4. All that stuff about the importance of a "liberal education" is just a poor excuse offered by men who make a racket out of education because they never had the gumption to deal with the world of the hard buck.

5. The entrance into this place I made to be not by a door, but by a short ladder to go over the top, which ladder, when I was in, I lifted over after me, and so I was completely fenced in, and fortified, as I thought, from all the world, and consequently slept secure in the night, which otherwise I could not have done.

6. Among other testimonies of the Lord's gracious presence with his own ordinances, there was a youth of fourteen years of age (being the son of one of the magistrates) so wrought upon by the ministry of the word, as, for divers months, he was held under such affliction of mind, as he could not be brought to apprehend any comfort in God, being much humbled and broken for his sins, (though he had been a dutiful child, and not given up to the lusts of youth) and especially for his blasphemous and wicked thoughts, whereby Satan buffeted him, so as he went mourning and languishing daily; yet, attending to the means, and not giving over prayer, and seeking counsel, etc., he came at length to be freed from his temptations, and to find comfort in God's promises, and so, being received into the congregation, upon good proof of his understanding in the things of God, he went on cheerfully in a Christian course, falling daily to labor, as a servant, and as a younger brother of his did, who was no whit short of him in the knowledge of God's will, though his youth kept him from daring to offer himself to the congregation.

Exercise 8 Written assignment. As your instructor advises, apply the "positive" and "negative" tests for effective style to the following paragraphs. As your method, use the six steps recommended in the Critical Focus for determining a style.

1. Let anybody travel, as I did last year, through the valley of the Connecticut, and observe the houses. All clean and white and neat and well-to-do, with their turfy yards and their breezy great elms, but all shut up from basement to attic, as if the inmates had

all sold out and gone to China. Not a window-blind open above or below. Is the house inhabited? No—yes—there is a faint stream of blue smoke from the kitchen chimney, and half a window-blind open in some distant back part of the house. They are living there in the dim shadows bleaching like potato-sprouts in the cellar. . . . [Don't they know] every window should be a picture—sun and trees and clouds and green grass should never be far from us?

2. Consider the subtleness of the sea; how its most dreaded creatures glide under water, unapparent for the most part, and treacherously hidden beneath the loveliest tints of azure. Consider also the devilish brilliance and beauty of many of its most remorseless tribes, the dainty embellished shape of many species of sharks. Consider, once more, the universal cannibalism of the sea; all whose creatures prey upon each other carrying on eternal war since the world began. Consider all this; and then turn to this green, gentle, and most docile earth; consider them both, the sea and the land, and do you not find a strange analogy to something in yourself? For as this appalling ocean surrounds the verdant land, so in the soul of man lies an insular Tahiti, full of peace and joy, but encompassed by all the horrors of the half known life. God help thee! Push not off from that isle, thou canst never return.

3. *Mad*'s symbol, the insipidly smiling Alfred E. Neuman, who maintains his ghoulishly cheerful expression while the most appalling things go on around him, stands for American culture itself as the adolescent experiences it. This idiotically smiling figure implies that all is for the best in the best of all possible worlds, in spite of overwhelming evidence to the contrary. Alfred E. Neuman is the American *Candide*, but with one difference: he never mentions God and religion. Even *Mad* could not get away with that.

4. Sometimes I have seen burying places of several miles, belonging to very inconsiderable villages, which were formerly great towns, and retain no other mark of their ancient grandeur, than this dismal one. On no occasion do they ever remove a stone that serves for a monument. Some of them are costly enough, being of very fine marble. They set up a pillar with a carved turban on the top of it to the memory of a man; and as the turbans, by their different shapes, show the quality of profession, 'tis in a manner putting up the arms of the deceased. Besides, the pillar commonly bears an inscription in gold letters. The ladies have simple pillars, without other ornament, except those that die unmarried, who have a rose on the top of their monument. The sepulchers of particular fami-

lies are railed in, and planted round with trees. Those of the sultans, and some great men, have lamps constantly burning in them.

5. There was a girl whose complexion was Snow White, whose hair made ravens despair. She lived in a forest of tall buildings and television aerials and yearned for a knight on a white super-charger to carry her away. One day she came upon a shop with a swinging sign that said: "Magic Spoken Here," and she entered. The shop was crammed from Chock to Bursting with pills, potions, spells and wishingwells. But on the counter, gleaming brighter than a gold tinderbox, was a slim gold cylinder. It was longer than a match and smaller than a magic wand. In it was a color that was redder than poppy, riper than persimmon, richer than rubies and brighter than rain! The girl said, "Does this mean the end of my search?" And the proprietress twinkled and said, "No, this is the way to begin your story. It starts, you see, Once Upon a Red. . . ."

6. And he would remember: himself and his uncle standing beside the sheriff's car in the alley beside the jail watching Lucas and the sheriff emerge from the jail's side door and cross the dark yard toward them. It was quite dark in fact since the street light at the corner didn't reach this far nor any sound either; only a little after ten oclock and on Monday night too yet the sky's dark bowl cupped as though in a vacuum like the old bride's bouquet under its glass bell the town, the Square which was more than dead: abandoned: because he had gone on to look at it, without stopping leaving his uncle standing at the corner of the alley who said after him: "Where are you going?" but not even answering, walking the last silent and empty block, ringing his footfalls deliberate and un-secret into the hollow silence, unhurried and solitary but nothing at all of forlorn, instead with a sense a feeling not possessive but proprietary, viceregal, with humility still, himself not potent but at least the vessel of a potency like the actor looking from wings or perhaps empty balcony down upon the waiting stage vacant yet garnished and empty yet, nevertheless where in a moment now he will walk and posture in the last act's absolute cynosure, himself in himself nothing and maybe no world-beater of a play either but at least his to finish it, round it and put it away intact and un-assailable, complete; and so onto into the dark and empty Square stopping as soon as he could perceive at effortless once that whole dark lifeless rectangle with but one light anywhere and that in the cafe which stayed open all night on account of the long-haul

trucks whose (the cafe's) real purpose some said, the real reason
for the grant of its license by the town was to keep Willy Ingrum's
nocturnal counterpart awake who although the town had walled
him off a little cubbyhole of an office in an alley with a stove and
a telephone he wouldn't stay there but used the cafe where there
was somebody to talk to and he could be telephoned there of
course. . . .

STYLE AND EIGHT VARIATIONS OF IRONY

Quarrels and fights often begin from verbal misunderstandings; they
can even play prominent roles, one notes, in political campaigns. But
we are concerned here with writers who by temperament like to say
one thing and mean just its opposite. They delight, as do their readers,
in recognizing the fact that nothing in life seems to be what it appears
on the surface. This suggesting the very opposite of what one says is a
form of *irony*, a term derived from the Greek *eiron*, meaning "a dis-
sembler in speech."

The critical reader prides himself on being able to detect irony
in anybody's style, and the critical reader is the kind that a novelist like
Charles Dickens welcomes and expects. His *Pickwick Papers* provides
us with an entertaining introduction to irony as a means of giving a
style character.

One of Mr. Pickwick's piquant experiences features a situation
of *dramatic irony*. Pickwick, a corpulent bachelor, is considering hiring
Sam Weller as a servant, and asks his landlady, Mrs. Bardell, a series of
questions which the widow and mother completely misunderstands.
When the reader sees that Pickwick does not realize how the questions
are being interpreted, the reader has the pleasure of knowing something that neither of the characters does. He is witnessing dramatic
irony, here one of comedy.

> "Mrs. Bardell," said Mr. Pickwick, at last, as that amiable female
> approached the termination of a prolonged dusting of the apart-
> ment—
> "Sir," said Mrs. Bardell.
> "Your little boy is a very long time gone."
> "Why, it's a good long way to the Borough, sir," remonstrated Mrs.
> Bardell.
> "Ah," said Mr. Pickwick, "very true; so it is."

Mr. Pickwick relapsed into silence, and Mrs. Bardell resumed her dusting.

"Mrs. Bardell," said Mr. Pickwick, at the expiration of a few minutes.

"Sir," said Mrs. Bardell again.

"Do you think it a much greater expense to keep two people, than to keep one?"

"La, Mr. Pickwick," said Mrs. Bardell, colouring up to the very border of her cap, as she fancied she observed a species of matrimonial twinkle in the eyes of her lodger; "La, Mr. Pickwick, what a question!"

"Well, but *do* you?" inquired Mr. Pickwick.

"That depends—" said Mrs. Bardell, approaching the duster very near to Mr. Pickwick's elbow, which was planted on the table— "that depends a good deal upon the person, you know, Mr. Pickwick; and whether it's a saving and careful person, sir."

"That's very true," said Mr. Pickwick, "but the person I have in my eye (here he looked very hard at Mrs. Bardell) I think possesses these qualities; and has, moreover, a considerable knowledge of the world, and a great deal of sharpness, Mrs. Bardell; which may be of material use to me."

"La, Mr. Pickwick," said Mrs. Bardell; the crimson rising to her cap-border again.

"I do," said Mr. Pickwick, growing energetic, as was his wont in speaking of a subject which interested him, "I do, indeed; and to tell you the truth, Mrs. Bardell, I have made up my mind."

"Dear me, sir," exclaimed Mrs. Bardell.

"You'll think it very strange now," said the amiable Mr. Pickwick, with a good-humoured glance at his companion, "that I never consulted you about this matter, and never even mentioned it, till I sent your little boy out this morning—eh?"

Mrs. Bardell could only reply by a look. She had long worshipped Mr. Pickwick at a distance, but here she was, all at once, raised to a pinnacle to which her wildest and most extravagant hopes had never dared to aspire. Mr. Pickwick was going to propose—a deliberate plan, too—sent her little boy to the Borough, to get him out of the way—how thoughtful—how considerate!

"Well," said Mr. Pickwick, "what do you think?"

"Oh, Mr. Pickwick," said Mrs. Bardell, trembling with agitation, "you're very kind, sir."

"It'll save you a good deal of trouble, won't it?" said Mr. Pickwick.

"Oh, I never thought anything of the trouble, sir," replied Mrs.

Bardell; "and, of course, I should take more trouble to please you then, than ever; but it is so kind of you, Mr. Pickwick, to have so much consideration for my loneliness."

"Ah, to be sure," said Mr. Pickwick; "I never thought of that. When I am in town, you'll always have somebody to sit with you. To be sure, so you will."

"I'm sure I ought to be a very happy woman," said Mrs. Bardell.

"And your little boy—" said Mr. Pickwick.

"Bless his heart!" interposed Mrs. Bardell, with a maternal sob.

"He, too, will have a companion," resumed Mr. Pickwick, "a lively one, who'll teach him, I'll be bound, more tricks in a week than he would ever learn in a year." And Mr. Pickwick smiled placidly.

"Oh you dear—" said Mrs. Bardell.

Mr. Pickwick started.

"Oh you kind, good, playful dear," said Mrs. Bardell; and without more ado, she rose from her chair, and flung her arms round Mr. Pickwick's neck, with a cataract of tears and a chorus of sobs.

"Bless my soul," cried the astonished Mr. Pickwick;—"Mrs. Bardell my good woman—dear me, what a situation—pray consider.—Mrs. Bardell, don't—if anybody should come—"

"Oh, let them come," exclaimed Mrs. Bardell, frantically; "I'll never leave you—dear, kind, good, soul;" and, with these words, Mrs. Bardell clung the tighter.

"Mercy upon me," said Mr. Pickwick, struggling violently, "I hear somebody coming up the stairs. Don't, don't, there's a good creature, don't." But entreaty and remonstrance were alike unavailing; for Mrs. Bardell had fainted in Mr. Pickwick's arms; and before he could gain time to deposit her on a chair, Master Bardell entered the room, ushering in Mr. Tupman, Mr. Winkle, and Mr. Snodgrass.

Mr. Pickwick was struck motionless and speechless. He stood with his lovely burden in his arms, gazing vacantly on the countenances of his friends. . . .

This final scene depicting the bewildered Mr. Pickwick caught holding his limp landlady in his arms illustrates also the *irony of circumstance*. The innocent old gentleman appears to be in the wrong even to his three friends, and the irony of the situation is heightened by the author's verbal irony as matters take a worse turn immediately for Mr. Pickwick:

The astonishment of the Pickwickians was so absorbing, and the perplexity of Mr. Pickwick was so extreme, that they might have remained in exactly the same relative situations until the suspended animation of the lady was restored, had it not been for a most beautiful and touching expression of filial affection on the part of her youthful son. Clad in a tight suit of corderoy, spangled with brass buttons of a very considerable size, he at first stood at the door astounded and uncertain; but by degrees, the impression that his mother must have suffered some personal damage, pervaded his partially developed mind, and considering Mr. Pickwick as the aggressor, he set up an appalling and semi-earthly kind of howling, and butting forward with his head, commenced assailing that immortal gentleman about the back and legs, with such blows and pinches as the strength of his arm, and the violence of his excitement, allowed.

After Mr. Pickwick has hired Sam Weller and rigged him out in splendid fashion at a secondhand emporium, Sam is in a proper mood for *Socratic irony.* The term is derived from Plato's *Dialogues,* in which Socrates, in order to continue a discussion with a companion, asked questons that seemed to make himself appear ignorant. Sam likewise compliments himself by seeming to denigrate himself:

> "Well," said that suddenly-transformed individual, as he took his seat on the outside of the Eatanswill coach next morning; "I wonder whether I'm meant to be a footman, or a groom, or a gamekeeper, or a seedsman. I looks like a sort of compo of every one on 'em. Never mind; there's a change of air, plenty to see, and little to do; and all this suits my complaint uncommon; so long life to the Pickvicks, says I!"

And the reader is happy to second those sentiments, as he imagines what a mixture of outfits Sam must be wearing.

But Mrs. Bardell, the landlady, went to a law firm to sue Pickwick for a breach of promise. Dickens finds the episode an occasion for other ironies. At the law office, Sam makes a model remark of *verbal irony* when he overhears one of the law partners, "Mr. Fogg," describe it a "Christian act" to teach a poor man with a big family and a small income the lesson not to get into debt; and to teach him by having his weekly pay deducted: "Nice men these here, sir," Sam whispered to his master. "Wery nice notion of fun they has, sir."

Dickens seems also to have had no lofty regard for prohibition of alcoholic spirits, as this following example of *sarcasm* suggests. (Sarcasm relies upon the ambivalent strength of the ironic statement, but cuts and bites fiercely in its language.) Here are excerpts from "Report of the Committe of the Brick Lane Branch of the United Grand Junction Ebenezer Temperance Association":

"H. Walker, tailor, wife and two children. When in better circumstances, owns to having been in the constant habit of drinking ale and beer; says he is not certain whether he did not twice a week, for twenty years, taste 'dog's nose,' which your committee find upon inquiry, to be compounded of warm porter, moist sugar, gin, and nutmeg (a groan, and 'So it is!' from an elderly female). Is now out of work and pennyless; thinks it must be the porter (cheers) or the loss of the use of his right hand; is not certain which, but thinks it very likely that, if he had drank nothing but water all his life, his fellow work-man would never have stuck a rusty needle in him, and thereby occasioned his accident (tremendous cheering). Has nothing but cold water to drink, and never feels thirsty (great applause). . . .

"Thomas Burton is purveyor of cat's meat to the Lord Mayor and Sheriffs, and several members of the Common Council (the announcement of this gentleman's name was received with breathless interest). Has a wooden leg; finds a wooden leg expensive, going over the stones; used to wear second-hand wooden legs, and drink a glass of hot gin and water regularly every night—sometimes two (deep sighs). Found the second-hand wooden legs split and rot very quickly; is firmly persuaded that their constitution was undermined by the gin and water (prolonged cheering). Buys new wooden legs now, and drinks nothing but water and weak tea. The new legs last twice as long as the others used to do, and he attributes this solely to his temperate habits (triumphant cheers)."

The biting humor of these passages from the "Report" take on additional irony when behind the narrator—here the secretary whose minutes we are reading—we clearly discern Charles Dickens grinning with us at this impossible logic.

Anticlimax has already been shown, but as is to be expected of a device wherein a lofty or serious tone falls off into an undignified one so as to produce laughter, or at least a smile, Dickens takes frequent advantage of it. At an ice-skating party Pickwick breaks through the ice and is finally rescued:

"Oh, he'll catch his death of cold," said Emily.

"Dear old thing!" said Arabella. "Let me wrap this shawl round you, Mr. Pickwick."

"Ah, that's the best thing you can do," said Wardle; "and when you've got it on, run home as fast as your legs can carry you, and jump into bed directly."

A dozen shawls were offered on the instant. Three or four of the thickest having been selected, Mr. Pickwick was wrapped up, and started off, under the guidance of Mr. Weller: presenting the singular phenomenon of an elderly gentleman, dripping wet, and without a hat, with his arms bound down to his sides, skimming over the ground, without any clearly defined purpose, at the rate of six good English miles an hour.

Thus a serious situation ends up with an offhand comment on the rate of speed.

Romantic irony contains the reversal from high and tender beauty to ridiculous reality. Lord Byron is one of best illustrators of it in "Don Juan." Here is the shipwrecked youth being discovered half-drowned by a pirate's beautiful young daughter, Haidée:

And she bent o'er him, and he lay beneath,
  Hushed as the babe upon its mother's breast,
Drooped as the willow when no winds can breathe,
  Lulled like the depth of ocean when at rest,
Fair as the crowning rose of the whole wreath,
  Soft as the callow cygnet in its nest;
In short, he was a very pretty fellow,
Although his woes had turned him rather yellow.

One other form of irony, the *paradox,* shows a lively intelligence at work and a critical, penetrating eye. A paradox is a statement that appears to be self-contradictory, but which contains a reference that reconciles these contrasting aspects. As an essayist, G. K. Chesterton made the paradox the basis of his style:

Faith is the power of believing that which we know to be untrue.
Charity is the power of defending that which we know to be indefensible.
Hope is the power of being cheerful in circumstances which we know to be desperate.

Thus the resources of language and thought serve every writer to express his experiences and opinions in whatever style he finds congenial to his talents and his needs. The better the writer, the more he seeks the critical reader who can evaluate as well as share vision and purpose.

CRITICAL FOCUS

Irony works in comedy and tragedy to give a style tensile strength.
Among its variations are these: dramatic irony, irony of circumstance,
Socratic irony, verbal irony, sarcasm, anticlimax, romantic
irony, and paradox.

Exercise 9   Essay assignment. Develop by analysis and example as well as by detail and comparison this general topic: Ironies that go largely unnoticed in the life and world around us.

Exercise 10   Report assignment. Study a short story by one of the following writers—or others recommended by your instructor—and report on the various forms of irony you find in it. Summarize and classify your findings.

Stephen Crane	Ernest Hemingway	Caroline Gordon
Sherwood Anderson	Eudora Welty	Frank O'Connor
James Thurber	Dorothy Parker	John Cheever

Exercise 11   Written analysis. In *The Scarlet Letter* Nathaniel Hawthorne presents a famous scene of dramatic irony when the Reverend Mr. Dimmesdale, who is the father of Hester Prynne's illegitimate child, has to witness her shame before the public eye and to address her himself. No one, not even the reader, knows the truth of the situation. Read and study that scene and discuss what diction, what narrative details, what tone Hawthorne employs to present this scene so that the reader, after later learning Hester's secret, would think back on this scene and ask himself: "Could I have guessed it?"

Exercise 12   Written analysis. In *The History of Mr. Polly*, H. G. Wells was one of the first of the English novelists to present the emergence of the common man in a changing society. It abounds with comic irony. Discuss sentence by sentence what ironies you find in the passage quoted below.

> Miriam combined earnestness of spirit with great practical incapacity. The house was never clean nor tidy, but always being frightfully disarranged for cleaning or tidying up, and she cooked because food had to be cooked, and with a sound moralist's entire disregard of the quality or the consequences. The food came from her hands

done rather than improved, and looking as uncomfortable as savages clothed under duress by a missionary with a stock of out-sizes. Such food is too apt to behave resentfully, rebel, and work Obi. She ceased to listen to her husband's talk from the day she married him, and ceased to unwrinkle the kink in her brow at his presence, giving herself up to mental states that had a quality of preoccupation. And she developed an idea, for which, perhaps, there was legitimate excuse, that he was lazy. He seemed to stand about a great deal, to read—an indolent habit—and presently to seek company for talking. He began to attend the bar-parlour of the God's Providence Inn with some frequency, and would have done so regularly in the evening if cards, which bored him to death, had not arrested conversation. But the perpetual foolish variation of the permutations and combinations of two-and-fifty cards taken five at a time, and the meagre surprises and excitements that ensue, had no charm for Mr. Polly's mind, which was at once too vivid in its impressions and too easily fatigued.

It was soon manifest the shop paid only in the most exacting sense, and Miriam did not conceal her opinion that he ought to bestir himself and "do things," though what he was to do was hard to say. You see, when you have once sunken your capital in a shop you do not very easily get it out again. If customers will not come to you cheerfully and freely, the law sets limits upon the compulsion you may exercise. You cannot pursue people about the streets of a watering-place, compelling them either by threats or importunity to buy flannel trousers. Additional sources of income for a tradesman are not always easy to find. Wintershed, at the bicycle and gramophone shop to the right, played the organ in the church, and Clamp of the toy-shop was pew-opener and so forth; Gambell, the greengrocer, waited at table and his wife cooked, and Carter, the watchmaker, left things to his wife while he went about the world winding clocks; but Mr. Polly had none of these arts, and wouldn't, in spite of Miriam's quietly persistent protests, get any other. And on summer evenings he would ride his bicycle about the country, and if he discovered a sale where there were books, he would as often as not waste half the next day in going again to acquire a job lot of them haphazard, and bring them home tied about with string, and hide them from Miriam under the counter in the shop. That is a heart-breaking thing for any wife with a serious investigatory turn of mind to discover. She was always thinking of burning these finds, but her natural turn for economy prevailed with her.

chapter 10

HOW TO READ A BOOK

An author merely collects notes for a certain suggested
work and every reader then writes the book for himself.
Sir Hugh Walpole

Spy out what is half there—the page-under-the-page.
Wyndham Lewis

No one can prescribe how anyone—not even in this
age of "standardized products"—should read a book.
For no matter how hard he may try to avoid it, everyone is an individual with his own set of values, however in process of change, and his own personal backgrounds. These individual differences make it obvious
that everyone reads a "different" book, although its
title and author be identical. He brings an individual
critical or appreciative intelligence to the denotations
and connotations of the writer's language.

But, as it has been the purpose throughout this
book to make clear, means do exist to take one beyond the merely personal, emotional reaction to what
he reads. Certain methods permit a high degree of
objective evaluation and appreciation, among which
are the examination of any piece of writing for its
diction, logic, structure, tone, and style. All the Critical Focus summaries have suggested possible means
for such a critical approach.

Now we hope to apply these methods to full-
length books. Let us begin with those that explain,
comment, and interpret.

NONFICTION: BIOGRAPHY, HISTORY, SCIENCE, AND SOCIAL SCIENCE

Since a major emphasis of this text has been upon the analysis of exposition and argument in these various areas of study, we can draw upon the previously established principles and facts to suggest a check list for reading books in any of these fields. But before coming to the outline, let us review several fundamentals about such expository and persuasive writing.

Almost all books in these disciplines try to explain or establish a viewpoint, a thesis, or a proposition. The author may or may not have been adequately prepared to cope with the task he set himself in preparing and writing that book. He may have had an exaggerated opinion of his ability and knowledge. Through indolence or lack of true scholarly responsibility, he may have been too willing to settle for easy answers to the significant problems that any serious book inevitably raises by the nature of its subject matter. Or he may have been obsessed with the certainty of a conclusion which he has long entertained and which has finally driven him to writing the book. In such circumstances, he may refuse to face data and theories that might negate his emotionally charged thesis. He would feel that doubt could bleed his energy and shake the conviction impelling him to complete the book.

The biographer, for example, or the historian must work with some highly nonobjective data and evidence for the construction of a book that relates a life or an event and seeks to make it meaningful. The biographer approaches his task of interpretation by searching out what he considers to be the complex of character traits that are to make his personage understandable, at least to the author. It is true that he may have studied volumes of letters, memoranda, perhaps even diaries and journals, as well as published works—all prime materials. Unfortunately, these items often disclose very little of the most secret life of the subject. In fact, the subject of the biography probably was as biased in speaking of himself as were those of his times who wrote or spoke of him. After the conscientious scholar has amassed and collated such information, he still must decide what views he can take of it. The historian who tackles such tremendously involved historic events as revolutions, economic and social epochs, and wars has an even greater task of weighing evidence, sorting out existing theories, criticizing available commentaries, and eventually trying to find a cohesive structure and viewpoint whereby he can bring order to what is in reality too often a chaos.

What are the motives that prompt the biographer, the historian, the scientist, or the social scientist to undertake the laborious task of writing a book? Their motives may be those of any other writers. They may be trying to arrive at a truth, a "fact," as to the best of their ability and knowledge they can formulate it. They may be satisfying an academic demand required for professional advancement; they may be moved largely by personal vanity; they may hope for monetary returns. Motives alone will not generally determine the quality of the book.

For whatever his professional backgrounds, the author must also have some capabilities as a writer. Through training and practice he must have arrived at some competence in meeting the particular demands of expression in his own area of specialty as well as those of general good writing. We expect of biographer and philosopher of science alike that their books show the unity, the organization, and the clarity we have come to expect of good writing. Readers obey the *law of economy:* they will not ordinarily waste their time trying to decipher what the expository author has failed to make clear with one reading.

After these reminders, we come now to the outline based on all that we have learned about expository writing.

A Critical Reader's Check List for Books of Biography,
History, Science, and Social Science

1. What is the structural organization of the book?
   a. Read the Table of Contents.
   b. Note the proportion of space given the respective topics.
2. What is the author's thesis or purpose?
   a. Study the Foreword or Preface:
      (1) For statement of purpose and plan
      (2) For background the author considers essential to intelligent reading
      (3) For possible explanation of method or techniques used
   b. Read the first chapter critically.
3. What are the sources drawn on for the book?
   a. Examine the footnotes, notes, and bibliography.
   b. Study the opening chapter for views on sources.
4. What is the author's tone?
   a. Determine his attitude and outlook toward his subject: his objectivity or subjectivity, his respect and consideration for its complexity and difficulties.
   b. Try to find his attitude toward the reader.

5. What is his style?
   a. Test for unity, coherence, and emphasis, making for easy and interesting reading.
   b. Appraise the suitability of his diction and general tone to his method of approach and handling of specific problems.
   c. Look for general consistency of manner, tone, and logic.
6. What is the book worth?
   a. Find in the index a topic on which you have some information and read that section most critically.
   b. Measure his degree of success in doing throughout the book what he set out to do in the beginning.
   c. Read reviews and note points made in light of your own conclusions.
   d. Evaluate the book's significance as a contribution to its subject.
   e. Decide on your own pleasure or displeasure as a reader.

FICTION: THE NOVEL

No matter how they may disagree with one another on other aspects of the novel, critics all admit it should be a long work of fiction, taking considerable time to read. Whether the form is said to have originated with *Arcadia, Don Quixote, The Princess of Cleves, Robinson Crusoe,* or *Pamela* depends upon which critic one is reading. His criteria for a novel will also determine whether Sterne's *A Sentimental Journey* or Alain Robbe-Grillet's *The Voyeur* should be included in this genre. Fortunately, one can read a novel with pleasure and understanding without first having settled such points. Yet one who wishes to discuss and weigh any novel can well profit from critics' approaches to novels, at least as a suggestion of *what to look for in general.*

In written fiction of any length, somebody is telling the story. He is the *narrator,* or the voice through which the author tells the story. The narrator often lies concealed behind various *points of view.* He may be the first-person *I* who reports as the one undergoing the experience, as in *Robinson Crusoe* and *Gulliver's Travels.* He may be the *central intelligence* characteristic of Henry James's novels, also termed *the roving narrator:* a single superior mind that is placed in the center of the dramatic action and observes with clear insight more than any one of the characters himself can know. This roving narrator reaches perfection in James Joyce's short story "The Dead." Shifts in narrator are common in the modern novel and make some of them difficult to follow. Novelists such as Nathalie Sarraute shift from one character and point of view to the other without warning, in order to create an impression of immediacy, of the orderly chaos of social life, for example, around a dinner table.

Earlier novelists such as Henry Fielding and Samuel Richardson entered the story in their own voices, much as the narrator did in E. M. Forster's *Howards End,* but whether this direct voice is really that of the author as author or as a person who has adopted the "mask" of authorship is difficult to say. Since the times of Turgenev and Henry James, authors have made their tone more and more objective, and their narrators increasingly difficult to detect. Some try to keep themselves as authors as anonymous as possible. But some voice still must tell us what any one or all of the characters do, think, and feel. Miss the voice of the narrator, and you miss the best clue to the narrative.

Theme is not synonymous with *moral* or *message,* we have said, for works of literary art are more than teaching exemplars. Theme does relate to meaning and purpose, in the sense that every novelist worthy of consideration has at least several points to make, several "facts" to underscore through the patterned action he narrates. For example, what does *theme* mean when related to Herman Melville's *Moby Dick?* The book's many symbols and allusions to religious and other myths suggest numerous insights and purposes that Melville had while writing the novel and which the story embodies—ideas dealing with the nature of man and *the problem of evil.* Theme, then, represents all of the many things the author has to say about the various aspects of life that he shows his reader, and statements of theme can be arrived at only through the inductive process. Above all, no one speech, symbol, or expression can safely be taken by itself as embodying the full purpose of the novelist.

In great novels the people represented as living may assume the real proportions of human beings, but, of course, none is as complex as any living person is. *The characters* may seem complicated and many-sided, but this appearance is part of the author's magic of illusion. For the narrator is always governed by an economy of design that rules out trying to have characters do, think, and feel all of the aimless or functional things that make up daily human acts. Nor has he space or need to show all of the self-contradictions and aberrations of behavior that make individual human acts mysterious and unpredictable. Some existentialist novelists who are also *nihilists*—for example, Samuel Beckett in *Watt* and his other novels—attempt to present completely aimless, instinctive lives troubled by consciousness. But like the more traditional novelists, the existentialists have to restrict themselves to certain traits or aspects of the human personality.

Few authors try to give the depth to their characterizations that Tolstoy does to Pierre and Prince Andrew in *War and Peace,* and to show them, furthermore, as changing in outlook and behavior as they undergo realistic experiences. Dostoyevsky goes even more into analyzing the dark recesses of character, but even he must be satisfied to give his characters comparatively few traits and motives.

What *motivation* prompts people to do the noble as well as the evil or weak acts that newspapers record, and the many more no one ever hears about? What makes us behave as we do? Psychology, sociology, anthropology, all the other sciences, and religion attempt answers. These explanations may help some novelists to work out an efficient cause and effect fictional world, but the study of motives absorbs writers other than those of crime-detection tales.

As in real life, book characters are prompted to act by the ambitions, desires, physical urges, obsessions, etc., that their author has "found" at work in them, as their persons take shape in his imagination. Also, they generally react to their physical and social environment as would people in real life whom they resemble, or as the reader is willing to grant that such people act. They live in a world of *verisimilitude,* one resembling life. This cultural world in which the book people live is given various terms: *atmosphere, cultural atmosphere, setting, social environment,* or *milieu.* Perhaps the last term is the most fitting one for this context.

Milieu includes the intellectual, moral, social, economic, political, religious, educational, artistic, etc., world of any story. The narrator must choose some kind of place-time set of circumstances in which the characters follow out the patterns of their lives—patterns perhaps not visible either to them or to the reader until the end. Whether it be a band of boys running wild on an island, as in William Golding's *Lord of the Flies,* or a youth come to New York from his preparatory school, as in J. D. Salinger's *The Catcher in the Rye,* the novel's characters speak, think, and act as their education, temperament, and rearing—or lack of it—would lead the reader to expect. How free or determined they are by that physical world and its milieu of culture are questions the critical reader will want to decide for himself. So each novel has its own ethical tone, by means of which the reader can identify himself if he finds in it elements to his liking or with which he is familiar.

Empathy is the projection of one's sympathies or consciousness into things outside and beyond himself. It is this gift of the human personality that leads some critics to regard novels as being almost "seductive," and it also explains the suspicion under which the novel lay for centuries. Coleridge called this pleasure in reading, in surrendering to story, "the willing suspension of disbelief." Certain authors more than others can arouse in us a sense of close relationship; we recognize their individual voices in the overtones of their narrators. Readers fascinated by love and death, thus, enjoy the novels of Ernest Hemingway, and others prefer a Charlotte Brontë or a John O'Hara. Still others find empathy in comic-strip characters.

Action as the sum of the events, patterned in a design set by the author, entices the reader and holds his attention. The sorrows and tribulations of people in realistic situations struggling through one difficulty after the other to attain some hoped for goal is a common formula of *action*. "Boy gets girl," "girl gets boy" are plot actions still enabling readers to suffer and win vicariously with heroes and heroines. In this sense action means *plot:* a series of closely linked incidents, beginning with an opening situation of conflict and, chapter by chapter, plunging the hero into one ordeal after the other until, after reaching a climax of effort and suspense, the hero either wins or loses. By means of dramatic scene and summary, each incident can be given scenario realism.

But in the modern and contemporary novel *action* has acquired new meanings. Joyce, Proust, and Kafka discarded old formulas and discovered fresh narrative designs projecting the troubled consciousness of their authors. The "new" novel continues this experimentation in form to depict the changing condition of man as it is now regarded in terms of history, psychology, philosophy, and science. And more than ever before, artists require the critical reader to become also the creative reader, thinker, and even writer.

A Critical Reader's Check List for Novels

1. **Who are the main characters?**
   a. **Note the degree of complexity of their behavior, thought, and feeling; their appearances, habits, mannerisms, speech, attitudes, values.**

    b. Note especially what changes, if any, they undergo in growth or deterioration in keeping with their personalities and temperaments.

2. What is the milieu?

    a. Be able to describe the social forces and institutions that shape the characters and their lives: political, social, economic, philosophic, religious, educational, etc.

    b. Determine to what extent they are influenced by nature in the sense of the air, water, light, open country, field, woods, etc., that surround them.

3. What is the design of the action?

    a. Find the conventional plot if such exists: a basic conflict or struggle gradually being worked out to a resolution favorable or unfavorable to the main characters.

    b. Define the order of time of the narrated acts: flashback, summary, story within story, etc.

4. What is the theme (or themes)?

    a. Compare the fate of each character to the others'.

    b. Appraise the characters' lives for freedom of choice in the courses of action they took.

    c. Determine the relationship of the tone to these lives.

    d. Weigh any and all speeches that seem to be statements of values, philosophy, or morality.

    e. Discern the author's feeling toward the milieu of his characters.

    f. Try to learn the author's relationships to his narrator or narrators to note possible approval or disapproval of what is said or done.

    g. Examine the diction for symbols, myths, allusions to other books or history, but stay in context.

5. Who is the narrator (or narrators)?

    a. Locate the voice that tells the story.

    b. If it is concealed, search out the *intelligence*, the consciousness through which we are "viewing" or "hearing."

    c. Look for first-person narrator, an omniscient narrator (one who knows all and tells all), a *central observer* who seems to be looking over a main character's shoulder and seeing more than the character possibly can.

    d. Decide whether the narrator assists the story or needlessly confuses it.

6. What are the tone, the style?

    a. Decide whether the author is being subjective or objective (present in the story or absent).

    b. Define the general mood of the novel as one of optimism, pessimism, tragedy, comedy, or farce. (These terms require careful definition.)

c. Note any presence of the various kinds of irony.

d. Carefully determine all shades of tone in relation to the characters and events of the novel.

e. Appraise the *style* as the sum of the impressions that diction, design of action, theme, attitude toward milieu, and all the more indefinable features make upon you.

7. What type of novel is it?

It may be any one of these (definitions of which may be found in a literary handbook): of manners, of ideas, picaresque, sentimental, romantic, realistic, naturalistic, epic, psychological, autobiographical, satirical, historical.

8. Did you enjoy reading it?

GLOSSARY

Abstract: As the opposite of *concrete*, those terms that denote general qualities or concepts rather than specific objects, terms such as *charity, strangeness,* and *malice.* Concrete words denote objects perceivable by the senses, though words such as *table* and *gun* may also serve as general concepts.

Action: The basic structure of any narrative, the sum of the imitations of real-life acts that provides the framework of the narrative. In the conventional drama, *action* is considered as follows: Act I, introduction of action; Act II, rising action; Act III, climax; Act IV, falling action; Act V, resolution of action. In the short story or the novel, the configuration of the action, comprised of the basic events of the narrative, is often referred to as *plot.* (See *Plot.*)

Analogy: The suggesting, by comparisons, of previously unrecognized similarities in two or more things or situations that admittedly resemble each other in some respect. For good analogy, the points of similarity between the things or situations compared must be stronger than the points of difference.

Antithesis: The rhetorical practice of adopting parallel or side-by-side structure for ideas or things that are contrasting or opposite. (See *Parallelism.*) The use of similar grammatical forms in employing antithesis is forceful and economical. For example: "Fair is foul, and foul is fair."

Argumentation: The kind of writing, unlike exposition, that deals with pertinent *issues* in order to prove and to persuade rather than merely to explain. There are several types of arguments, such as change of policy, analogy, cause and effect, and fact. (See *Issue.*)

265

Assumption: A statement or premise the credibility of which is assumed or taken for granted. Assumptions form the basis for many everyday arguments and very frequently lack foundation in fact.

Circumlocution: Expression consisting of indirect, roundabout phrases or sentences that do not come directly and clearly to the point. Circumlocution wastes words and the reader's time and patience.

Cliché: Any trite, hackneyed expression that has lost, through overuse, the force it may have originally had. For example: *tired but happy, sadder and wiser, in this modern (atomic, fast-moving) age, heady wine, the smell of success.*

Connotation: The implied or suggested meanings a word has whereby it can create images, arouse memories, or start a series of free associations in the mind of the reader. Connotation may be either private or general: *private* in the sense that every person can have unique associations aroused by a word; *general* in that almost everyone shares some images or suggested meanings a word evokes. For example: *alley* or *laundry* may well have special meanings for some people, but all people probably share some images suggested by these terms.

Context: The sentences or paragraphs which come before and after the term in question. At times, the whole discourse may be required to determine the meaning of the term or expression. There may be also a psychological context created by previous writers or speakers using the same general term or expression, which prepares the reader or audience to interpret the meaning in a special way.

Deductive reasoning: The process of logical thinking which begins with a general principle or assumption and applies it to a particular case or instance. As a result, the particular is given the acceptance previously granted to the general principle. (See *Syllogism.*)

Definition: The lexical meaning of a word, represented by its entry in the dictionary.

Denotation: In contrast to *connotation,* the explicit, nonemotionally colored meaning of a word or term.

Diction: The choice of words. Good diction is the judicious selection of language having the denotations or connotations appropriate to the writer's intents and purpose.

Didactic: The character, qualities, or tone of teaching or preaching. Writing that is more concerned with driving home a point or illustrating a lesson or moral than with communicating an understanding is considered didactic. Only highly talented writers, deeply moved by profound insights, can give such a *message* the character of high art.

Editorialized news: News stories appearing on the regular news pages ordinarily devoted to objective reports have editorial content if they include interpretive comments or personal opinions.

Empathy: The projection of one's feelings and thoughts into persons or objects outside of himself. In reading poetry or watching a drama, for example, one may consent to let part of himself go out into the world of wonder or realism created by the writer or the actor. Similarly, one may permit his imagination to identify places and things as parts of himself, or himself as part of them.

Enthymeme: A syllogism in which one of the premises is omitted or unexpressed. For example: "There he goes in his little foreign car. Hope he's got enough life insurance." This clipped syllogism can be formally stated thus: All who drive little foreign cars may very well be killed in an accident. He drives a little foreign car. Therefore, he may very well be killed in an accident.

Euphemism: The substitution of a term having a more mild, inoffensive association for one that is harshly direct. For example: *senior citizens* for *old people.*

Exposition: A basic kind of writing, as distinguished from argumentation, description, and narration, which deals primarily with explanation, but may require the skills of the other three basic types. Exposition explains by identifying, defining, analyzing, classifying, showing cause, illustrating, exemplifying, comparing, and contrasting.

Fallacy: An error in reasoning or a kind of faulty logic. The most common fallacies are these: hasty generalization, false analogy, ignoring the issue, begging the question, argument against the person (character assassination), the loaded question, the dilemma, and rationalization.

Figurative language: The figures of speech—simile, metaphor, metonymy, personification, synecdoche, and so forth. These figures or *tropes,* when apt and suitable to their context, give the reader pleasure through their manner of saying one thing in terms of another. (See *Symbol, Myth,* and *Irony.*)

Humor: The recognition of the incongruity of elements in a situation that normally does not have such incongruous aspects. An example of verbal humor:

Robber: "Your money or your life!"
Victim: "Take my life. I'm saving my money for my old age!"

Image: The sensation suggested by a connotative term in a description (sight, sound, smell, taste, feeling). In advertising and commercial publications, it means a representative example, something or someone that embodies traits and features typical of a class of consumers, a product, a corporation, or a public figure.

Inductive logic: The process of reasoning wherein first a particular, individual fact is established, and from this particular it is inferred that a conclusion can be drawn regarding the operation of things similar to this initial fact. If one has had a bad experience with a "blind date," he may inductively assume that all blind dates will result in the same kind of unhappy experience.

Inference: The process of deriving conclusions from evidence or syllogistic premises. For example: If all college graduates have no trouble finding jobs, we can infer that any particular person we know who is graduating from college will soon find a position. To infer is to deduce what is true in the particular from what is true in general.

Intuition: Knowledge arrived at without any conscious process of reasoning. Awareness of this new insight or discovery of meaning may produce emotional thought and excitement. Poets and scientists both rely upon such unsought knowledge as possible illumination of what has been previously obscure.

Irony: A state of affairs in which the implicit meaning, either verbal or situational, is different from, or opposite to, the apparent meaning. Irony thus introduces opposites or contraries in order to produce a degree of tension in the reader or audience. The resolving of these opposites releases that tension and produces the laughter of comedy, the painful emotions of tragedy, or the wry smile of wit recognized. There are at least eight variations of irony: dramatic, Socratic, verbal, circumstantial, sarcasm, anticlimax, romantic, paradox.

Issue: A main point of difference between opposing views in an argument. Other points may be accepted by both sides concerning the topic being argued, but by definition, there must be certain basic points of disagreement, on which the argument will be lost or won. (See *Argumentation.*)

Jargon: All the technical terms and prevailing slang expressions peculiar to a profession or calling; a highly specialized vocabulary. It fails as a language for general writing since its terms and meanings are strictly tied to the context of the profession or trade wherein the expressions pass for current speech. It accounts for difficult prose styles that try to interlard jargon with abstract terms having only vague referents.

Language: Any system of symbols, verbal or written, which a people use in a more or less uniform or conventional manner to communicate meanings to one another. In a growing society the language is a flexible, responsive agency of communication which includes new and changing terms and meanings while at the same time preserving the old.

Lead summary: The reporter's term for the opening sentence of his news story. It contains the gist of the whole report by supplying the essential who-what-when-where-why information. Since the lead summary does represent the reporter's understanding of what is most significant about the event he is reporting, it involves a personal judgment to some extent. Its journalistic validity depends upon the skill and talent of the reporter.

Linguistics: The science of language.

Literary criticism: The study of literature as art. It traces its origins to Aristotle's *Poetics* and the discussion of such terms as *imitation, tragedy, comedy,* and *catharsis.* As is to be expected, there are various critical schools or theories as to what elements and practices constitute the highest forms of literary art.

Logic: The science of reasoning. As such, it deals with arriving at conclusions and solving of problems. It is ordinarily divided into deductive and inductive reasoning.

Meaning: See *Semantics* and *Syntactic.*

Media: The means through or by which something is accomplished. Hence the general term for all agencies of public communication—radio, television, newspapers, magazines, and books.

Metaphor: A figure of speech involving a comparison in which no words indicating similarity—*as, as if, as though, like*—appear. For example: "In this life, what you sow, you reap." A metaphor which runs to considerable detail and is applied at some length is called an *extended metaphor.*

Milieu: The intellectual, moral, social, economic, political, religious, and educational conditions and forces that make up the world of any narrative or history.

Motivation: The combination of character traits and circumstances that leads characters in fictional narratives to act as they do. It provides a kind of cause-effect order that creates the illusion of verisimilitude for the reader or audience. Biographers and historians must also try to find the reasons for the behavior of their historic figures.

Myth: The stories and characters of a people, usually as related to their historic past or early origins. Novelists and poets such as James Joyce and William Butler Yeats have given myth prominence in modern literature.

Narrative substance: The incident in nature, the act of a person, the imaginative fantasy, the half-buried memory, or sudden perception out of which a fully developed narrative can be created by a skillful author.

Narrator: The "voice" that the author has chosen to "tell" the reader the narrative he has created out of the narrative substance. As the storyteller, the narrator is permitted by the author to say only what the author wishes him to reveal at any given point in the narrative. The narrator may be the main character or a minor one relating either his own or someone else's experiences. He may also be almost indiscernible. (See *Point of view.*)

Objective: The critical term given to writing that conceals or effaces the identity and views of the author. In contrast to *subjective,* it pertains to the impersonal statement that appears to be a detached report or narrative, which in no way seems to reveal the interests or reactions of the author doing the relating or stating.

Paradox: A statement seeming to offer an inherent contradiction, but which, when thought through, reveals no such irreconcilable opposites. For example: The more he studied, the more he investigated, the less he knew.

Parallelism: The rhetorical principle that holds that similar ideas should be expressed in similar word patterns or syntactic forms for the sake of smoothness and economy.

Personification: The figure of speech wherein human qualities or attributes are given to abstract or inanimate things. Imaginative writers who are deeply moved by what they wish to say may resort to personification to express their identification or empathy with inanimate things. For example: Fog shrouded every street, muffled every wheel and voice, and held in its clammy clutch all the warm life of the city. John Ruskin called personification that grows out of sentimentality, *the pathetic fallacy;* rain clouds, for example, could be said to be weeping if one happened to feel mournful himself.

Plot: The action of the narrative considered as an interrelation of incidents and episodes to form a story pattern. It ordinarily means the parts of the story, the various stages of the protagonist's conflict leading to some climax and following denouement or conclusion. Some modern "plotless" narratives still have story parts, but the design of their arrangement differs radically from the old chronological order.

Point of view: The author's chosen narrator must maintain some position in relation to the characters in the story that he tells. His view may be *omniscient,* wherein he knows everything about everybody and presides as a kind of god over the world of people and things he narrates. He may be the first-person narrator (the "I") who tells only what he himself has seen, done, or observed. He may be the concealed *central intelligence* of the Henry James narratives, and as such see and hear and know just a little more than the character singled out as the central personage can see or know. These are only a few of the possible viewpoints for the narrator.

Propaganda: Historically, the communicating or spreading of "the truth" through every available means. But through the deliberate exploitation of all media to support a national cause or program, propaganda now has a "bad" meaning. Its devices include the golden promise, prestige borrowing, identification with the crowd, the red herring, public demonstration of unity, and join-the-winner.

Proposition: The thesis in an argument. It forms the basic statement of contention in a debate. In a syllogism, each of the three statements—the two premises and the conclusion—is a proposition; in each, something is affirmed or denied about a subject.

Rationalization: The kind of thinking by which one seeks to explain his actions, or to excuse his failures or shortcomings on the basis of creditable motives rather than by analyzing his true motivation. By making some excuse or the other in the form of "good reason," the person so excusing himself may feel that he need not consider himself guilty for any inadequacy.

Referent: The semantic term for the object or thing which a word represents, denotes, or symbolizes.

Rhetoric: As defined by Aristotle, "The power to see the possible ways of persuading people about any given subject." It now includes all arts and crafts of writing and composition.

Satire: Literary compositions, in prose or in verse, that hold up for scorn and ridicule the weaknesses and foibles of human nature. It is generally associated with the comic, but unlike the comic, which arouses more or less sympathetic laughter, satire seeks to revile and even to destroy what it attacks by exposing it to laughter that may be savagely bitter.

Semantics: The study of meanings and changes of meanings in a language. It is concerned with denotation and connotation as affected by the historical and cultural changes the society undergoes.

Sentimentality: Self-indulgent emotions or emotional thinking that goes to lengths unjustified by the circumstances, giving rise to some gush of sympathy or pity. It becomes mawkish or maudlin when lavished upon objects wholly undeserving of excesses of self-elevating pity.

Sign: Any object or phenomenon evident to the senses that serves nonverbally to communicate a meaning. Philosophers of language and linguistic scholars do not always agree on the definition of this and similar terms.

Simile: The figure of comparison that employs such terms as *like, as if, as, as though.* For example: The salesman went through town like a cyclone.

Stereotype: Any expression applied as a "formula" answer to a situation or problem that is essentially complex and highly variable. Stereotypes consist of phrases and sentences that have so often been applied to such a wide variety of situations that they no longer have any specific relevance.

Structure: All forms of compositional organization and units of development, such as the sentence, the paragraph, the essay or article in the various forms of narration, exposition, description, and argumentation. Structure forms the backbone of any piece of writing; it is the systematic arrangement and development giving design to a work.

Style: A highly complex term having many meanings because of its long history. It is still closely related to four concepts: style as ornament, style as the man, style as sincerity, and style as grace. It may also be thought of as formal (high), middle, and informal. *Good style* is often considered now to be one exhibiting economy and concreteness of diction, tone of conviction, and effective structure. It is a style not burdened with faulty and trite diction, needless abstractions, tautology (wordiness), circumlocution, obscurity of expression, and syntactic errors.

Subjective: As the opposite of *objective,* a term that describes the kind of writing that is highly personal and appears to reveal clearly the interests and tastes of the author, who considers it proper to voice his feelings and views on what he is relating or explaining.

Summary: An abridgment or statement in brief of a previous discourse. It contains in as concise language as possible all of the main points and their chief supporting details in the composition. The ability to summarize accurately is one measure of one's skill in comprehension.

Syllogism: The traditional formula or schema of deductive reasoning. A syllogism consists of two premises—major and minor—and a conclusion. To be *valid,* a syllogism must comply with the rules that govern it. For example: Graduating seniors do not have to worry about finding jobs. Mary and Bill are graduating seniors. Mary and Bill do not have to worry about finding jobs.

Symbol: Like *sign,* that which represents or stands for something else, but considered to have more meaning than *sign.* Language, strictly speaking, is a system of symbols, for words are symbols. When *symbol* becomes *symbolism,* it takes on a special significance. For example: *Japanese cherry tree* as a term joins the world of reality with one of fantasy and imagination, if that term unites the physical tree with the legend and ritual of Japanese culture.

Syntactic: Pertaining to *syntax* meaning, or the meaning of a pattern of words in the light of their grammatical relationship as part of a sentence.

Tautology: Verbosity, the excessive or repetitive use of words and phrases to make a statement. For example: He was a lazy, indolent, unambitious sort of fellow who didn't ever seem to want to work much.

Theme: The essential meaning of a work, its basic pattern of significance, sometimes thought of as its *message.* The theme may be directly stated or be most obliquely concealed within the literary work. One apparent theme may suggest several others also present in a poem, short story, drama, or novel; these themes may even seem to be in conflict. It is the reader's task and delight to try to read the work of a master with the same insights that seem to have moved the author in writing it. An essay itself can be spoken of as a *theme,* as can the thesis or central idea of an essay.

Thesis: The central idea, the main purpose, the theme. These are often considered as synonyms; in general, however, the thesis is the one-sentence statement, appearing either in the opening part of the essay or in the conclusion, that expresses the main point of the exposition.

Tone: That characteristic of a piece of writing that through its diction, logic, and structure suggests the possible attitudes that the author has toward both his subject matter and his audience. Tone reflects the mood and purpose of the author—his compassion, uneasiness, bitterness, or friendliness.

Verisimilitude: The quality of credible reality that authors seek to give their fiction. It consists in presenting sufficient images of familiar, recognizable details for the audience to visualize the milieu and accept as lifelike the characters who enact there the patterned design of their lives. It enables the reader to feel empathy.

SOURCES AND
ACKNOWLEDGMENTS

Page 2   Leo Spitzer, "Language of Poetry," in Ruth Nanda Anshen (ed.), *Language: Its Meaning and Function,* Harper & Rowe, Publishers, Incorporated, New York, 1957, p. 205.

4   Exercise 3. Ernest Gellner, *Words and Things,* Victor Gollancz, Ltd., London, 1959, p. 27.

4   Exercise 4. "A Ballad of New Words." By permission. From *Word Study,* copyright by G. & C. Merriam Co., publishers of the Merriam-Webster Dictionaries, Springfield, Mass.

5   Exercise 7. William J. Entwistle, *Aspects of Language,* Faber and Faber, Ltd., London, 1953, p. 11.

6   Exercise 9. Susanne K. Langer, *Philosophy in a New Key,* Harvard University Press, Cambridge, Mass., 1942, pp. 290–291.

11   Tom Carter, "Maturing, But at What Cost?" *The Vanguard,* Portland State College, Portland, Oregon, Nov. 15, 1963.

14   Jane Austen, *Sense and Sensibility,* E. P. Dutton & Co., Inc., New York, 1906.

15   Max Savelle, "Nationalism and Other Loyalties in the American Revolution," *The American Historical Review,* vol. 67, pp. 901–902, July, 1962.

17   Exercise 13. Eric Heller, *The Disinherited Mind,* Bowes and Bowes Publishers Ltd., Lon-

Page   don, 1957, pp. 26–27. Published in the United States by Farrar, Straus and Giroux, Inc.

18   Exercise 15. (1) (2) Arnold J. Toynbee, "Nationalism as a Threat to Man," ©1963 The New York Times Company. Reprinted by permission also of Arnold J. Toynbee.

19   Exercise 17. Herman Melville, *Billy Budd,* E. P. Dutton & Co., Inc., New York, 1958, pp. 304–305.

21   Exercise 19. Jane Austen, *Pride and Prejudice,* E. P. Dutton & Co., New York, 1906.

23   George Lamming, *In the Castle of My Skin,* McGraw-Hill Book Company, New York, 1953, pp. 127–128.

26   Donald Day, *Uncle Sam's Uncle Josh,* Little, Brown and Company, Boston, 1953, pp. 120–121. Copyright 1953 by Donald Day.

30   Exercise 25. H. L. Mencken, *The American Language, Supplement 1,* Alfred A. Knopf, Inc., New York, 1945, p. 283. By permission of Alfred A. Knopf, Inc.

32   Exercise 29. Walter Houston Clark, "Religion as a Response to the Search for Meaning," *The Journal of Social Psychology,* vol. 60, pp. 127–128, June, 1963.

33   Exercise 32. John A. Monro, Dean of Students, Harvard College, "Letters," *Look,* p. 7, Dec. 17, 1963. By permission of Dean John A. Monro.

36   *Consumer Magazine and Farm Publications,* vol. 45, pp. 346, 131, 139, Apr. 27, 1963.

37   Gabriel Kolko, *Wealth and Power in America,* Frederick A. Praeger, Inc., New York, 1962, pp. 56–57.

37   *How Many Trees Can a Chipmunk Eat?* By permission of the Weyerhaeuser Company.

40   Exercise 6. *Attention, Belief, and Believing Action.* By permission of *Good Housekeeping.*

41   Exercise 7. *The Fundamental Freedom.* By permission of Union Oil Company of California.

Page 42   David Caplovitz, *The Poor Pay More,* The Free Press of Glencoe, New York, 1963, p. 29.

42   C. West Churchman, *Measurement of Consumer Interest,* University of Pennsylvania Press, Philadelphia, 1947, pp. 122–123.

43   Edward L. Brink and William T. Kelley, *The Management of Promotion: Consumer and Demand Stimulation,* Prentice-Hall, Inc., Englewood Cliffs, N.J., p. 50. ©1963.

44   Elmer G. Leterman, *The New Art of Selling,* Harper & Row, Publishers, Incorporated, New York, 1957, p. 123.

45   Lawrence M. Hughes, "Making Big Advertising Pay," *Sales Management,* vol. 90, p. 40, Mar. 1, 1963.

45   Stephen White, "The Creative Man at Work," *Horizon,* pp. 112–113, March, 1962.

46   Sebastian de Gruzia, *Of Time, Work, and Leisure,* The Twentieth Century Fund, New York, 1962, p. 363.

47   Exercise 12. "The Leo Ritter Test," advertisement in *Town & Country,* July, 1964.

49   (1) "Beauty Bulletin," reprinted from *Vogue;* ©1963 by the Condé Nast Publications, Inc., Greenwich, Conn.

50   (2) Elsie Pell, *François Mauriac,* Philosophical Library, Inc., New York, 1947, p. 35.

50   (3) Marshall W. Fishwick, "Diagnosing the American Dream," *Saturday Review,* p. 9, Dec. 21, 1963.

50   (4) "The Name Industry," *Time,* p. 79, Dec. 20, 1963.

55   R. C. Brewster, "More Psychology in Spelling," *Harvard Business Review,* pp. 95, July-August, 1953.

55   Bernard Kilgore, "The Challenge of Communication in Economics," *Journalism Quarterly, Special Supplement,* p. 434, Summer, 1963. By permission of *Journalism Quarterly.*

56   Norman Jacobson, "Political Science and Political Education," *The American Political Science Review,* vol. 57,

Page   p. 562, September, 1963. By permission of *The American Political Science Review.*

60   Exercise 8. William H. Blanchard, "National Myth, National Character, and National Policy," *The Journal of Conflict Resolutions,* vol. 6, pp. 144, 147, June, 1962.

61   Robert S. Boyd, "Humor Remains Free," *The Oregonian,* p. 3, Dec. 26, 1963. By permission of Chicago Daily News Service and *The Oregonian.*

62   Excerpts from a Governor Nelson A. Rockefeller television Oregon presidential primary broadcast, May, 1964.

63   Albert Camus, *The Rebel,* Alfred A. Knopf, Inc., New York, 1956, pp. 78–79. By permission of Alfred A. Knopf. Inc.

65–66   P. C. Jain, "What Are Our Propagandists Up To?" *National Review,* 150 East 35th Street, New York 10016, vol. 13, pp. 307–308, Oct. 23, 1962.

66   Data from J. W. Young, "Do We Need a College of Propaganda?" *Saturday Review,* vol. 44, p. 85, Feb. 11, 1961.

67   Walter Lippmann, *A Preface to Morals,* The Macmillan Company, New York, 1921, p. 281.

72   Exercise 17. V. Larkin (mechanic at Rostov Farm Machinery Plant), "Boring vs. Jolly," *Izvestia,* p. 2, Sept. 30, 1963. Reprinted in the *Current Digest of the Soviet Press,* vol. 14, no. 39. Translation from the *Current Digest of the Soviet Press,* published weekly at Columbia University by the Joint Committee on Slavic Studies, appointed by the American Council of Learned Societies and the Social Science Research Council. Copyright 1963. By permission.

74   Exercise 18. Preaching Print, Inc. (advertisement), "Born into a Tax-burdened World," *The Oregonian,* p. 24, Dec. 25, 1963. By permission of Preaching Print, Inc.

75   Exercise 21. *Time,* July 3, 1964, p. 60.

78   Taken from John Tebbel, *The Compact History of the American Newspaper,* pp. 262–263. Copyright ©1963 by Hawthorn Books, Inc., New York.

79   Exercise 3. Lord Windlesham, "The Mirrors of the South,"

Page   *The Listener,* Oct. 31, 1963. This quotation and others to follow later in this chapter do so by permission of The British Broadcasting Corporation and Lord Windlesham.

80   "Harwell Enumerates Qualities of a Reporter," *Editor & Publisher,* p. 38, May 4, 1963. By permission of *Editor & Publisher.*

81   Data from Philip M. Wagner, "What Makes a Really Good Newspaper and Why They Are So Few," *Harper's Magazine,* pp. 13–16, June, 1962. By permission of Philip W. Wagner.

82   Ben H. Bagdikian, "The President Nonspeaks," *Columbia Journalism Review,* pp. 44–45, Spring, 1963. By permission of *Columbia Journalism Review.*

83   Phil Kerby, "Setting the Record Straight," *Frontier,* December, 1963. By permission of Phil Kerby, editor.

84–85   Karl E. Meyers, *The New America: Politics and Society in the Age of the Smooth Deal,* Basic Books, Inc., New York, 1961. By permission of Basic Books, Inc.

86   Exercise 9. Herbert A. Otto, "Sex and Violence on U.S. Newsstands," *Journalism Quarterly,* p. 24, Winter, 1963. By permission of *Journalism Quarterly.*

87   Ben H. Bagdikian, *op. cit.*

88   *Newsweek,* p. 17, July 13, 1964.

89   *U.S. News & World Report,* p. 44, July 20, 1964.

89   *Time,* p. 26, July 10, 1964.

90   "Readings—Something to Write Home About," *Time,* p. 62, July 3, 1964. By permission of *Time,* Inc.

91   "Night of the Iguana," *Newsweek,* p. 85, July 13, 1964. By permission of *Newsweek.*

92   Dallas S. Townsend, Jr., "Procrustes' Bed," *Columbia Journalism Review,* p. 39, Summer, 1963.

92–93   "Senator Fulbright Bares Press Services to Foreign Agents," *Editor & Publisher,* June 22, 1963; p. 9, Apr. 6, 1963.

Page 93   "Automation Expert Pictures Press of 1973," *Editor & Publisher*, p. 51, Apr. 27, 1963.

93   Howard R. Long, "The Golden Age of Weeklies," *Grassroots Editor*, p. 2, October, 1963.

95   Exercise 15. (1)–(4) Lord Windlesham, *op. cit.* (5) Alan Barth in Nieman Chair Lecture, 1962, Marquette University College of Journalism, as quoted in *Journalism Quarterly*, p. 26, Winter, 1963. By permission of *Journalism Quarterly*. (6) Thomas M. Storke, in *Editor & Publisher*, p. 34, June 1, 1963.

102   "Not in Here, 301," *The Oregonian*, p. 28, Nov. 11, 1963. By permission of *The Oregonian*.

105–
107   Exercise 3. (1) Glenn Leggett, "The Female in Academe," *American Association of University Professors Bulletin*, p. 228, Autumn, 1963. By permission of *AAUP Bulletin*. (2) Edward Rosenheim, "Letter to a New Dean," *ibid.*, p. 228. By permission of *AAUP Bulletin*. (3) "Faculty Participation in College and University Government," *ibid.*, p. 253. By permission of *AAUP Bulletin*. (4) "Architects Say Northwest Tower's Yellow Pain Wreaking Havoc," *The Oregonian*, 1963, Nov. 11. (5) Byron E. Logie, "Letters," *Look*, Dec. 17, 1963. By permission of Mr. Logie. (6) Robert O. Shipman, Assistant Dean, Graduate School of Journalism, Columbia University, "Letters," *Look*, p. 18, Nov. 5, 1963. By permission of Dean Shipman. (7) Mrs. Robert Wilhite, *ibid.*, p. 18. By permission of Mrs. Robert Wilhite. (8) Donald D. Landon, *ibid.*, p. 18. By permission of Mr. Donald D. Landon. (9) Quoted in *Parade*, Jan. 5, 1964. By permission of *Parade*. (10) *The Last News*, vol. 3, no. 1, Gospel Publishing House, Springfield, Mo., p. 4. By permission of Gospel Publishing House.

109   Exercise 8. "Hang Tight on Loose," *Oregon Journal*, p. 12, July 8, 1964. By permission of *Oregon Journal*.

110–
111   H. L. A. Hart, "Holmes's Common Law," *The New York Review of Books*, pp. 15–16, Oct. 17, 1963.

114   David Hapgood, "Africa's New Elites," *Harper's Magazine*, p. 46, December, 1963. By permission of David Hapgood.

Page 114–   Exercise 10. From *Ludas Matyi,* Budapest, by Laszlo Palasti
115   in *Atlas,* pp. 305–306, November, 1963. By permission of
     Laszlo Palasti and *Atlas,* who translated the article.

116–   "Critic Claims Professors Lazy," *The Sunday Oregonian,* p. 21,
117   Oct. 6, 1963.

121   James Boswell, *Boswell's London Journal, 1762–1763,* Fred-
     erick A. Pottle (ed.), McGraw-Hill Book Company, New
     York, 1950, p. 171.

121–   Congressman Usher L. Burdick, *Congressional Record, Ap-*
122   *pendix,* 1950, p. A237.

123   "Nothing New," Letter to the Editor, *Oregon Journal,* July 9,
     1964.

123   Martin Gardner, *Fads and Fallacies in the Name of Science,*
     Dover Publications, New York, 1952, pp. 28–33.

124   *Time,* p. 56, Nov. 1, 1963.

124–   Albert Bandura, Ph. D., "What TV Violence Can Do to Your
125   Child," *Look,* pp. 46–48, Oct. 22, 1963. By permission of
     Look.

126   Michel de Montaigne, *The Essays of Michel de Montaigne,*
     A. L. Burt, Publisher, New York, 1894.

126   Oscar Wilde, *De Profundis,* Doubleday & Company, Inc.,
     New York, 1927, p. 41.

127   William C. Coles, Jr., "The Way Johnny Can't Read,"
     American Association of University Professors Bulletin, p. 242,
     Autumn, 1963. By permission of *AAUP Bulletin.*

128–   Exercise 15. (9) Union Oil advertisement originally in *The*
129   *Wall Street Journal,* July 7, 1963. (10) (11) (12) Book
     advertisements in *The New York Review of Books,* vol. 1,
     no. 8, Dec. 12, 1963. (15) R. Taton, *Reason and Chance in*
     Scientific Discovery, A. J. Pomerans (trans.), Science Edi-
     tions, New York, 1962, p. 57. (16) CBS News Broadcast,
     Jan. 8, 1963. (19) Ives Hendrick, *Facts and Theories of*
     Psychoanalysis, Alfred A. Knopf, Inc., 1958.

130   Exercise 17. Arthur Schopenhauer, "Preliminary: Logic and
     Dialectic," in *The Essential Schopenhauer,* by permission of
     George Allen & Unwin, Ltd., London.

Page 131   *Webster's New Collegiate Dictionary.*

131   Attributed to Arthur Wellesley, Duke of Wellington.

132   "How Not to Read a Book," editorial, *The New York Times,* ©1963 The New York Times Company. Reprinted by permission.

133   F. R. Leavis, "A Rejoinder," in Eric Bentley (ed.), *The Importance of Scrutiny,* Grove Press, Inc., New York, 1948, p. 21. By permission of F. R. Leavis.

134   Oswald Spengler, *The Decline of the West,* Alfred A. Knopf, Inc., New York, 1932, p. 29. By permission of Alfred A. Knopf, Inc.

134–   Fyodor Dostoyevsky, *Notes from the Underground,* The
135   New American Library of World Literature, Inc., New York, 1961, p. 153.

136   Exercise 18. (2) M. Brewster Smith, "Mental Health Reconsidered," *American Psychologist,* pp. 301–302, June, 1961. (3) Dostoyevsky, *op. cit.,* p. 183. (4) Senator Wayne Morse, "Is the Present United States–Cuban Policy Adequate?" *Congressional Digest,* p. 268, November, 1962. By permission of *Congressional Digest.*

138   Exercise 23. (2) Ellen Moers, "The Angry Young Women," *Harper's Magazine,* p. 91, December, 1963.

138–   Exercise 24. (8) "Gleanings from the Writings and Speeches
139   of John F. Kennedy," *Saturday Review,* p. 26, Dec. 7, 1963. (9) *Time,* p. 45, Dec. 20, 1963. (10) Robert Graves, "A Poet's Investigations of Science," *ibid.,* by permission of *Saturday Review.* (11) (12) *Time,* Dec. 20, 1963. (14) Advertisement in *Saturday Review,* Dec. 7, 1963. (15) James Baldwin, "Talk to Teachers," *ibid.,* Dec. 21, 1963. By permission of *Saturday Review.* (16) Michael A. Musmanno, Justice Supreme Court of Pennsylvania, in "Letters from Readers," *Commentary,* p. 253, September, 1962. By permission of Justice Musmanno.

142   R. S. Crane, *The Language of Criticism and the Structure of Poetry,* University of Toronto Press, Toronto, 1953, p. 92.

147   "The Surface" is reprinted with the permission of Charles Scribner's Sons from *To Mix with Time* by May Swenson. Copyright ©1963 May Swenson.

Page 151   Exercise 1. Robert Browning, "Meeting at Night."

152–   Exercise 3. William Stafford, "Locality," *The Critical*
153   *Quarterly,* vol. 5, no. 3, p. 214, Autumn, 1963. By permission
of William Stafford.

156   Anton Pavlovich Chekhov, "Heartache," *The Portable Chekhov,* Avrahm Yarmolinsky (ed.), The Viking Press, Inc., New York, 1944.

157–   Reprinted from Thomas Wolfe, *Look Homeward, Angel,*
158   p. 494. Copyright 1929 Charles Scribner's Sons; renewal copyright ©1957 by Edward C. Aswell.

160–   Kevin Andrews, *The Flight of Ikaros,* Houghton Mifflin
161   Company, Boston, 1959, pp. 104–105. By permission of Houghton Mifflin Company.

163   Exercise 7. (1) Student theme. (2) Thomas De Quincey, "Dream-fugue Founded on the Preceding Theme of Sudden Death."

164   Exercise 9. William Wordsworth, "Poverty."

165–   (1) Nathaniel Hawthorne, "Egotism: Or, the Bosom's Ser-
166   pent," Houghton Mifflin Company, Boston, 1900. (2) Joseph Conrad, "Amy Foster," *Collected Tales,* Doubleday & Company, Inc., 1921.

167–   Joseph Conrad, Preface to *The Nigger of the Narcissus,* 2d ed.,
168   Doubleday & Company, Inc., Garden City, New York, 1914. By permission of J. M. Dent & Sons Ltd., London, and the Trustees of the Joseph Conrad Estate.

177   Russell L. Ackoff, *Scientific Method,* John Wiley & Sons, Inc., New York, 1962, p. 22. By permission of John Wiley & Sons, Inc.

177–   Data by permission from Homer W. Smith, *From Fish to*
178   *Philosopher,* Little, Brown and Company, Boston, pp. 151– 152.

178–   Bentley Glass, "Information Crisis in Biology," *Bulletin of the*
179   *Atomic Scientists,* October, 1962. Reprinted with permission. Copyright October 1962 by the Educational Foundation for Nuclear Science, Inc.

Page 179   Ritchie Calder, "A Science Reporter Speaks of 'Babelology,'" *The UNESCO Courier*, p. 46, July, 1961.

180   R. C. Bibby, "The Concept of Culture," *Nature*, p. 1145, June 20, 1964.

181   Exercise 3. "The People Speak," *Oregon Journal*, July 4, 1964.

182   Exercise 4. *A Concordance to the Poems of W. B. Yeats*, Cornell University Press, Ithaca, New York. By permission of Cornell University Press.

185   Wolf von Eckardt, "New Towns in America," *The New Republic*, p. 17, Oct. 26, 1963. By permission of Wolf von Eckardt.

186   Niccolo Machiavelli, *The Prince*, Henry Regnery Company, Chicago; The Bodley Head, London, 1952, p. 53.

186–   Robert A. Dahl, *Modern Political Analysis*. ©1963, by per-
187   mission of Prentice-Hall, Inc., Englewood Cliffs, N.J.

188–   Hugh Dalziel Duncan, *Communication and Social Order*,
189   Totawa, N.J., 1962, pp. *xv–xxviii*.

189–   Paul Tillich, *Dynamics of Faith*, Harper Torchbooks, Harper
190   & Row, Publishers, Incorporated, New York, 1958, pp. 85–89. By permission of Harper & Row, Publishers, Incorporated.

190–   Exercise 9. (1) H. Helson, R. R. Blake, and J. S. Mouton, "An
191   Experimental Investigation of the Effectiveness of the 'Big Lie' in Shifting Attitudes," *Journal of Social Psychology*, vol. 48, p. 57, The Journal Press, Provincetown, Mass., August, 1958. By permission of The Journal Press. (2) Quoted in Reece McGee, *Social Disorganization in America*, Chandler Publishing Company, San Francisco, 1962, p. 79.

191   Exercise 10. Samuel Johnson, *Rasselas*, Ginn & Company, Boston, 1904.

193   Herbert Read, *English Prose Style*, Beacon Press, Boston, 1955, p. 90. Copyright 1952, Pantheon Press, New York.

195–   Wright Morris, *The Territory Ahead*, Harcourt, Brace &
197   World, Inc., New York, 1958. By permission of Wright Morris.

Page 200   William Hazlitt, "On Application to Study."

201   Exercise 1. Osbert Lancaster, *Classical Landscape with Figures,* Houghton Mifflin Company, Boston, 1948, p. 53. By permission of Houghton Mifflin Company and John Murray, Publishers, Ltd., London.

202   Exercise 2. H. L. Davis, *Honey in the Horn,* William Morrow Company, Inc., New York, 1935, p. 148. By permission of William Morrow Company, Inc.

202–
203   Exercise 3. (1) Rudolf Arnheim, *Film as Art,* University of California Press, Berkeley, 1957, pp. 67–68. By permission of Rudolf Arnheim. (2) *Screen Stars,* p. 57, April, 1964. By permission of Magazine Management Co.

203–
204   Exercise 4. "Big-daddy of Waters," NBC advertisement appearing in *The New Yorker.* By permission of the National Broadcasting Company.

206   Exercise 7. "An American Hero," *Look* advertisement, Jan. 28, 1964. Reproduced through the courtesy of Investor-Owned Electric Light and Power Companies.

210–
212   Exercise 10. "Columnists," *Time,* p. 43, Jan. 24, 1964. By permission of *Time,* Inc.

212   Exercise 11. "How to Build a Boy," *Life,* Jan. 7, 1964. This advertisement created for The Advertising Council, Inc., by J. Walter Thompson Company.

212–
214   Exercise 13. "Udall Takes His Stand," *The New Republic,* pp. 10–11, Jan. 8, 1964. By permission of The Honorable Morris K. Udall, 2nd District of Arizona.

215–
218   Bertrand Russell, *Human Knowledge: Its Scope and Limits,* Simon and Schuster, Inc., New York, 1948, pp. 308–311. By permission of Simon and Schuster, Inc. and George Allen & Unwin, Ltd., London.

219   Rainer Maria Rilke, *Letters to a Young Poet,* M. D. Herter (trans.), W. W. Norton & Company, Inc., New York, 1934, pp. 74–76. By permission of W. W. Norton & Company, Inc.

225–
226   Excerpt from F. Scott Fitzgerald, *The Great Gatsby,* pp. 85–86. Copyright 1925 Charles Scribner's Sons; renewal

Page

copyright 1953 Frances Scott Fitzgerald Lanahan. Reprinted with the permission of Charles Scribner's Sons.

227   Exercise 15. Dylan Thomas, "Just Like Little Dogs," *Portrait of the Artist as a Young Dog.* Copyright 1940 by New Directions.

227– Exercise 16. Henry James, *The Wings of the Dove,* Dell
228   Publishing Co., Inc., New York, 1958, pp. 359–360.

229– M. H. Abrams, *The Mirror and the Lamp,* Oxford University
231   Press, Fair Lawn, N.J., pp. 229–240. By permission of Oxford University Press.

233– Will Durant and Ariel Durant, *The Age of Reason Begins,*
234   Simon and Schuster, Inc., New York, 1961, p. 404. By permission of Simon and Schuster, Inc.

234– F. O. Matthiessen, *The James Family,* Alfred A. Knopf, Inc.,
235   New York, 1947, p. 224. By permission of Alfred A. Knopf, Inc.

237   Kingsley Amis, *Lucky Jim,* Doubleday & Company, Inc., Garden City, New York, 1954. By permission of Doubleday & Company, Inc.

239– E. M. Forster, *Howards End,* Alfred A. Knopf, Inc., New
240   York, 1921. By permission of Alfred A. Knopf, Inc.

242   Exercise 3. (1) Joseph Conrad, *The Secret Sharer,* Doubleday & Company, Inc., 1921. (2) John Ruskin, *The Stones of Venice,* Smith, Elder, and Co., London, 1873. (3) Attributed to Paul Elmer More. (4) Henry David Thoreau, *Walden,* Houghton Mifflin Company, Boston, 1910. (5) Cyril Scott, *Music,* The David McKay Company, Philadelphia, n.d., p. 104. (6) G. K. Chesterton, *Heretics,* John Lane Company, New York, 1905, p. 54.

242– Exercise 4. (1) William Morris, "An Apology," *The Earthly*
243   *Paradise,* Longmans, Green & Company, New York, 1896. (2) William Ernest Henley, "Invictus." (3) John Keats, "When I Have Fears." (4) Edward Lear, "The Jumblies," *The Complete Nonsense Book,* Dodd, Mead & Co., 1912.

244   Exercise 5. Dick Sanders, "Editorial," *Portland State Review of Student Writing,* Spring, 1956.

Page 244–
245

Exercise 7. (1) Frank Norris, *The Octopus.* (2) James Russell Lowell, "Dante," *Among My Books.* (3) Walter Savage Landor, *Reflective and Discursive Essays.* (5) Daniel Defoe, *Robinson Crusoe.* (6) John Winthrop, *John Winthrop's Journal, 1634,* James Kendall Hosmer (ed.), Charles Scribner's Sons, New York, 1908, p. 120.

245–
247

Exercise 8. (1) Harriet Beecher Stowe, *Household Papers,* Houghton Mifflin Company, Boston, 1896. (2) Herman Melville, *Moby Dick,* Grosset & Dunlap, Inc., New York, 1925. (3) Laurence Wylie, "Youth in France and the United States," *Daedalus,* p. 208, Winter, 1962. By permission of the American Academy of Arts and Sciences. (4) Lady Mary Wortley Montague, *Letters Written during Her Travels in Europe, Asia, and Africa,* London, 1743, pp. 33–34. (5) "Once upon a Red," *Vogue,* Nov. 1, 1963, Max Factor advertisement. By permission of Max Factor & Co. (6) William Faulkner, *Intruder in the Dust,* pp. 211–212. Copyright 1948 by Random House, Inc.

253

G. K. Chesterton, *op. cit.*

INDEX